Edwin Freshfield

Minutes of the Vestry Meetings

and other records of the parish of St. Christopher le Stocks, in the city of

London

Edwin Freshfield

Minutes of the Vestry Meetings
and other records of the parish of St. Christopher le Stocks, in the city of London

ISBN/EAN: 9783337848606

Printed in Europe, USA, Canada, Australia, Japan

Cover: Foto ©Lupo / pixelio.de

More available books at **www.hansebooks.com**

PRIVATELY PRINTED.

MINUTES OF THE VESTRY MEETINGS

AND

OTHER RECORDS

OF

The Parish of St. Christopher le Stocks,

IN THE

CITY OF LONDON.

EDITED BY

EDWIN FRESHFIELD, *Doctor of Laws,*

Vice-President of the Society of Antiquaries of London, and one of the Churchwardens of the Parish.

LONDON:

PRINTED BY RIXON AND ARNOLD, 29, POULTRY, E.C.

1886.

INTRODUCTION.

The Documents printed in this volume are to be found in two large folio books, one called the Book of Records, and the other the Vestry Minute Book. Both these books are now in fair condition. The Book of Records, which has been beautifully repaired, was, about 16 years ago, in a miserable condition.

I had intended to make a complete transcript of the Book of Records, but I found that this would seriously interfere with the continuity of the Minutes of the Vestry Meetings, which was, to my mind, the principal object I had to keep in view.

The Book of Records was originally prepared in 1486, for the purpose of containing—not the Records of the proceedings of the Vestry meetings—but a list of the property appertaining to the Parish and the evidences relating to it. It had been intended that the book should begin with an Index. The first pages are cut so as to allow of the insertion of an Alphabetical Index, but I do not think that this intention was ever even partially carried out.

The first document entered in the Book was a complete list of all the goods belonging to the parish, then follow various Wills relating to the parish property, memoranda of leases, and of a variety of other matters interesting to the parish. These memoranda have, from time to time, been added to up to the close of the seventeenth century. In the space which had been set apart for the Index, the earlier Vestry Minutes were entered, extending from the year 1559 to the year 1591. From the year 1591 to 1593 the entries are made in a different part of the book, and after the latter date they are entered in the second volume, which contains only Vestry Minutes. It seemed to me, therefore, that if I interposed between the earlier Vestry Minutes, the whole or a considerable part of the contents of the Book of Records, I should be destroying the continuity of the parish history. I have preferred, therefore, to place at the end of the Vestry Minutes, in an appendix, such documents from the Book of Records as I thought were immediately connected with or interesting for the present volume, reserving my intention of printing the whole or such parts of the rest of the contents of the Book of Records as I think necessary. A certain portion of it, which consists of copies of leases, I do not think will be necessary, nor am I sure that any good object will be attained by transcribing the whole of the Wills, though I propose hereafter to give an abstract of the most interesting portions of them.

The items which will, I think, be considered most interesting are those to be found in the earlier portion of the Vestry Minutes, and in the various inventories and miscellaneous articles taken from the Book of Records. Commencing with these later, I think the list of jewels, goods, and ornaments, the Articles agreed upon at a Vestry held in 1507, the assessment for the Pews in 1554, and for the Clerk's wages in 1561, will be considered among the most curious documents.

The Inventory of Church goods in 1488 has already been printed in the publications of the Society of Antiquaries, but I thought it well to print it again here, as when publishing the Parish documents, there were additions to it which it became necessary to make, but which were not necessary in the previous publication. The Inventory is interesting both to the student of antiquities and also as shewing the wealth of so small a parish as St. Christopher must always have been.

From the Articles drawn up in 1507, some instructive particulars may be gathered. It appears that the Curfew was rung at St. Christopher's at eight o'clock in the evening. The Articles prescribe regulations for the closing of the alley gate of the churchyard, and the times when it shall be opened. They prescribe that the Chaplain or Chauntry Priest shall not let his house, or any part of it; the manner and times at which the various services are to be performed in the Church; that none of the Chaplains shall go to any Trental; and that the Chaplains shall not go to their mass two at once, but shall go to their masses immediately the one after the other. It is probable that these Articles were entered in an earlier Vestry Minute Book, which is lost, because the particular entries are manifestly only copies. The memorandum of the assessment of the pews, made in the year 1524, is also very interesting and instructive.

It would seem that what are termed the Clerk's wages were collected by an assessment upon the pews, and the memorandum provides for the punishment to be inflicted upon any person who rebelled, so that he would not sit or pay according as was appointed by the assessors. The change of religion made no difference in these regulations, for in the year 1574, upon the occasion of a further sessment for "the byll of the Clarke's wages," it is provided as follows: "It is furdar agreed in this Vestery, that all suche as shall refuse to pay as they ar sessed for this iij years, the churche wardens shall show the sessors thereof, & they shall be cauled beffour them, and yf they wyll not be parswaded by them to pay as they are sesed, then the churchwardens shall shew them in the ordynarys court, at the coust and charges of the parysh, a cording to an ausyentt or Dar hear in this boak wretten."

This, no doubt, refers to the order made in 1524, just 50 years before.

It appears from other sources in the books that the whole of the money was not applied to the payment of the Clerk's wages, but went towards the general Ecclesiastical purposes of the parish; in fact, it was practically a church rate, in a form of a payment for the pews, but no part of the money raised in this way went, as far as I have been able to gather, towards the clergyman.

The description given of the pews is interesting. It will be gathered from it that there were certain pews in the body of the church set apart for women. Among them, one is described as being on the north side, "next pew before the shryving hous." It seems to have been usual to have such an article in the church though it went by different names. In the accounts of St. Michael's, Cornhill, printed by my friend, Mr. Alfred J. Waterlow, the first person who seriously undertook the work of re-producing those interesting documents, there is this entry in the year 1548:—

"Item paid to the joyner for takynge downe the shryvyng pew, and making another pew, in the same place, iij^s."

It would appear that the custom of having separate pews for women was common in London, because in the Minute Book of St. Michael's, under date 2nd February, 1583, is an entry in which these are alluded to. This entry is as follows: "Also it is agreed that ye Churchwardens shall make stayne foote paces at the women's pues in the church for their mayde s̄vants to stand and knele on, & the lycke paces to be made in ye quyre."

There are also minutes referring to subsequent assessments for the Clerk's wages in the years 1561 and 1562.

At page 74 there is a declaration of the value of certain Ecclesiastical property belonging to the parish, made in the first year of King Edward the 6th. It is stated that the premises were situated in the parish of St. Dunstan's in the West, that they were of the clear yearly value of 110 shillings. They were sold at 16 years' purchase to Mr. John Croke, of Chilton, in the County of Berkshire, subject to a lease to Mr. T. Witton, for 60 years from 35, Henry VIII. I presume that Mr. John Croke must have purchased on behalf of the parish as there is abundant subsequent evidence in the Records that the property early in Queen Elizabeth's reign, was again in the hands of the parish who were receiving the rents and profits, and as I remarked in the introduction to the parish accounts, it formed the subject of an interesting law-suit with the tenant Witton.

The minutes proper began in 1561, and I have extracted them as far as 1685. Taking them with the account books and registers they make a very complete history of the parish. From them we learn (page 2) that there was a water-fall and course in the churchyard, where no doubt the Wall-brook ran as an open stream.

The parish had a clock which caused them a great deal of trouble. In 1566, the churchwardens were ordered to "se the cloke pvsed" by the advice of a man of knowledge, and also mended, or new made, as nede shall require, so yt yt may be a good and pffytt cloke."

This not being successful, it would seem the parish determined to sell the clock, but before it was sold, viz. in 1572, "it was fardar agreed that wher as it was apoynted, that the clocke shudd have byne sowld, yt is now agreed that it shall be kepte, & one too be apoynted too kepe yt goinge, and to have for the keeping yt, vi$^{s.}$ viij$^{d.}$ by the yere."

In 1574, the parishoners again got tired of the clock, for it was agreed that the Churchwardens "shall do their best ffor the sellyg of the organs, the clocke, and the egle of brasse, to the most benefitt of the prshe."

But neither did this succeed, for, in 1577, it was "agreed that some skylfull man have the sighte of the cloke, and ether to mend yt, or chang yt, or sell yt."

It was also "agreed that the cop. egell and the organs shall be solde."

It was also agreed "that these persons that hathe the doynges for the cloke shall have the barres of the chansell to be cote done, & to be sold for the most provete, and to be done in the beste forme and maner, and the pwlpete to be altered by theire dyscressyon, and to berne stēn. old papest bookse wh. remayned in ye vestery."

In the year 1578, in the list of goods, there appear:

Item, 1 payer of Organs.

Item, 1 Egle of Brasse, or lattin.

This is the last time they appear in the Minute Book. Their next appearance is in the Account Book, in 1581:

Rd. for the Egle of Lattin or brasse .	xlj$^{s.}$	vi$^{d.}$
Rd. for the pillers of the pticun sawne downe	xiij$^{s.}$	iiij$^{d.}$
Rd. for the Orgaynes, w$^{h.}$ certaine old cubbords	xlviij$^{s.}$	vj$^{d.}$
Rd. for the Clocke, being very olde and worne ...	x$^{s.}$	

And this is the end of them.

In the year 1573, there is an entry which is of some interest. At this time, Mr. Bartholomew Busfield was the Rector. It was "agreed that the parson, yf he can help the paryshe to recover all the money that John Baker, clarke to the Court of Consyences, hauth in his hands, of the parryshes, that the parson shall hav the on haufe thereof, barying haufe the charges and standyng bond, as the paryshe by the ockacyon therof shall."

This was a Court established by an order of the Court of Common Council, in the 9th King Henry VIII., for the recovery of small debts under 40s. in the City of London, by a summary and inexpensive process. It was afterwards confirmed by Act of Parliament, in King James' reign, 1 James I. c. xiv. and was called the Court of Requests. The City of London, in respect of law reform, as in respect of every other improvement, was far in advance of the so-called superior law courts of the realm, and frequently incurred the odium of the lawyers practising in those Courts, for its cheap and expeditious manner of enforcing the rights of the citizens, notably, in the instance of this Court, which they tried to supersede, and the excellent Court of Arbitration on claims on policies of marine insurance, which they succeeded in abolishing

It appears that the day upon which the Churchwardens were elected in the City parishes varied from time to time. I believe they were originally elected with the Common Council, upon St. Thomas's Day. They were all elected according to the custom of London, and I believe that the custom in St. Christopher's Parish, and in the whole of London, was, in Queen Elizabeth's reign, to elect Churchwardens to serve from Christmas to Christmas. Each Churchwarden, in turn, was elected as Junior Churchwarden, to take the place of the Churchwarden then going out of office. He was elected to serve for two years, so that in the second year he would be Senior Churchwarden, and the newly elected parishioner would be the Junior Warden.

As I have said, the elections took place at various times, but in and after the year 1580, they were held on the first Sunday in December, and the minutes usually mention the fact that the newly elected Warden was to remain Churchwarden for the period of two years, according to the accustomed order of the parish, or according to the ancient custom, and in one place it is said to be according to anneyentt custom, always used in the parish, to hold the election on the next Sunday after St. Andrew's Day, to hold office from the following Christmas.

The Churchwardens seem to have made up their accounts to Christmas, and this arrangement was eminently practical and convenient.

In the year 1605, the time of electing Churchwardens was changed to Easter Sunday, and this appears to have been the practice until 1635, when, under the auspices of Mr. John Macarnesse, the then Rector, upon the 15th April, "It was ordered and agreed by the Parson & the major part of the parish then psent, that, from henceforth, no Vestree shall be called or held in the parish upon the Saboth Day, and that the choosing of Churchwardens and other officers for the parish shall, every yere, be upon Easter Monday."

Notwithstanding that the custom of electing in December is stated to be antient, this is not borne out by the Vestry Minute Book. In 1559, the Churchwardens were chosen on the 10th March. In 1562, they were chosen upon "St. Matheyas Day, for the yer ensewing, and so an notha afta acordyng to the awnsyent custom." In 1564, the election was held on the 25th March, being our Lady Day. The elections seem to have been at various dates in February and March, until the year 1580, when, as I said before, they were made in December.

In St. Michael's, Cornhill, they were, by an ancient ordinance, to have held office for a year, from the Feast of the Purification, but from 1456 to 1556 they seem to have made up their accounts to All Saints' Day.

I would willingly dwell at length upon some of the other topics of interest in this book, but must content myself by mentioning one other.

At page 73, under date 5th June, 1561, is the following entry :—"Also 2d. ob is to be gathered every Sundaye by the Sexton, wch was wont to serve for holy breade, and nowe to serve for wyne for the comunion table, and if any overplus be left then the same to be geven to the por of the prisshe."

Although I have never seen it mentioned in any book, it seems clear to me that originally it was the practice in England, as it is still in other Christian countries, for the parishioners to offer the bread to be used at the Holy Communion. No doubt this was done at a time when the parishioners ordinarily communicated with the Priest. The parishioners seem to have had a course by which they, in turn, provided the loaf. In the course of years, the bread thus offered for the Communion was distributed after the service. This distribution, which is common in the East, is called the Antidoron, and was, I believe, called in the French *pain beni*. I am not sure if this distribution was made in England at the time of the Reformation, or if the loaf was represented by a money payment only. The money payment was twopence, which was collected every week from the families whose turn it was to offer the loaf. The collection was made by the Parish Clerk.

We find an allusion to this practice in an obscure passage in the Clerk's duties in the Parish books of St. Stephen's, Coleman Street. I call it obscure because it is written over an erasure, and is barely legible.

This passage reads as follows :—"Item. They shall be redy ev'y sonuonday after matens be sayd, to orden water and salte, and to cutte the holi loffe, s, ijd ob and a ob loofe for the cantille sub pena of a ob to the chirch to be payd. Item. They shall see the pfett of the curate in offeringys, in wax, in wyne, in brede."

It would seem from this that it was part of the Clerk's duty to cut the "holi loffe," the price of which was twopence ; but whether the loaf or the twopence was provided, is not clear.

The reformers of the Church of England adopted and availed of existing customs and institutions. The distribution of the bread was not made part of the custom of the Church of England, but an actual Communion was enforced, as appears from the rubrics of the first prayer book of Edward VI.

First there is a rubric plainly implying that the Holy Communion was to be celebrated daily except Wednesdays and Fridays ; afterwards the following direction—

"Likewise in chapels annexed and all other places there shall be no celebration of the Lord's Supper except there be some to communicate with the Priest and in such chapels annexed where the people hath not been accustomed to pay any holy bread there they must either make some charitable provision for the bearing of the charges of the Communion or else for receiving of the same resort to the parish Church."

There is then a provision made as to the description of the bread for the Communion ; the rubric then proceeds, "and for so much as the pastors and curates within this Realm shall continually find at their costs and charges in their cures sufficient bread and wine for the Holy Communion as oft as their parishioners shall be disposed for their spiritual comfort to receive the same. It is therefore ordered that in recompence of such costs and charges, the parishioners of every parish shall offer every Sunday at the time of the offertory the just value and price of the holy loaf with all such money and other things as were wont to be offered with the same to the use of their pastors and curates, and that in such order and course as they were wont to find and pay the said holy loaf ; also that the receiving of the Sacrament of the Blessed Body and Blood of Christ may be most agreeable to the institution thereof and to the usage of the primitive church, in all Cathedral and Collegiate Churches there shall always some communicate with the Priest that ministereth, and that the same may be also observed everywhere abroad in the country, someone at the least of that house in every parish to whom by course after the ordinance herein made it appertaineth to offer for the charges of the Communion or some other whom they shall provide to offer for them shall receive Holy Communion of the Priest, the which may be the better done for that they know before when their course cometh and may therefore dispose themselves to the worthy receiving of the Sacrament, and that him or them, who doeth so offer the charges of the Communion and other who be then Godly disposed thereunto shall likewise receive Communion, and by this means the minister having always some to communicate with him may accordingly solemnize so high and holy mysteries with all the suffrages and due order appointed for the same, and the Priest on the week day shall forebear to celebrate communion except he have some that will communicate with him."

This rubric is not repeated in the second Prayer Book of King Edward VI. 1552, but the practice of the contribution by houses is referred to thus :—"The bread and wine for the Communion shall be provided by the curate and the churchwardens at the charges of the parish, and the parish shall be discharged of such sums of money or other duties which hitherto they have paid for the same by order of their houses every Sunday." In Queen Mary's reign all this was altered, but on Queen Elizabeth's accession the order of the second Prayer Book of King Edward VI., in this respect, was re-enacted.

It was, no doubt, this alteration in the rubric which caused the parish to determine "that the ii$^{d.}$ ob is to be gathered every Sundaye by the sexton wch was won to serve for holy breade and nowe to serve for wyne for the communion table." There is the following minute which shows that the collection of the 2$^{d.}$ was afterwards discontinued and the bread and wine paid for out of the parish funds. A.D. 1570. "It was further agreed yt ye charge of the communio^{n} bred and wyne should be at ye cost of ye pishe hereafter, and to be in ye accōptes of ye church wardes."

The only other minute in this connexion is one fixing the times for the Holy Communion. This will be found at page 10. "At the same vestry it was condescended and agreed that once wth in the space of sixe weekes thear shal be a communion."

In other parishes in the city the Holy Communion was celebrated once a month, and the information afforded by the Records with regard to the church services and the time and mode of performing them is often very interesting.

I would instance this by two quotations from the minutes of St. Michael's, Cornhill, which I have before quoted. In the year 1563 the parish determined that "the first Sunday of every month the communion of Christ's body and blood should be read out and ministered." "The second Sunday children and servants after evening prayer to be catechised."

In 1568 the parish determined as follows :—" All Hallowes Day." "Att this vestre itt was agreed that upō evere Sonday there showld be a destens betwixthe the morning prayer and the pistill and gospell, and the lattine of the spayce of one ower or there abowtts, to the ede thatt such svantts and otheres as could nott to cū fyrste morning prayer att the leeste they might cu untto ye pystill gospell and littany."

Other illustrations might be given, but I have not yet come across any other instance of an allusion to a collection for the holy leaf or for holy bread.

In 1662 in the revised Prayer Book the rubric was altered to a simple direction that the bread and wine at the Communion shall be provided by the curate and the Churchwardens at the charges of the parish.

I must defer a longer notice of the contents of these books until I can make it more comprehensive and general, than can be done in an introduction.

I cannot conclude without expressing again my obligations to my friend, Mr. Welch, of the Guildhall Library, for the valuable assistance he has afforded me.

5, Bank Buildings, London,
February, 1886.

ST. CHRISTOPHER LE STOCKS.

MINUTES OF VESTRY MEETINGS.

The iij day of februare the obeet of John Gedney . . . . . spent in the quier & the Rest to the . . . in the bode of the cherche

A^{o} D 1579 26 of february

. . . . . ced of straungers beynge sicke in my p̃ishe as licenced to eate [flesh ac]cordyng to ye s^{d} acte of parlemẽt helde at westminster . . . day of January In ye fyveth yeare of ye queenes ma^{ts} R^{n}

By me Bartholomew bowsfell p̃son of S^{t}
[Christoph]er by ye Stockes in londõ

It is condysendyd and ag[reed] . . . . . of a vestrye the ix . . . . thatt whereas goodman overton . . . . . hathe broken a serten cloth . . . . gold . . . . . clothe y^{t} ye goodman o[ver]ton . . . . . for xij ownes at v^{s} [the] owne . . . . the gold comyng thereof . . . . . ys content to geve it . . . . . the losse yff anye losere and sa . . . the . . . . . com̃vnyon cupe the [they] are cõtentt . . . . . for eu'ye [every] ownce thereof . . . . . Rayte as a nother goldsmythe wyll . . . . . the lyke also they are agreyd thatt . . . . . shall allowe for the challys for . . . . . d and halfe q^{t} iiij^{s} x^{d} for eu'y . . . . .

Also the vestrye hathe greyd the . . . . . thatt Hen fridantt yoman shall have . . . . . wagys for one yere to begyne at . . . . . next iij^{li} and xviij^{d} a weeke tyll . . . . . begyn

m^{d} that the xiiij daye of dessemb[er] the goodman overton browght in his akownt before the m̃ of the presshe and by the same akownt hyt dowthe appere that the seyd over[ton] dothe owe vnto the presshe the som̃ of vj^{li} vj^{s} vij^{d} of the wch sũ the masters of the parreshe are contented to abat him xlij^{s} aponne kondes[ion] that w^{t} in viij dayes after this dat the seyd ŵ overton dow bryng in and paye vnto m^{r} forrman for the yewse of the parresshe iiij^{li} iiij^{s} vij^{d} and yf the seyd overton dow not paye the seyd mone akordeng as above seyd then hyt is hereby agred by the consent of all the m̃ of the paresshe that the seyd ovarton shall paye thes holle som̃ wch he owes w^{t} owt anye rebatmẽt wch is vj^{li} vj^{s} vij^{d}

harry becher — per me george ffreman
thomas benneste' — thoms lavrns
thomas basford
wyngot

Thes be the p̃sells . . . goods and ornaments of the churche of seynt Chrystophers fownde yn the same churche the xxiiijth day of Julye A^{o} 1559 taken ynto the warde & kepyng of John Whithed & gyles Event wardens at that tyme of the same churche ij a.

In pms a chalyce & a patent weynge viij oncs e[ach] & e[ach] p^{t} p[ar]c[ell] gylt
It a ~~cross of coper & gylt w^{t} the foote allso gylt~~
It a ~~payer of laten candellstycks~~
It a ~~sen̄s of laten~~ — thes pcells ar sold
It iij ~~bells of laten to sett tap̃s yn for the roode lofte~~
... a ~~holy wãt stocke of pewter~~
... a pyxe of pewt^{r}
... a ~~chrismatory of pewter~~
It on̄ altare clothe of nettyłł clothe & ij towells of nettyłł clothe
It ij playne [tabell] ~~alltare~~ clothes & ij playne towells
It on̄ old [tabell] ~~alltar~~ clothe of dyaper
It a vestyment w^{t} ij tunycles of clothe of gold ~~w^{t} an albe~~
It a red vestyment of saten of bruges ~~w^{t} an albe~~ *brok*
It a cope of blew vellvet w^{t} flowres of golde
It ~~ij~~ j herse clothes of clothe of golde
It an olde herse clothe w^{t} a red cross
It iiij alltare clothes on̄ of them ys crymsyn vellvet & an̄ other of them red velvet bothe be sett w^{t} flowrys of gold & on of red damaske w^{t} flowres of golde & on̄ of them ys fustyân apes w^{t} flowres of gold
~~It a corporas case & a corporas clothe~~
It a turky carpet to lay vnder foote before ye Alter
~~It a vayle of lynnen to drawe ov'thwarte the pyx~~ solde
It vij surpluses for men & ij for chylderne
~~It ij grayles & iiij antyphonaryes on of them yñ prente~~
~~It ij masse books & ij hympnalls & v p̃cessyon booke & a manuełł~~
~~It ij gret legends & ij psalters~~
~~It a lynen clothe paynted w^{t} the takyng downe of chryst frõ ye cros~~ brent
~~It iij baner clothes for crosses paynted & gylded~~ brent
~~It a lampe of laten y^{t} hong yn the body of ye chirche~~ solde
It a deske of laten

by me gyles Everet

~~*Item a com̃unyon . . .*~~
~~*It iij lit woll clothes on of tawny(?) wol & on of fustyan & a . . . .*~~

The xth of m'che in a^{o} 1559 Jhõn overton was chosen churche w[arden] . . . . gyles Everet & for Audytors ys chosen m^{r} forman m^{r} Ja . . . . . wormałł & Jhon Kelke si l.

The vij[th] of Decem̄ . . .

Md at the next meting to talke of the . . . . . that remayneth in m[r] Jaks the Churchewardens . . . . . is retourned home

The xxv[th] of february 1561 acc the c[om]putacōn of Englonde

The daye and yeare aboue in a comon vestry yt was agreed that the parishe shall haue and receyve to ther vse the rent of a shedde in the Churche yard w[th] whitley Carpenter occupiethe *att v s the yerly rent therof*

Item that the pson shall haue and receyve to his v[se th]e yerlie rent of a certaine comodite of ground to [keepe] bourds in, in the occuping of m[r] whiteheade

The Parishe also are condescended, that in consideracōn that M[r] Beacher shall at his proper costs and charg[es] beare all suche costs and charges, as shall from tyme to tyme be necessary for the repayring and amending of a certaine water fall & course in the churche yard comyng throwgh his ground they shall yerlie pay in acknowledging of a rente xij[d], and towching such reparacōns as shalbe necessary for the Mouthe of the same water fall in the Churcheyard yt is agreed, that the parishe shall beare the one halfe, and M[r] Beacher shall beare the other.

Item that the person shall pay to the vse of the churche for a vale, that he had, vj[s] viij[d] for a frame of the Organes, vj[s] viij[d] ... ... } xiij[s] [iiij[d]]

Yt is also agreed that suche Ornaments as are remayning in the Churche shalbe sold by M[r] Beacher, and suche as he shall adioyne wth hym, for the most pffitt that can be ~~wth the consent of the paryshe~~

M Rd of m[r] phelpott by me Harry becher for hes dett above wrytten the wyche ys put In to my acowmpt of thys yer a[o] 1562 as In the sam̄ aperythe ... ... } xiij[s] iiij[d]

The xij day of July 1562 att a vestrey kept wer chosen awdetturs for John Jacks acowmpt thes psons her namyd
m[r] forman
m[r] yonge
m[r] bassford
John Kelke

The xxvij[th] day of sept'bar 1562 at a vestrye kept the sayd day wer elecktyd & chosen Colecktors for the powa' to saye
Robartt Horne groc'
w[m] Weldon habdasher
for thes yer nyxt Insewyng

M[d] that m[r] phelpott pson hathe the kaye of the cherchyard of the grett dore, and of the wyckett, mynte and the taylar & cortys hathe etha' of them a kaye &c[r]

The xxiiij day of febrewary 1562 apon sent matheyas daye A vestrey keptt

Thomas barens merc' clecktyd & chosen cherchewardyn for the yer Insewyng & so an notha' afta' acordyng to the awnsyent ordar
m[r] forman
John kelke
m[r] welden
m[r] lorans

M[d] a festrye kept the xxx day of maye 1563. iij b

M wher ytt was Condesendyd and agreyd that wher as adam wormall & stephen barrowe ar In dettyd to the pyshe of sent Crystofars In the som of iij[li] for that they stond bond for John ova'ton latt of thes pyshe that an acsyon shall be Comensed agaynst them for the sayd dett for that they wythe owtt acksyon do Refews to paye the sam wyche dett aperyth apon the fott of harry bechars acownpt delyv'yd vp thes day to thomas larens &ct'

M allso then agreyd thatt John menty hes wages shalbe awgmentyd vn to the som̄ of lvjs ayer wyche ys xiiijs the qta' be seds the xijd aqtar for washeyng the lennyn to be gen at owr lady day last past and so to Contenew apon hes good behavor & at the goodwyll & plesur of the pyshe &c'

a vestrey keptt the xxv day of marche beyng our lady day a[o] 1564

Thomas Bassford chosen cherchewardyn for thes yer to Com from sent mathews daye past to sve afta' the old Costom of the pysh In the sam Rom
awdytturs chosen for m[r] barnes acowmptt
m[r] forman
m[r] lorans
m[r] garna'
thomas heron

M xx pamhetts [payments] of cherchewardyns acownpts dd to m[r] bassford the sam' daye & the cherche bocke

m[d] that the povr mans boxe was broken oupe for takyng of ij keyes the xxx daye of m'che an[o] 1564 In the p[r]sence of ow[r] mynyster m[r] lythall m[r] george forman m[r] thomas larrans to be destrybutyd to the powre In the p[r]ryshe the some beynge there In was fownde to be xxxix[s] Juste by me thomas basford and forwthe w[t] [forthwith] was bestowyde by m[r] forman & m[r] larrans & master yonge &c

the xviij daye of June An[o] 1564 a vestery kepte the sayde daye were chossen & eleckyte collectors for the poore for y[e]ere to cō ii a
thomas wylkes
wyllyam hyckmote

the keyes of the churche boxe are In the kypynge of John lythawll mynyster ij of them & theye other ij of me thomas basforde agreede apon y[t] yf y[e] keyes be loste the kypers to paye for them

The accowmpt of vs John kelke and ffelix Laurens collectors for the pore of crystys hospytall for the pishe of saynt crystovers geven vpe in octob[r] a[o] 1564

Recs̄ as foloweth

It of S[r] w[m] garret for xij monethes at vj[s] viij[d] the moneth Some	iiij[li]
of thomas wylks for xij monethes at iiij[d] the moneth ...	iiij[s]
of Edward sothworth for xij monethes at viij[d] p moneth ...	viij[s]
of w[m] welden for xij monethes at xvj[d] p moneth	xvj[s]
of thomas mons for xij monethes nothyng	
of m[r] cromton for xij monethes nothyng	
of thomas hearne for xij monethes at viij[d] p moneth	viij[s]
of m[r] harry becher for xij monethes at viij[s] p moneth	iiij[li] xvj[s]
of John gardenar for xij monethes at ij[s] p monethe	xxiiij[s]
of John kelke for xij monethes at viij[d] p monethe	viij[s]
of thomas Adams for xij monethes at iiij[d] p monethe ...	iiij[s]

of thomas wheatley for xij monethes at iiij^{d} p̄ moneth ... iiij^{s}
of thomas Laurens for xij monethes at viij^{d} p̄ moneth ... viij^{s}
of Robart thornton for x monethes at iiij^{d} p̄ moneth iij^{s} iiij^{d}
of Rychard merryot for xij monethes at iiij^{d} p̄ moneth ... iiij^{s}
of thomas basford for xij monethes at viij^{d} p̄ monethe ... viij^{s}
of adam wormall for ij monethes at vj^{d} p̄ mothe ... ... xij^{d}
of steven barrow for viij monethes at iiij^{d} p̄ moneth ... ... ij^{s} viij^{d}
of John whyt hed for xij monethes at iiij^{d} p̄ moneth ... ... iiij^{s}
of w^{m} colle for x monethes at iiij^{d} p̄ moneth ... ... iij^{s} iiij^{d}
of m^{r} forman for xij monethes at xx^{d} p̄ monethe ... ... xx^{s}
of m^{r} thomas barrow for xij monethes at xvj^{d} p̄ moneth ... xvj^{s}
of felix Laurens for xij monethes at iiij^{d} p̄ monethe ... ... iiij^{s}
of w^{m} hyckmot for xij monethes at iiij^{d} p̄ moneth ... ... iiij^{s}
of w^{m} throwgood for xij monethes at iiij^{d} p̄ moneth ... ... iiij^{s}
iv b. of John smythe for vj monethes at iiij^{d} p̄ moneth ... ... ij^{s}
of John yong for xij monethes at viij^{d} p̄ moneth ... ... viij^{s}
of m^{r} Banest^{r} for xij monethes at xvj^{d} p̄ moneth ... ... xvj^{s}
of gylls Evenet for ij monethes at iiij^{d} p̄ moneth ... ... viij^{d}
of John Jacks for xij monethes at xij p̄ moneth ... ... xij^{s}
of m^{rs} Jacks widow for xij monethes at iiij^{d} p̄ moneth ... iiij^{s}
of henry Roshall for iij monethes at iiij^{d} p̄ moneth ... ... xij^{d}
of antony whyt for xij monethes at viij^{d} p̄ moneth ... ... viij^{s}
of Raff Boswell for iiij monethes at iiij^{d} p̄ moneth ... ... xvj^{d}
of w^{m} poolle for xij monethes at iiij^{d} p̄ moneth ... ... iiij^{s}
of georg wooddrof for ij monethes at iiij^{d} p̄ moneth ... ... viij^{d}
of Rychard swarland for xij monethes nothing

Some of all the Reseytts by vs Rec^{d} as afore aperythe ... ... } xix^{li} x^{s}

Wherof is pd to the pore of owre p̄ishe as vnd^{r} aperythe fyrst to Jonne carlett widow for iij monethes at ij^{s} the monethe } vj^{s}
To Edward bawne for xij monethes at ij^{s} p̄ moneth ... ... xxiiij^{s}
To Wedow clebrowcke for xij monethes at xij^{d} p̄ moneth ... xij^{s}
To John mynton for xij monethes at viij^{d} p̄ monethe ... viij^{s}

The some of all that is p^{d} by vs to the pore of this p̄ishe as above sayde is } ij^{li} x^{s}

More p^{d} to the clarcke of thospitall as by his quyttans dothe apere the Rest of the some above gatheryd wth is ... } xvij^{li}

v a. In the p̄yshe off Seynt Crestoffers

m^{d} the xxj day of desemba^{r} 1562 the powa^{r} mens boxe wos openyd In the p^{r}sens of the p̄tys onda^{r} wrytten, wherIn ther wos fond In mony the so$\bar{m}$ of xxij^{s} ix^{d} wherof ther wos destrebewtyd the sam day vnto thes powa^{r} of thes sayd paryshe of sent crystofars and destrebewtyd by the hands of harry bechar & John Jacks cherche wardyns for that tym to saye som^{a} ... ... } xxij^{s} ix^{d}

to fatha^{r} bawne ... ... ij^{s}
to motha^{r} Carnell ... ... ij^{s}
to myntey the powa^{r} sexten of the sa$\bar{m}$ p̄yshe ... ij^{s}
to Claybrocks wydowe ... ... ij^{s}
to anthony a blynde powa^{r} man ... ... iij^{s} iiij^{d}
to Cowrtys wyffe In Cornyll whos husband wos p^{r}sona^{r} ... ... v^{s}
to Cowrtys wyffe In the cherche yard chargyd w chyldarn ... ... ij^{s}
} xviij^{s} iiij^{d}

so Restythe In the hands of harry bechar on of the sayd cherche wardyns that longythe vnto the powa^{r} the sayd day above sayd to be destrebewtyd when ytt shalbe apoyntyd by the sayd cherchewardyns & othars of the pyshe ... ... } iiij^{s} v^{d}

Wettneses to thes doyngs the sayd xxj day of desēba^{r} 1562
m^{r} fylpott p̄son John yonge
m^{r} forman w^{m} weldon
& harry bechar & John Jacks cherche wardyns

Rd the xviij day January 1562 at a commewnyon that wos gevyn for the vesse [use] of the powa^{r} ... } v^{s} v^{d}

apoyntyd for kepeng of the fower keyes of the cherche boxe to saye
harry bechar to keyes
thomas lorans to keyes

m^{d} the 3 day of aprell 1563 wos put In to the cherche boxe the mony that aperythe to Remayn above that longs to the powa^{r} in the p^{r}sents of m^{r} forman m^{r} yonge & m^{r} lorans ... ... } ix^{s} x^{d}
m^{d} that ther wos Rd at a co$\bar{m}$ynyon the 27 day of marche ... iij^{s}
m^{d} that ther wos Rd at a co$\bar{m}$ynyon the 4 day of aprell j^{s} vj^{d} ob
~~m^{d} that ther wos Rd at a comewnyon the 9 of maye 1563 som iiij^{s} vij^{d}~~

Som^{a} xiiij^{s} iiij^{d} ob

m^{d} transporttyd thes som that Remayethe vnto the nyxt sed·of thes leffe

The ix day of Aprell 1563 was gevyn to the powa^{r} of the pyshe off the boxe mony befor wrytten as owa^{r} v b.
To anthony the blynd man ... ... xvj^{d}
To old Bane ... ... xij^{d}
To motha^{r} Carell ... ... xij^{d}
To thomas Raynam ... ... xij^{d}
To Claybrocke wydow ... ... xij^{d}
To Corttys wyffe In cherche yard ... xij^{d}
To menty sextyn ... ... xij^{d}
To mothar spencke ... ... xij^{d}

Som viij^{s} viij^{d}

gevyn by Consent of harry bechar gorge forman & thomas lorans
so Rest In boxe v^{s} viij^{d} ob

Rd apon esta^{r} day at a comynyon 1563 som iij^{s} xj^{d}
Rd at a Comywnyon apon the 9 day of maye pott In boxe iiij^{s} vij^{d}
Rd at a comvnyon the vj daye of ffebruary 1564 for the powre mans boxe & there remaynythe stylle ... ... } ij^{s}

Resseuyde the x daye december An^{o} 1564 ow^{t} of ye powr mans boxe In the p^{r}sence of m^{r} george forman m^{r} lythall parson m^{r} larrance & m^{r} thomas basforde churche warden & destrybutyde as followythe
to father bawme ... ... xvj^{d}
to ye goodman slawter ... ... xij^{d}
to ye goodman dragon ... ... xvj^{d}
to the goodman mynton ... ... xvj^{d}
to the goodwyffe kelke wyddowe ... ... xvj^{d}
to the goodwyffe cleybrowke wydowe ... ... xvj^{d}
to the goodman Raynam taylowre ... ... xvj^{d}
to the goodwyffe tomson ... ... xx^{d}
to the goodman tomson ... ... xij^{d}
to the goodman felde ... ... xij^{d}
to the goodwyffe warcope ... ... viij^{d}
to the goodman holford ... ... x^{d} q^{r}
to the goodwyffe bentle wydowe ... ... viij^{d}

19^{s} 10^{d} q^{r}

In a westery kepte the xv daye of ap'll an^{o} 1565 whereIn ys electyd & chossyn m^{r} thomas banyster churchewarden to Joyn w^{t} thomas basford for ye yere to cō

Audytors chosen & apoynted at thys same vestery for thomas basford acovnte ~~master gardener~~ master kelke / thomas horne of ye old, m^{r} ~~Jakes~~ forman / m^{r} yonge the nve

A furder order takyn for ye stocke belongynge to ye churche and p'ryshe to be put fourthe to w^{m} weldon hande apon suffysyente suerties to be Repayed ageyne at iij monthes warnynge yf any shuche thynge hapyn to ye vse of ye p'ryshe ether ells at ye yers ende to be broughte In

A vestery kepte the xv daye of Jully An^{o} 1565 where In ys electyd & chossen w^{m} weldon churchewarden to Joyne w^{t} thomas basforde for thys yere to cō

more at thys vestery ys chossen colectors for the povre m^{r} hearne & Robard colson for ye yere to cō

at thys vestery yt ys agreed y^{t} w^{m} weldon shall make hys bond to ~~m^{r} bycher m^{r} forman~~ m^{r} alderman m^{r} bycher & to m^{r} forman

The xxij daie of December a^{o} 1565 The poore mens boxe was oppenyd in the pressence of John Leythall pson thomas basford & w^{m} weltdon churche wardens whearein was xix^{s} wch was the same daye distributed to thes poore people of the pishe whose names ffollowe after

It in prim^{s} father bawne had ... ... xviij^{d}

w^{m} slater had ... ... xij^{d}

xpover Battie had ... ... xij^{d}

Good man Dragon had ... ... xij^{d}

John myntyn had ... ... xx^{d}

Good man howson had ... ... xij^{d}

widdowe kelke had ... ... xij^{d}

widdowe hewes had ... ... xij^{d}

widdowe bentley had ... ... xij^{d}

Thomas exstall had ... ... xij^{d}

willm Tyerer shomaker had ... ... xij^{d}

Thomas curtys xij^{d} his mother in Law widdow Raynam xij^{d} ... ij^{s}

widdowe claybroke xij^{d} Robt thompson founder xij^{d} ... ij^{s}

John flowd xij^{d} willm sild xij tomson ye Carpinter vj^{d} ... ij^{s} vj^{d}

Som^{a} Geaven to them xix^{s}

Thaccompt of willm weltden and Robart horne collectors ffor the poore of christs hospitall ff Gatherid in the pishe of S^{t} xpovers next the Stocks ~~in the yeere of our~~ begon at mighellmas A^{o} Dñi 1562 vntill the feast of S^{t} myghuell A^{o} 1563 as pticullarly ffoloythe

It in prim^{s} of S^{r} w^{m} Garrard ffor a yeare ... ... iiij^{li}

of thomas mounes for x monethes at ij^{d} the monethe ... xx^{d}

of Ric stevenson for xij monethes after ij the monethe ... ij^{s}

of Edward Southwo'the for xij monethes after 4^{d} ... ... iiij^{s}

of willm yarryngton for iiij monethes after ij^{d} ye monthe ... viij^{d}

of willm weltden for xij monethes after 16^{d} ye monethe ... xvj^{s}

of thomas herne for xij monethes after viij^{d} ye monethe ... viij^{s}

of John kelke for xij monethes after vj^{d} the monethe, of adam wo'mall 6^{s} ... ... xij^{s}

of m^{r} henry Beacher for xij monethes after viij^{s} the monethe iiij^{li} xvj^{s}

of Thomas Brayfilde for iiij monethes after ij^{d} the monthe ... viij^{d}

of John Gardner for ix monethes after ij^{s} the moneth xviij^{s}

of Robart thorneton, Thomas addams, adam wheatley, widdow case Ric merryott, Stephen barrowe John whitthed w^{m} whickmote, willm thorrowgood, Jno yonge, m^{rs} Jakes widdowe, henry Russhall ffor xij monethes after iiij^{d} the monethe am^{ts} vnto ... ... } xlviij^{s}

of thomas Lawrence for xij monethes after viij^{d} & of thomas basford & anthony whitt for xij monethes & of Robt horne for x monethe am^{ts} to ... ... } xxx^{s} viij^{d}

of georg forman for xij monethes after xx^{d} the monethe ... xx^{s}

of Thomas Barnes for xij monethes after xvj^{d} the monethe ... xvj^{s}

of John smyth for x monethes of thomas curtys for ij mōthes after iiij^{d} ... ... iiij^{s}

of Thomas Banester for xij monethes after xvj^{d} ... ... xvj^{s}

of Giles evenett, m^{r} satturley, w^{m} poole, & Jno boswell fo^{r} 12 mōthes afte^{r} ij^{d} ... ... viij^{s}

of John Jackes for ix monethes after xij^{d} of gatton ij^{s} ... xj^{s}

Som^{a} Rc^{d} by me w^{m} Weltden am^{ts} to } xix^{li} xij^{s} viij^{d}

Whearof pd to the poore of our pishe as after followithe

first to Joane Carlill widdow for xij monethes after ij^{s} the monethe ... ... xxiiij^{s}

to Edward Bawne for xij monethes after ij^{s} the monethe ... xxiiij^{s}

to Anthony Argam for vij monethes after ij^{s} ye monethe ... xiiij^{s}

to wyddow claybroke for xij monethes after xij^{d} the monethe xij^{s}

to John Myntyn flor xij monethes after viij^{d} the monethe ... viij^{s}

Som^{a} pd vnto the poore of this pishe am^{ts} to } iiij^{li} ij^{s}

Payd vnto the Clarcke of thospittall ffor the Rest Gatherryd in this pishe as apperethe by the treasorers . . .. } xv^{li} x^{s} viij^{d}

A vestrie holden the xxiiijth of m^{r}che A^{o} 1565

It in this vestrie yt is agreed y^{t} the Glass windowe ou^{r} the pticicon betwene the quyer & bodie of the churche to be mendid at the pishes cost

m^{d} Thomas Banester is elected & chosen for churchwarden for this yere to come

Audito^{rs} for Thaccopt of w^{m} weltden

m^{r} herne, m^{r} yong } old m^{r} barnes, m^{r} Gardner } the newe { & they To sytt on Sattarday next

yt is agread y^{t} the churche w'dens shall make certyn Setes or formes aboute the comonyon table

yt is also agreed y^{t} the wall at the northe Dore of the churche shalbe heythened as moche as nede shall Requyer & y^{t} m^{r} pson shall mend the Dore of the churche y'd at his Coste

A vestrie kept the xxiijth Daie of Junij 1565

at this vestrie is elected & chosen collectores for the pore for this yeare to Come, Jno Gardiner and Thomas tyrrell Grocers, and to take their Charge at maghellmas next according to the order

and it is further agreed thatt thomas addams shall haue the vawte vnder the churche ffor v^{s} Rent by the yeare So far as Convenyent place may be founde for the Laying of the Deade mens bones in, and to begyn now att Mydsom^{r} A^{o} Dñi 1566.

A vestrye the xxiiijth of february 1566

Att this vestrye was Electid and chosen m^{r} George forman for this ij yeares to be churche warden

Also yt is agreed thatt the churche wardens and Jno yonge & Thomas Basforde to vewe ye bill of clarks wages & bring their Report therof to m^{r} alderman garrard & m^{r} alderman beacher to fynishe yt also awdito^{rs} for the Accompt of m^{r} banyster

Thomas barnes, John gardner } old — John hutton, fraunces Lambarde } new

Also yt is agreed y^{t} the churche wardens shall se the cloke p̄vsed by the advice of a man of knowledge & also mendid or new made as nede shall Requier so y^{t} yt may be a good & p̄ffytt cloke.

also y^{t} m^{r} fforman shall putt in sewerties for the churche stocke accordinge to the order taken at the Receving of the same bettwene this & whittsontide next

b. at vestry cawled & samhede [? summoned] the vijth day of Jwly it whas agrede that Jhon howtton & thomas adamys Do be the colactars for this yer Insewynge from the feste of synte Myelle fforwarde it ffordars agreide at present tyme That whyllām whelldon & adam whattle & mastare sowtton to be sswarn & to sarche thru the thry years of the chawrge for amendmente Thar of and fordar to Inqwyar and sartyfe at the nexte vestrye ffor the makynge of Convenynte syttes abowght the Comynyon The tabelle

A^{o} Di 1568, 25 of marche

Chvrchewardens for ye yeare fololowyng George formā Edwarde Sutheworth

Auditours for ye accompte for ye churche

John Hutto^{n} felix lawrence Thomas Tyryll & to make an ende of theire accompte betwixte this & whitson tyde next

forther yt is agreed in this vestere y^{t} Addā whettlye shall have in lease for xxjth yeares ye sheed in ye corner by ye p̄son[age] paying for ye same to ye p̄ishe yearely x^{s} & to be bounde wthin ye space of ij yeares next foloweyng to bylde yt

A^{o} D. 1568 Septēb 5

yt was agreed in a vestrie y^{t} Thomas Basford w^{m} weldo^{n} Jhon yonge Thomas Adams Richard Byllingesley together wth ye churche-wardēs George formā Edward southeworth shall uewe [view] & make reporte cōcerning ye sheed by ye p̄sonage in ye churche way & howe muche grounde more he shall have vnto ye same, & reporte to be made hereof to ye aldermē vpō S^{t} mathewe his day next

A vestry holden the xxiiijth of february A^{o} 1568

Att this vestry John yonge is chosen churchewarden for thes two yeares to Come wth Edward southworthe thother churche warden

Auditours for m^{r} formans accompt for thes two yeres past

Thomas barnes, Thomas basford } thold — felix Lawrens, Thomas Tyrrell } the newe

And yt is agreed that thawditors shall awdit the said Accompts before maye Daie next and thatt at or befforc may daie m^{r} forman shall dellyu^{r} the stocke of the p̄ishe to his successor.

a. A vestrye holden The xxiiijth of february A^{o} 1569
Et An^{o} R^{ni} Rne Elizabethe &c xij^{mo}

At this vestry Thomas Addams skynn^{r} ys ellectyd and chosen to be Churche warden for two yeares to Come wth m^{r} yonge thother church warden. And it is agreed that the said Addams accordinge to the fform^{r} order Taken shall putt in twoo sufficient sewerties ffor the Churche stocke and Geave a cart loade of great coales to the poore As others befforc by thagrement of the hole p̄ishe haue Done & promesed To doe.

Allso This daie w^{m} weltden did dellyu^{r} vnto the Churche wardens his monny ffor to brye a lode of Coles ffor the poore according to his fform^{r} promesse wch was behynde vnpaid ffor the Tyme that he had The said churche stocke

Awdytars for m^{r} yongs Acownt

Thomas tvrryll, ffelix Lawrens } thold — Edwarde sothworthe, w^{m} welden } the new

A vestry holden The xxth daie of Junii A^{o} 1570

At This vestrye Robart yoarde & John Mathewe ar chozen Collectors ffor the poore of thospitall and they to begyn their Collectyon the first sonday of october next according to the old accustomed order

In this vestry yt is agreed by generall Consent y^{t} ffrom henceffortlie who so eu^{r} shall byd or desiere the p̄ishon's to goe To offer at an offerrynge wheare any marryadge is wthin the Cyttie the same p̄son shall geave twoo pence to the poore mens boxe of this p̄ishe and the churche wardens to call ffor the same & se yt be putt into the said poores boxe

A^{o} D 1570 24 of february

It was agreed by a vestre y^{t} foelix lawrēce should be ye churchwarden in m^{r} yonge his place

It was forther agreed y^{t} ye charge of ye cōmuniō bred & wyne should be at ye cost of ye p̄ishe hereafter & to be in ye accōptes of ye churchwardēs

The auditors for m^{r} Adams accōptes

1 Edward Suthewicke
2 willeā weldē
3 George foreman
4 Clemēt kelke

M^{d} That thear ys to be Received yearely out of the m'chant Taylo^{rs} haull at the hands of the wardens of the same Company the some of Tenne shillings wch is of the Gyfte of m^{rs} p̄sons wyddowe and is to be Received at the feast of Chrystmas } x^{s}

Item The Comvnyon Cupp and the Cover of Sylver all Gilte weyinge nynetene ounes Restynge in Implement

A Vestry holden the 17 of Jvne 1571

At this Vestry Edward Dowtye and thomas sprage are chosen collettors for the pore of the ospytall and they to begyn there coleccyon the fyrste sonday in octobr nexte Acordyng to the old costom

A Vestry holden the 25 of Jvly a^{o} 1571

At this vestry are chosen to be sessars for the clarcks wages these p̄tes folowen

m^{r} forman
m^{r} sothwell
m^{r} clement celke
m^{r} welden
felix Lawrens m^{r} barnes
thomas adams
} To be Ended & don beffore the xxvth of m'che next

A Vestry holden the xxv[th] of february A° 1571

At this vestrye yt agreed That for so moche as ffelix Lawrens ys deptid out of this Lyffe thatt Thomas addams shall supplye his Rome ffor the yere To come, and That Addam wheatly shalbe thother church warden ffor these two next yeres to com

Att this Vestrey is chosen ffor Auditors of felix Lawrens Accompt These p̄sons following

m[r] fforman
Clement kelke
henry bowyer
Rowland Elryngton

It is agreed that the organs & the cloke shalbe sold by the churchwardens and twoo other of the p̄ishoners that ys m[r] yong & w[m] weltden.

Item yt is agreed thatt m[r] beacher wth thassent of m[r] p̄son and the churche wardenss may sett vpp a tombe ffor his ffather wheare he & they shall thinck yt meete for the same to stond in ye churche

psōns pñt at this vestry

m[r] Duffild p̄son	Tho Tyrrell	John Mathew
m[r] Tho Barnes	Tho addams	Ric' Smallwood
m[r] henry Beacher	adam wheatley	Thomas wilks
Clement kelke	henry bowyer	Thomas Cotton
Jn° yonge	henry allwarde	John Leaves
Thomas Basfourd	w[m] thorowgood	Ric' howson
w[m] weltden	Roger Rigson	

a A vestrye holden the xj[th] daie of Maij A° 1522

The bill of the clarcks wages Last sessid was Redd at this vestrye and theare Conffirmed accordinge to the said sessinge thearof w[ch] was Don & made the xx[th] daie of aprill Last past.

In this vestry also yt was agreed that for as moche as the Leades Coverrynge the churche is verry moche in decay & by often sowdrynge of yt is ffounde to be the worrsse & n[ot] the bettar thatt the churche wardens shall Cawse a plumber to newe cast ffve six or se[ven] sheetes of the same & so to Laye the same againe that theareby the p̄ishe may vnderstand what the charges wilbe to new cast and Cover the whoale churche and thearafter to vse the same.

A vestry holden the xxix[th] of Junij A° 1572

Att this vestrye ys chosen to be Collectours ffor the poore ffor this next yeare To Come Raphaell Smythe and henry allwarde And they to begyn their Collection at the sonday next after migellmas next according to the accustomed order

A vestrey holden the xxiiij[th] daye of ffebruary in Anno 1572

Att this vestrye Thomas Turrell groc' is chosen churche warden fo' Towe yeres too come withe Addame whettlowe thoth' cherchewarden

yet is fardar agreed at this vestry that wher as yt was apoynted that the clocke should have byne Sowld yt is nowe agred that yt shalbe kepte, and one too be apoynted too kepe yt goinge and to have for the keping of yt vj' viij[d] by the yere.

Allso yt is agreed that ther shall be a new bibell bowght. And the owld bibell is Sowld to John yonge for xiij' iiij[d]

A vestry holden the v day of July 1573

at thys vestrey Rowland Elryngton and harry bowyar ar chossen collecturs for the pore of the ospytall and they to begyne there collecyon the fyrst sonday in october next ackordyng to y[e] custume

A Vestrey holden the xj day of october 1573

at thys Vestrey ar Chossen ffor the awdytt of addam whettleys a Cowntt ffor thys yeres Charge these p̄ssons ffollying

m[r] goreg fforman
m[r] harry bechar
Rowland Elryngton
Edward dowghtey

A Vestery houlden the xxvij day of Dessēbar an° 1573 ix b.

at this vestery yt is agreed that the paryshe shall paie the Charges of the Repa'yng of the shed . . . . yng vs wch adam whelley Churchwarden mvst pay toward yt & that from hensfourth he shall Repayer the Sayd Shed at his Chorst & chargis & Soo for his Rent to Contyne tenant wch is fyve shyllings a year to be payd to the paryshe

It ys agreed that the parson yf he Can help the paryshe to Recovar all the moñy that John Baker clarke to the Court of Cōsyences* hauth in his hands of the parryshes that the parson shall hau the on haufe therof barying haufe the charges & standyng bond as the pa'yshe by the ockacyon therof shall

It ys agreed that mente ou' sexton hauth a yeares lebarty to provyd for him a house nerar to the paryshe

a vestrey holden the vij day of marche 1573 where at theire wase Chossen Rychard swarland Churche warden ffor too yeres to Come wth thomas tyrrell the other church warden.

A vestry holden the xxvj[th] of september 1574

At this vestry m[r] harry beache' & Ric Rygbye ar chosen collectours for the poore ffor One yere next Comynge & to begynne the first sonday of october accordinge to the accustomed order.

A vestrie holden the xiiij[th] of novemb[er] A° 1574

Att this vestry is Chosen Collectours ffor Thomas Tyrrells accompt by them to be auditted beffore the

Edward Dowghtie
Ric Candler
John yonge
henry bysshopp

Yt ys agreed that the churchwards wth the helpe of adam wheatley shall take order ffor the Repayryng of the Leades ouer the quyer and the churche wardens to Disbourse the mony that shalbe Laied out vppon the same w[ch] m[r] p̄son hathe agreed & is Content to Repay the same againe by xx' yearly vntill it be pd

yt is furthe' agreed thatt the churche wardens wth adam wheatly shall Lykewise take order ffor the Repayrynge of the Leades & stone worke of the steeple

yt is agreed that the churche wardens shall do their best ffor the sellyg of the organs the cloke and the Egle of brasse to the most beneffitt of the p̄ishe

yt is agreed thatt m[r] fforman m[r] hutton m[r] yong & m[r] busshopp wth m[r] p̄son shall do their endevo' ffor the getting of the money out of Jn° Bakers hands by order of the busshopp or otherwise, and allso . . . . [illegible]

It is agreed at this vestrey thatt the bill ffor the clarcks wages shalbe seased againe by these p̄sons ffollowinge x a.

George fforman	
~~John yonge~~	m[r] Beacher
m[r] Busshopp	Rowland elryngton
Tho Turrell	willm weltdon
Jn° hutton	Richarde Candler

* A photograph of this entry is given, as this the most important word is doubtful.

Md yt is further agreed thatt thold Dewties for clarks wags dewe vntill . . . . . . Last shalbe pd accordinge to the formr seasement

A vestrey holden the xx day of ffebruary 1574

At thys vestrey ys Chossen willyam thowrogood churche warden ffor too yeres to Come wth Rychard swarland the other churche ward[en] allso yt ys ordred that the churche wardens shall suffer no body to drey no Clothes in the church leeds

Md a Vestry houlden the xx day of marche ano dni 1574

yt is agreed that the byll of the clarkes wages beying newly Sessed by mr gorge forman mr becher mr busshoup mr weldon thomas teryll Rouland eldarton John hutton & Rychar Candlar & shall stand from Crysmas Last past for there [three] years to com and aftar the iij yeares all such as haue byn Raysed by thes sessers to be pulled down to the pims they ware afour

It is furdar agreed in this Vestery that all suche as shall refuse to pay as they ar Sessed for this iij yeares the churche wardens shall show the sessors therof & they shalbe Cauled beffour them and yf they wyll not be parswaded by them to pay as they ar sessed then the churchwardens shall shew them in the ordynarys Court at the Coust & charges of the parysh a Cordyng to an ansyentt or Dar hear in this boak wretten

at this Vestery ar chosen for the audett of Rychard swarland a Countt for his yeares charges thes parsones foloweng

mr welden	Rychard candelar
~~mr bushope~~	thomas teryll & mr allyn

the a Count to be mayd the last day of august 1576.

The Inuytory of all the Impell ments yn the churche of Saynt xhrystofar' left in the hands John mente Clarke of the paryshe & then delyvered vnto him by the hands of wm thorowgood Curche warden the 22 day of march ano dni 1574 as foloweth

Item a comvnyon tabull
Itē j Dyap tabull Clouth
Itē ij towells of Calacow clouth
Itē j towell playn of holand
Itē 2 pattens of pewtare
Itē j peutar pottell wyn poutt
Itē j peutar quart wyn poutt
Itē j gathered surples
Itē j playn Surples
~~Itē a Clouk w'oute any led to yt~~
Itē a payer of orgaynes
Itē 2 ladars
Itē j playn forme
Itē j shovell & 2 Couffens
Itē j Couffen for a chynd
Itē 2 futt passes
Itē j lytell Cobard standyng in the Chansell
Itē j bouke of beryeng & xkrystenyng
Item an ould turkett tabull Clouthe
Itē j tabull clouth of fustyan anapes spangled wt gould

Itē j other of Red Velvett spangled wt gould
Itē j tabull clouth of Calacow egeg abouth wt sylke
Itē a tabull Clouth of holland
Itē ij Joynd formes wth matts to them
Itē ij bybells j parrafyses 2 Sarves boukes
Itē 4 Sautters & j lytell Sarves bouke
Itē an egell of brasse
Itē j heares Cloath of tesshew Clouth
Itē j other of Red Damaske spangled wth gould
Itē a Cover payn of holand that mr forman gave
Itē a tabull of the x comāndements of Clouth of sylver
Itē a tabull of the Comāndements prynted
Itē a forme to lyfft vp & Downe wt ij fett of yearn [iron]

Itē ij bard chest a yearn & iij wanskott cobards in the Vestery
Itē ij bouxses to gather for the poure

Itē a box wt iij kayes standyng at the enteryng in to the Curch to putt in mony for the poure

Item a Comvnyon Cupe wt a kever of Syllver & gyllt & pattē of Sylver and gylte Remaynes in the hands of the Corche warden wm thorowgood

A vestry houlden the x day of June ano 1575 for the Chosseng of the Collectors for the ospytall whar it is agreed that Wyllyam Rydar & nycolas barnsly ar Chossen for this yeare } wm rydar nycolas barnsly

A Vestery houlden the xv day of Jenary ano 1575 for the chosen of the syd men where yt is agreed that hary boyar & gorge paradyne & mr candelar & Rychard heyes

allso yt is furdar agreed at this Vesstery that the parson & mr Candelar & the ij curche wardens shall se the a Count of the Colectours for the pour wo payes & wo pay not & what they haue Ressevcd

A vestrye Howlden the 25 february 1575 for the chewssynge of the churche warden where yt ys agreede mr Henry Bechere He to serve for 2 yeres to come wth willyam thoroughgoode

at this Vestrey houlden the 20 day of august ano 1576 ar Chosen Colettours for the poure gorge paradyn & Robart Coudny for this year to Com

allso it is agreed at this Vestrey by the Consent of the houll paryshe that a poure woman in this paryshe named Wedow Claybroke shall haue the Rent of her house in the ally that she Dwalls in Payd for her every year quartarly vnto the landlord so long as she leveth by the paryshe wch is xiijs iiijd a year

At the vestrie holden the 16 daye of Decembar Anno 1576 there [are] chosen for the Awditt of Willm Thorowgood account ffor the last yere past Being Churche warden viz

Thomas Tyrrell	ffrauncis Gountter
mr allen	nicholas Barnsley

The same accompt to be ffynished beffore the last of Januarie next

At a vestrie holden the 20 daye of Januarie Anno 1576 Being present the worshipfull Mr Alderman Dixe and the hole parishe Ther was chosen for Churchwarden harry Boyer for ij yeares to come wth ~~henry~~ mr Beacher

At the same vestrie was also chosen for syde men ffor this present yere ffrauncis Gounter and Adame whetly mr Allen and mr Ramsey

At the same vestrie Request was maid that ther might be some learned man apoynted to Read a lecter in this prishe twise a weke and for the mayntenaunce therof A collection should be made of the benevolence of the prisheners to thentent it might be knowen what the same wold Amount vnto ffor the doing wherof ther was apoynted Mr Boyd and Mr Allen to travall wth the prishners and to sett downe in writting what everyman is willing of his owen benevolence to geve yerly towards the same

At the vestery holden the xxjth of Aprell 1577 there was chosen for the audett of Harry bechr his acco for the yeare last paste beinge churche warden vyz

ffrauncs Guntr }	Willm Througoode
nycolas barneslye }	Harry Aylworthe

the same accompt to be fynyshed by the last of this monthe

At the same vestrie yt ys agreed that m^{r} ffuller wth the two churche wardenes shall take care to apoynt some learned man for the readinge of a lecture from mychelmas next to Ester followinge & to bestowe vpon the said lecturer as to them shalbe thought convenyent

ffurder yt ys apoynted that these men followinge shall make a new sessemẽt of the Clarks wags vyz the first gatheringe for the first q̃rt^{r} to begynne at mydsom̃er

m^{r} Allen	m^{r} Guntter
m^{r} Tyrrell	Harry bech^{r}

At the Vesterye Holden the 19 of Janũ 1577 was chosen sessers to sees the skevengers bille m^{r} welden m^{r} whetleye m^{r} swarland

It ys agreed to haue a newe booke boughte for the kepinge of the regester of maryeges chrysnynge & beryalles accordyng to the statute & to be newryten & to begyne at chrysmas laste & to be wryten by m^{r} layland ouer cewrate & over syne by the churchwardens

It ys agreed that some skylfull man haue the sighte of the cloke & ether to mend yt or chang yt or sell yt & be chusen for the same parpose ye churchwarden & m^{r} Allen & m^{r} Eldryngton & to bryng in there reports

It ys agreed that the cop[per] Egell & the orgens shall be solde by the churche wardens and m^{r} Allen

There ys chosen for cherchwarden wth Henry bowyer m^{r} Elderyngton

It ys agreed that these psones that hathe ye doynges for the cloke shall haue the barres of the chansell to be cote done & to be solde for the moste provete & to be done in the beste forme & maner, & the pwlpete to be altered by theire dyscressyon, & to berne s'ten olde papest bookes wch remayned in ye vestery.

It ys agreed to gather goodmens Devossyon at s'ten sarmons wch shall be thought good by the dyscressyon of the churchwardens & collecters of the pore

At a ffestery holden the seconde of ffebruary 1577 was chossen Awdeters for the churche wardens accompte m^{r} Ryder m^{r} candeler m^{r} hotten m^{r} wheteley

ffor sydmen Ric' gylmer
Jno notshalle

A vestry howlden the xviijth day of January Anno 1578

yt is agreed that soche mony as Rowland elryngton hathe in his hands being the Remaynar of soche mony as was in hys hands when a was Collectter for the poore wth mony is agreed shalbe putte into the power mens box in the churche

At this vestry m^{r} Tho allyn pewterer ys elected & chosen churche warden ffor this p'sent yere to come ffor Cornehill side in the place of m^{r} henry Bowyer whoase tyme is now owte & To Joyne wth m^{r} Elryngton.

At this vestry is ellected awditto^{rs} ffor m^{r} Elryngtons accompt

Ric Candler	George p'adyn
w^{m} Rider	m^{r} henry Beacher

At this vestry ys chosen ffor Sydemen
Humffry Streate And Ric hayes

yt is agreed at this vestry that mynten shall haue his qua'te' Rent dewe at o' lady day next

A vestry holden the xvth daie of february A^{o} 1578

At this vestry Thomas Cotton ys Elected & Chosen to be Clarcke of this p̃ishe. And shall have ffor his Sallarry ffower pounds yearely, and that he shall ffynde a suffycient p̃son to serve vnder hym at his cha'ge as sexten wheareby the p̃ishe may & shall be here after well & orderly Served, and his wages to begynne ffrom our Lady next viz the xxvth daie of m'che next

At this vestry ys agreed thatt mynten his widdow shall haue geaven her out of the pores boxe the some of fyve shillinges

The xvjth daye of ffebruarij A^{o} 1578

An Inuentory of all the Implements in the Churche of Sct xp̃ofor deliuered vnto Thomas Cotton by the hands of m^{r} Thom Allin churche warden

Item j Comunion Table w^{t} a frame
Itm ij formes wth foote paces joyned
Itm j playne fforme
Itm j dyap^{r} table cloth
Itm j table cloth of callico edged w^{t} silk
Itm j coverpayne of dyaper
Item ij Lytle olde Towells
Itm j patten of pewter
Itm j pottell pott of pewter
Itm j quart pot of pewter
Itm ij gatherd surpleses
Itm j playne surples old & torn
Itm j payer of organs
Itm ij ladders
Itm j lytle cobbart in ye chauncell
Itm ij coffins & j coffin for a chylde
Itm j book of christning & burying
Itm j olde turkey table cloth
Itm j table cloth of fustion a nap̃ls

Itm j table cloth of redd velvett spangled w^{t} gold
Itm j byle [bible] j paraphreses j sarvys booke
Item iiij olde salters & iij olde salme books
Itm ij s'vice books for ye xvijth of novẽber
Itm j hearse cloth of Tisshewe
Itm j cloth for the pulpet of damask spangled
Itm j table of the x com̃aundements of silver
Itm ij Iron barr chests in ye vestry
Itm j boxe w^{t} iij keys ent'ing to the churche
Itm ij boxes to gather monney
Item j shovell ij olde chests in the loft
Itm j Egle of Brasse or lattin
Itm̃ j homely Book
Itm̃ j sheete of leade & s'tayne old leade of ye glasse windows

At a vestry holden the xxviijth daye of June A^{o} 1579 xij

ffor the Chewsing of the collectors for the poore of christs hospitall at whiche vestry was chosen for the yeare following } Richard Candler, John Downes

m^{d} that thes was gedered in sent xoporfers prỹs towards the makyng of hastynge haven as yt apereth by a byll of enery mãgyst the som of … … … … } xx^{s} vij^{d}

At a vestry holden the xxvijth daye of September 1579 vpon complaynt made by dyvers of the p̃rish of great noyessances done by Roger Riggsbye by occacion of a sope howse newly Errected on the backsyde of the p'sonage as well to thar howses as in the waye leading from the p'sons howse vnto the streete whearvpon it is ordered by the concent of the whole p̃rishe the parson lykewyse havinge geven his concent to the same y^{t} ye great doore opening into the street shalbe kept locked & the key therof to remayne in the custody of the p̃rishe clark & y^{t} the tennants Dwelling w^{t}in the same Gate whoe have bin accustomed and vsed heartofore tyme owt of mynde to haue keyes of the same wicked ~~so that they may com in and owt at convenient~~ and none other p̃sons shall haue seuerall kaies of the lytle wycket to thintent that the same may be kept locked at convenient tyme

And moreou' it is Agreede at the same vestry y' Richard Robinson carpinter shall haue the sheadd in ye church yard syde by lease for the rent heartofore payde which lease is to be made vnto him by the p'son and churche wardens and vpon reasonable couenaunts to be Agreede vpon by the saide parson and churche wardens in ye name of ye whole prishe wth the advyse of maister ffvller

At a vestry holden the xj^th daye of October A° 1579 it was Ordeined & Decreede that non shall laye Any mann' of morter lome or any soile Agaynst the churche wall except that he or they first haue lycence of the churche wardens for otherwyse they shall paye to the churche wardens for eu'y suche tyme the som of Sixe shillings & eight pence in cūrrant money

At the same vestry it is Ordayned & decreed y' whereas Roger riggsbee by a vestry holden the xxvij^th of September shuld be debarred p'sently from ye way of the churche grounde going to his Sope howse that he the saide Roger riggsbee shall haue liberty to vse the same waye to bring in oyle or sope asshes & suche things for his occupying so that it bee done to as lytle noyance as maye be to the prishe or any othars and soe hee to haue and enJoye the same vntill Easter Even next commyng so farr furth as he wilbe bounde in the som of one hundreth pounds vnto the churche wardens for to Avoyde at the sayde tyme of Easter or ells the same graunt & tyme Lyberty to be voyde

S' xpofers at the stocks in London xiij^th day of Julij A° 1579

Item receaued for the first collection made in this prishe for A churche & hospitall newly repayered in Bathe } xxxv^s iiij^d
And more for the last collection made in this prishe ... xvj^d

At a vestry holden the xj^th day of marche A° 1579 was chosen Awdytors for the Accompt of Thomas Allyn church wa'den m' Ryder m' Candller m' Tapsfyld & m' Riggbey

xiij^th of m' 1579

Receaued of m' Alderman Dixsey for his lycens for eating fleshe to ye vse of the poore of the prshe ... ... } vj^s viij^d

At A vestry holden the xxvj^th daye of June A° 1580 for the choosyng of Collectors for the poore & for christs hospitall at whiche vestry was chosen for the yere following ... ... } henry tapsfeld & homphry stret

The xvij^th daye of July 1580 Richard Raynescroft & Arnold Richards chosen sydmen for ye yere following

The ix^th day of October 1580 at A vestry it was Agreede that the church wardens shuld paye the som of xiij^s iiij^d to m' Ramsay wch hee hathe payde by the Appointment of the pishe for widdow claybrok her howse rent behynd & vnpayd

The xviij^th day of December A° 1580 was chosen Churche warden wth M' Gunter in the Rowme of M' Thoms Allin, william Ryder to begenne his tyme at the feast of the birth of owre lorde god next ensewing

In the pishe of S' Christofers

At the vestry holden the xxix^th day of January 1580 There was a lease graunted vnto Nicholas Barnesly Cittizen and grocer of London of y' same iij tenamentes in ffleetstreete that were letten vnto Thomas Wytton as it doth and maye Appeare by writinge furthermore at large and the same Lease to bee geene at the birth of o' Lorde god Laste paste before theis p'sents for xxj yeares at vj^li xiij^s iiij^d yearely In wyttnes whereof theis psons beinge p'sent haue setto theire names

Ther is anew agrement afterwards on the other sid lefe

At A vestry holden the xxj^th day of maye A° 1581 was chosen Awditors for the Accompt of ffraunces Gunter churchewarden. m' Tirrell, maister Allyn, M' Tapsfyld & M' Riggbey

At this vestry it is Also condesended and Agreed that all suche howses in ye pishe as haue byn severall tenaments shall beare and paye all manner of cha'dges boothe to the churche & also ells what soeu' is to be chardged w' in ye warde & as they haue borne & payd A fore tyme

At a vestrye holden the xxix^th daye of Januarye anno Domini 1580 by the pson Churchwardens and the moste parte of the wo'shipfull pishoners of the pishe of S' xpofer at the Stocks in Loundoun yt is ordered condecended and fully decreed by the aforesaid pson Churchwardens and pisshoners of the pishe aforesayed that A Lease of iij tēnts nowe beinge iiij wth thapp'tenñts late in the tenure of Thomas Witton or his Assignes lyinge in the pishe of S' Dunstons in the West shoulde be made by the pson and Churchwardens aforesaid wth the consent of the moste parte of the pisshioners to Nicholas Barnesley cittizen and grocer of Londoun and to his Executors and assignes for the terme of ~~xxj~~ yeares to comence from the ~~birthe of o' lorde god laste paste~~ expiracon of the lease graunted to Thoms wytton and for the yearely rente of vj^li xiij^s iiij^d In consideration of the greate trauell and payne that the saide Nicholas hath alredy taken and hereafter shall take in ye recoveringe of the saide iij tents vnto the saide pisshe of S' xpofer aforesaide. It is also further ordered condecended and fully decreed by the aforesaide pson Churchwardens and pishioners that a lre of Attorney shallbe made to the said Nicholas or his Assignes for ye demaundinge of the quarters Rent wch is xxviij^s iiij^d due at the ffeaste of the birthe o' Lorde god laste paste before the date hearcof & for none paymennte of the said quarters rent the said Nicholas or his Assignes to reenter vppon the said iij tents to the vse of the aforesaid p'son Churchwardens and pishioners. In wittnesse of this our order & decree wee ye said p'son churchwardens & pishioners haue setto o' hanndes the daye & yeare firste aboue written

Wolstand Dixe Alderman
Bartholomew Busfeild p'son
Harry Beecher
Richard Candler
ffrauncis Gunter churchwarden
William Ryder churchwarden
William wellden
Henry Bowyer
Henry Toppsfeilde
Thomas Addames
Rafe Bosswell
Thomas wylks
John Leames
Ric Howson
p me Harry Sukyr
Thomas sprage

At A vestry holden the second day of July A° 1581 ther was chosen to be collecto^rs for the poore Henry Suker Richard Gylmour for this yeare following & to beginn the chardge and gathering the second sonday of September being the xth daye of the same moneth

At A vestry holden the xvijth daye of December 1581 was chosen Chirche warden with mr Ryder in the Rome of mr Gunter Nicholas Barnesley To begenne his tyme at the feast of the birth of owr Lord god next ensewinge &c.

The Last daye of December A° 1581 Henry Tapsfyld & Israell Owyn Chosen sydemen for this yere following at a vestry holden the same daye Above wrytten

At A vestry holden the xjth day of m'che A° 1581 it is agreed that the bill of the clarks wagis to be newly Seased by mr henry Beecher Mr welden mr Tirrell & mr Gunter shall stande from this tyme forward for the better mayntenance of all suche chardges & repracōns as shalbe needfull in & Abowte the churche & churche S'vice from tyme to tyme.

At A vestry holden the first of July A° 1582 ther was Chosen Collectors for the poore Thomas fforman & Richard Hayes for this yeare following & to begenne thear chardge & gathering The ixth of September & the second Sondaye of the same moneth

Also at the same vestry ther was Chosen Awditors for the Accompt of willm Ryder Churche warden Mr Tapsfyld & mr Rigby & also mr Candler & mr Alwarde

And more Over at the same vestry it was Agreede that ther should be A Table made with the Orders & Chardges of Buryalls & knylls & all other dewtys app'tayning to the Churche & officers of the same

At A vestry holden the ixth daye of December A° 1582 ther was Chosen Churche warden wth mr Barnesley in the Rome of mr Ryder Roger Rigby To begenne his tyme at the birth of owr lorde god next

Also at the same vestry it was Agreed That Mr Barnesley churche-waden shall Receave of mr Elrington a S'tayne Sum of monney yet Remayning in his hands since ye tyme that he was collector in ye p'ishe & mr Barnesiey to bring it in his Accompt & geve mr Elrington A Dischardg for ye same.

Att a vestrye holden The vijth daye of Octobr Anno 1582 ytt was ffullye Concluded & a greed a pon by the most p'te of the p'isheners of Saynt Crestophers Thatt a fayre Tabell or frame of wanscott shall be made to sett in Sarten ordynances & lawes made & agreed a pone in the same vestrye towchynge & Con-sarnynge all matters & dewtyes as well beloungynge & ap'tayn-ynge for the Clarke & sexstens offyce & dewtyes as allso whatt every p'ishner shall paye bothe to clarke & sexten & whatt theye shall paye to the Churchewardens to the vse of ye p'ishe to saye for Crystenyngs reed dyngs Chvrchyngs & buryells the grounde for the graves the grave makyngs, fynicly all manner of Ryghts & dewtyes a partaynynge theare vnto as maye a peere in the same tabell fayre drawyn owte wt greate letters in a joyners frame hangynge in the quyer of the same Churche of saynt Crestophers in wch vestrye all the sayde lawes & ordynances weare ofdye Rade to the p'isheners aforesayde as may a peere by a Coppye or draught theareof wt all or the most p'te of theare hands vnto yt Remayninge & a nyxsed into thys booke

Also at the same vestrye was Chosen Thomas Nebb to be sexton and to haue yeerly for his wagis the som of xls & to begenne from michaelmas last past

At A vestry holden the vjth daye of Januarij 1582 was Chosen to be sydemen for this yere following Henry Suker ~~& Edward Ryder Thomas Smith~~ But now John Thompson for yt mr smith goeth from ye prshe . . .

Also at the same vestry was Chosen to be the Awdytors of Nicholas Barnesley Churche warden his Accompt Mr Candler & Mr henry Alwarde & also mr streete & Mr suker

At A vestry holden the xxth daye of January Mr hutchinson then & that daye Read his Articles & tooke his full po[wars] . . . as p'son and also offered the whole Tythe of it vnto the p'rishe at a rate to be herafter talked of

By mee W: huchenson recto'

At a vestry holden the iijth daye of ffebruarij it was A poynnted that Mr Gunte' & Mr Ryder shulde bee Awdytors of all the Accompts of suche Collectors as is nowe com & named in A p'cept from Christes hospitall

At A vestry holden the xviijth of August 1583 Israell Owyn & Leaves wear chossen Collectors for the poore for this yere p'sent ensewing

At A vestry holden the xvth day of December A° 1583 Thear was Chosen Churche warden in the Rowme of Mr Barnsley, Thomas Spragg, & to begenne his Charge at the Byrth of owr Lorde god next ensewing the dat hearof

Also thear was Appoincted at the same Vestry to bee Awditors of the Accompt of Roger Rigbye Homphrey street Henry Suger ffraunes Gunter & Willm Ryde

At A vestry Holden the vjth daye of Januarij 1583 According to the Computacōn of England was Chozen to bee sydemen for this year ffollowing Edward Ryder and John Hooke To be sworne at the Archedecons his Visitacōn to be holden the xvth daye of this p'sent month at Sc̄t Magnus Churche

And at the same vestry it was condesended & Agreed that once wthin the space of sixe weekes thear shalbe A comunion

At A vestry holden the first daye of m'che A° 1583 it was Appointed that mr Street mr Wm Ride' mr' Barnesley mr Gonte' shold be ioyned to the parson and churchwardens to take a perfect auditt and accompt of the collecters for in arrerages for ye poore the 5 of march next folowinge accordinge to a p'cept from my Lo. Maio', to the alderman of ths ward

At a vestry Holden the 3 of Maij 1584 it was Condesended and Agreed yt James Woodshawe gentleman shuld goo forwarde with the sute hee hath in hande in the p'reshe behalfe this next tearme wch biginnethe ye vjth daie of maye for those tenamenntes which are in fleete streate healde in lease by mr wytten and ye saide Jeames woodshawe yf hee doo recover the lanndes or any pte thereof wth the arearages dew before ye lease was made to him of ye tenementes hee shalbe Alowed owte of those Arerages all his whole charges with reason and poundes more for A rewarde or Recompence our and aboue his saide Charges

At a vestry holden the vth daye of Julij 1584 was chosen to be Collector John Heath for this yeare next ensewing & Israell Owyn for to remayne wth him for the same year According to An order newly Taken by the Lorde Mayor &c

At A vestry holden the xiijth daye of December A^{o} 1584 Thear was Chosen Churche warden wth m^{r} Spragg in the Rowme of m^{r} Rigbie Homphrey Street To begenne his tyme at the birth of Owre lord and Saviow^{r} next coming

At A vestry holden the xth day of Januarij 1584 was Chosen to be sydemen for this yer following Thōms Parradyne and Jeffrey barnard

At A vestry holden the vijth daye of marche 1584 thear is Appoincted Awditors of the Accowmpts of Thoms Spragg Churche Warden ffrauncis Gunter Wm Ryder Nicholas Barnesley & Israell Owyn.

At A vestry houlden the xxixth of m^{r}che 1585 It is agreed betweene the p̄ishioners of S^{t} xpōfer nere the Stocks wth the consent of the p̄son & churchewardens that George witton & his heires & assignes shall haue such assurance of the Lands in controuersye as by nicholas ffuller shalbe thoughte convenient inconcidracon that the said George witton shall assure one Anuytie or yerelie rent charge of three pounds lawfull money of England to the said p̄ishe in p̄petuitie halfeyerelie to be paid and in defaulte of payemt by the space of one moneth to forfeyte eu'ye tyme for the breach xx^{s} nine pence wth a clawse of dystres for the principall rent & nine penc as aboue to be . . . the same assuraunce to be made betweene the date hereof & the first daie of the nexte terme by the counsell of mr ffuller

m^{d} at A vestry holden the xxvth of July it was graunted at the instant request and desyer of George wytton that he might haue tyme betweene this & Allhallowdaye next to make & finishe the assurance of the rent & Anuitie wch is all redy agrede vpon Aforesayde

W: huchenson
Thom^{s} Sprags W marke being churchewarden
homfreye Streete churchwarden
Nic̄hs ffuller
harry bech^{r}
Thomas tyrrell
Richard Candeler
ffrawncis Gunter
Wiłłm Ryder
Thoms fforman
Nycholas Barnsley
Jno Jaques
Jo: Thompson
Israell Owyn
Thom^{s} adams
By me John hethe
be me w^{m} wythenall
John Leaves
Salomon bright

At A vestry holden the iiijth daye of Julie thar was Chosen to be collector wth m^{r} heath, Arnold Richardsonn & to begenne his tyme According to the tyme Appointed

Also at the same vestry it was condesended & Agreed that Elizabeth the Childe of John Eglesfyld deceased shulde be p'ferred in to the hospitall According to the Order therin taken

At A vestry holden the iijth of October wer Chosen Awditors for the Collectors Accompt wth the Churchewardens M^{r} fforman & Thomas Addams

At A vestry holden the vijth daye of Decemb^{r} Anno 1585 was chosen Churche warden in the Rowme of Thoms Spragg Richard Candler his tyme begening from the birth of ou^{r} Lord god &c.

At A vestry holden the ixth day of Januarij 1585 was Chosen to be sydemen for this year ffollowing Thoms fforman & Thoms Turner & To be sworne at the Archdeconns visitacon to be holden the xviijth daye of this p^{r}sent month at St Magnus Churche

At A vestry holden the vjth day of marche A^{o} 1585 thear was Apointed Awditors fo^{r} the Accompt of homphrey Streete Church warden Nic̄hās Barnesley Izraell Owyn Thoms fforman & Richard Addams

At A vestry holden the xxixth daye of maye 1586 it was condesended & Agreede vpon cofference vpon the stat of wyttons lease whiche was first made from parson stanny & Churche wardens that A Lrē of Atturney be made vnto Thoms Smyth Scrivenor for demaunding of the Rent & for default of payment to Reenter for ye vse of ye pryshe & further it is Agreede for the Arrearages of the same rent that Ja[mes] Woodshawe shalbe called to know howe muche he hath Receaued therof to the vse of the p̄rishe & for the Resedew Thoms Smyth shall haue power by the sayde Lrē of Atturney for to dystrayne or other wyse for to recou^{r} the same for the vse of the sayd p̄esh

& more ou^{r} it is Agreede that yf this former Lease by not payment of the rent be made voyd that then ther shall be A new Lre of Atturney made to suche as the p̄rishe shall thinck good for to demaund the rent Resarued vpon the new Lease made vnto Nic̄hās Barnesley & James woodshawye & for not payment therof to Reenter to the vse of the p̄rishe

At A vestry holden the xxiijth of June A^{o} 1586 ther was Chosen Collector for the poore in the Roume of John Heath to Remayne with A'nold Richardson for this yeare ffollowing John Hooke whoe is to remayne for ij yeares According vnto the Order thearin taken

At the same vestry also ther was Appoincted to be seassors for the making p'vision of one othur comunion Cuppe Accordinge to an order in that behalfe made by the Ordenary The ij Church wardens Hom streete & Ric Chandler & m^{r} henry Beecher Nicholas Barnesley willm Ryder & Thomas fforman to be Levied & Rated vpon the parrisheners According to thear disscression

The Seasment of the ij^{o} & Last fyfetene graunted to the Queenes M^{tie} by Act of p'liament the xxvijth yeare of her maties Reigne In the ward of Brod streete seased the xxvjth daye of Aprill 1586 by the seasors hearunder named xvi

The p'sinct of Sc^{t} xpōfers p̄rishe

Barnard Wyndover	xij^{s}	Nicholas Barnesley ...	ij^{s}
wiłłm Towrhill	iiij^{d}	Robart Harrison	ij^{s}
Randall knevett	ij^{s}	Thoms Taylor	ij^{s}
John Harrison	iiij^{d}	widdow Kelk	o
Thomas doughty ...	ij^{d}	Henry Beeche^{r}	viij^{s}
Thoms Crayford ...	ij^{d}	Richard Candler	xx^{d}
John ffowler ...	o	Sallomon Bright	ij^{s}
Mark Pryme ...	o	m^{r} Sherriff Ratclif	x^{s}
Thoms Spragg	x^{d}	Arnold Richardson for m^{r} Jaques Backromes & watercowrse ...	xij^{s}
Thoms Howson	ij^{s}		
Richard Hills	iiij^{s}		
Robert Cudner	vj^{s}	John Leaues ...	ij^{d}
wiłłm yearington ...	o	Richard Raynescroft	vj^{d}

Jon Jaques for one tenament voyde	ijd	Jeffrey Leonard	ijd
Jerrom Bolton	iiijd	Thoms Turner	ijd
Richard Hayes	ijd	Henry Smallwod	vjd
Henry Suker	xvjd	Richard Addames backromes	viijd
mr ffullers Backromes	iijs iiijd	Thoms Parradins backromes	viijd
Hughe Dale	ijd	John Heath	viijd
willm withnall	viijd	Israell Owyn	vjd
Thoms Addams	ijd	Thoms Cotton	o
		Thoms fformans water cowrse	vjd

The Churche yard

Richard Robinson	iiijd	willm Martyn	ijd
Thoms Stone & Abraham Buck	viijd	Henry Smithe	ijd
John Hooke	iiijd	widdow Thornton	ijd
John Strahaune	iiijd	Timothy wheeler	ijd

Collectors { John Heath, John Hooke Nicholas Barnesley, Henry Suker } Seassors

Suma 3 — o — 8

14 At A vestry holden the xviijth of Septembr 1586 it was condesended & Agreed that thear shall be a letter of Atturney made vnto Thoms Smyth & Israell Owyn by the parson & Churche wardens to aske & demaund the rent of the Tenaments in fleete streete heald by George witton at the daye & Tyme mensioned in the Lease & for non payment thearof to make Reentry According to the effect & Tenour of the Lease mr John Jaques is Requyred to goe & bee A wytnes at the same Demaunding of the Rent or Reentry & Alsoe it is Agreed by the prishners that the same partyes shalbe saved harmles of & from Any damage that might happen therby

W. hutchinson
Nicℏs ffuller
henry bechr
Thomas tyrrell
Wiℏm Ryder
homfreye Streete
Richard Candeler

At A vestry holden the xviijth daye of December Ao 1586 It was Agreed & condesended by the consent of the prishe that Thoms fforman should be Churche warden in the Rome of homphry streete & wth Richard Candler the tyme begening at the feast of the Birth of owre Saviowr Jhūs Christe According to the Order as heartofore hath bin Accustomed By the Order of the prishe

At A vestry holden the viijth of Januarij Ao 1586 was Chosen Sydeman for & in ye Rowme mr fforman & T. Turner Robert Payrpoint and Thomas Tay'or & to S've this yer ffollowing & they must Appeare to take ther Chardg before the Archedeacon at St Magnus the xixth daye of this moneth

Md that the xvth of January 1586 George Wytton in consideracon of xijd to him geven by mr fforman the name of the pson & churche wardens did p'mise that if* he or John Shibnall his lessee would not discontynue or be nonesute in any accōn dependinge in his owne name or in the name of his said lessee concerning certen howses in ffletestrete wherevnto the pson & churchwardens of this pishe p'tende tytle ~~vnto~~ That then he would ~~forfytt~~ & resigne all his lease & interest that he hath in the same to the vse of the pishe

p me Georgiū Wytton

* The word "if" inserted subsequently to the original entry.

Att this vestrye were p'sent
mr Aldrm̄ Ratcliffe
mr ffuller
mr Becher
mr Tyrrell
mr Strete
mr Barnsley & dyu's others

At a vestry holden the xxixth daie of January Ao 1585 it was Agreede that mr Alderman Railyf mr henry Beacher mr Tirrell & mr Ryder shuld Accase the prishioners for A s'tayne Som of money to be Levyed ffor ffollowing of the Shewt for the lands in fleetestreat heald by Georg wytton

and mr Barnsley & mr Owyn to Collett the same monney wth all spead as Jaust Occasion & the sayd Lands be Recou'ed vnto the prashe yt then eu'y man shall haue his monney pd agayn vpon the Areareages thereof

At a vestry holden the xxvjth of marche Ao 1586 thear was apointed Auditors for the Accompt of Richard Candler Israell owyn Richard Addams mr streete & Thoms Taylor

At a vestrey holden the xviijth daye of June 1587 yt was agreed that mr alderman Ratclyff mr Harry Becher Mr Tyrrell and mr Rider shall ratte and make A new assessement vpon the prishioners ffor A Suply of A greate some of mony to be levied and gathered towards the sewt for the recovary of Certen land in flett stret for the prishe and the same money to be paid to mr fforman churche warden

At the same vestry was also chosen ffor colector for the pore for this yere wth John hook in the stead of Arnold Richardson, and to begynn his Colection the first of Septembr next Edward Ryder to contenew for 2 yers according to the custom

At a vestry holden The viijth daye of Octobr it was condesended concerning the Assessment next above mensioned that mr Streete & mr Suger shuld bee Collectors & the monney so colected to be dd vnto Thomas forman Church warden

At a vestry holden the xvth daye of October Ao 1587 ther was Appoincted to bee Seassors for the fyftyne graunted to the Queens Matie mr Henry Beecher mr Candler mr Barnesley mr Sugker and Colectors for the same

Wiℏm withnell and }
Henry Smallwod }

At the Guylde hall the xxiijo of Septembr 1587

The Seasment of the seconde and Last xvo Graunted the Queenes Matie by Acte of parliament the xxixo yeare of her Mats raigne, the warde of Brodstreete The prishe of St xpofor for ye presinct Seased the xvo October Anno domini p'd by they whose names ar heare vnder written

Mr Alderman Ratlife ...	xiijs iiijd	Thomas Taylor	ijs
Mr Alderman Skynnr ...	xiijs iiijd	Henry Becher	vj viijd
William Towrall	vjd	Richard Candler	xxd
Randall knevett	xxd	widdow Bright	xxd
Thomas Spragg	viijd	Arnolde Richardson bakroms	xijd
Thomas Craiforde	ijd	John Leaves	ijd
Nicholas Bacon	ijd	Richard Rainscroft	vjd
Robart Cudner	vjd	John Bolting	o
Nicholas Barnsley	ijs	Cornelis Speringe	xd
Robart Harryson	ijs	Richarde Hayes	ijd

Henry Suker	xij^{d}	Henry Smalwod	vj^{d}
John Bowsers bakgate	iij^{s} iiij^{d}	Richard Addams bakroms	vj^{d}
Hughe dale	ij^{d}	Thoms parradyns bakromes	viij^{d}
william withnall	viij^{d}	John Heathe	viij^{d}
Thomas Addames	oo	Israell Owins bakrom ...	vj^{d}
Jeffreye Leanarde	iiij^{d}	Thomas fformans water-cou'se	vj^{d}
Thomas Turner	xx^{d}		

In the Churche yearde

Richard Robinson	iiij^{d}	willm martin	ij^{d}
John Hooke	vj^{d}	Henry Smith	ij^{d}
Lewis Morgan	vj^{d}	Henry whitmore	ij^{d}
John Straughan	iiij^{d}	William Robartes	ij^{d}
widdow Thornton	o		

Sessors { m^{r} Henry Beecher, m^{r} Richard Candler, m^{r} Nicha^{s} Barnesley & Henry Suker } Regi Elizabet 29

Colectors { William Withnall & henry Smalwod } A^{o} 1587 Domini

An asse[s]ment made by the R worshipfull m^{r} Anthōi Ratlif Alde'mā m^{r} Henry Beeche' m^{r} Thoms Tirrell and m^{r} willm Ryder for S'taine Monney to be levied to follow A suete Depending in lawe for S'tayne howses Lying in fleetestret belonging in tyme past to owr ꝑishe of Sct xpofers whiche Sessors was Chosen the viijth day of October At a vestry holden in the same parrishe and the Colectors Chosen & Named &c Homphrey Streete & Henry Suker & they to deliu' the monney vnto m^{r} Thoms fformā Churche warden 1587.

Mr Alderman Ratlife	xx^{s}	Thomas Taylor	vj^{s} viij^{d}
Mr Alderman Skynn'	xx^{s}	John Hooke	xvj^{d}
m^{r} Henry Beecher	xv^{s}	Richard Robinson	xvj^{d}
m^{r} Richard Candlor	v^{s}	John Jaques	x^{s}
Arnold Richardson ...	iij^{s} iiij^{d}	Thoms Carpinter ...	ij^{s} vj^{d}
John Leaves	xvj^{d}	Thoms Smith	iij^{s} iiij^{d}
Richard Hayes	xvj^{d}	m^{r} Thoms Tyrrell	x^{s}
Henry Suker	vj^{s} viij^{d}	Robt Payrpointt	ij^{s}
willm withnall	iij^{s} iiij^{d}	Henry Aylword	ij^{s} vj^{d}
Thoms Addams	xvj^{d}	m^{r} John Bowser	vj^{s} viij^{d}
Jeffrey Leanard	ij^{s} vj^{d}	Thoms Paveley	ij^{s} vj^{d}
Thoms Turner	v^{s}	Homphrey Streete	x^{s}
Henry Smalwod	iij^{s} iiij^{d}	m^{r} William Ryder	x^{s}
John heath	iij^{s} iiij^{d}	Raphe Boswell	ij^{s} vj^{d}
William towrall	iij^{s} iiij^{d}	Edward Ryder	vj^{s} viij^{d}
Randall knevett	v^{s}	Richard Addams ...	ij^{s} vj^{d}
Thomas Spragg	iij^{s} iiij^{d}	Thoms Paradyne	v^{s}
Nichas Barnesley	x^{s}	Israell Owyn	vj^{s} viij^{d}
Robart Harrison ...	iij^{s} iiij^{d}	Thoms fforman	x^{s}

The vj of November payde vnto Thomas fforman by homphrey streete with m^{r} ffor mans owne x^{s} } x^{li} xviij^{s} viij^{d}

An assecement made by the worshipfull Mr Anthony Ratliff Alderman and Mr Henry Becher Mr Thomas Terrell and Mr William Ryder for Sarten mony to belevyed to follow a sute dependinge in lawe for Sarten howses lying in fleete streete belonging in time past to our ꝑishe of St Cristofers wch Sessors weare chosen at a vestry holden in the same ꝑish the 2nd of ffebruary 1586 the collectors heare of be Nicholas Barnsly and Israell Owyn

Mr Alderman Ratlyfe ...	xx^{s}	Nichas Barnesley	x^{s}
Mr Henry Beechar	xv^{s}	Robart Harryson ...	iij^{s} iiij^{d}
Mr Richard Candler	v^{s}	Thoms Tayler	vj^{s} viij^{d}
Mr Bright widdow	o	John Hooke	xvj^{d}
Arnold Richardson ...	iij^{s} iiij^{d}	Rychard Robynsonn	xvj^{d}
John Leaues	xvj^{d}	John Brogden	xvj^{d} cornhill
Richard Rayuescroft	o	John Jaques	x^{s}
John Bowlting	o	Thoms Carpinter ...	ij^{s} vj^{d}
Richard Hayes	xvj^{d}	Thoms Smith	iij^{s} iiij^{d}
Henry Suker	vj^{s} viij^{d}	Thoms Tyrrell	x^{s}
Hugh Dale	o	Robt Parpoint	ij^{s}
w^{m} withnall	iij^{s} iiij^{d}	Henry Allword	ij^{s} vj^{d}
Thoms Addams	xvj^{d}	Thoms Paveley	ij^{s} vj^{d}
Jeffrey leanarde	ij^{s} vj^{d}	Homphrey Street	x^{s}
Thomas Turner	v^{s}	William Ryder	x^{s}
Henry Smalwod	iij^{s} iiij^{d}	Raphe Boswell	ij^{s} vj^{d}
John Heathe	iij^{s} iiij^{d}	Edward Ryder	vj^{s} viij^{d}
Willm Towrall	iij^{s} iiij^{d}	Richard Addams ...	ij^{s} vj^{d}
Barnard windover ...	iij^{s} iiij^{d}	Thoms Paradyn	v^{s}
Randall knevett	v^{s}	Israell Owyn	vj^{s} viij^{d}
Thoms Spragg	iij^{s} iiij^{d}	Thoms fforman	x^{s}

A^{o} 1587

Att a vestry holden the xvijth of December was Chosen Churche warden in the Rome of m^{r} Richard Candler Robart Cudne' and to beginne from the feast of the byrth of owre Lorde god next comyng

At the same vestry was Chosen to bee sydemen for the same yer next ensuyng Richard Addams and Willm Withnall

The xviijth daye of December 1587

A note of the distrubucion of tenne shillings to the pore of this ꝑishe of the gifte of Mrs Parsons deceassed and paid yerly by the M^{r} and Wardens of the marchaunt Taylors of London to twenty pore of this Paryshe that is to saye six pence apece wch was nowe paid by Mr Walter Plomer Warden as followth

Widowe Whithead	vj^{d}	Thomas webbe	vj^{d}
Willm yerington elder and	vj^{d}	Amye webbe	vj^{d}
Willm yerington yonger ...	vj^{d}	Annys martyn	vj^{d}
Katherin Baune	vj^{d}	Marke Pryme	vj^{d}
Isabell Ansell	vj^{d}	John Savoye	vj^{d}
Wedow Johnson	vj^{d}	Thomas howson	vj^{d}
John ffowler	vj^{d}	Agnis egelsfild	vj^{d}
Agnis ffowler	vj^{d}	wedow Thorneton	vj^{d}
Thomas harris	vj^{d}	Thomas Cotton	vj^{d}
Widdow Philpott	vj^{d}	Keeth Cotton	vj^{d}

Some x^{s} Ri: Candeler

A note of xxxth saks of Coles geven to the pore of this ꝑishe of the gift of m^{rs} brass latte wiffe to phelix lawrence deceased distributed as followth the 4 of december 1587

Widow whithead	4	Thomas webbe ...	1
Willm yerington elder ...	4	Agnis m'tin	1
Katherin Bawne	1	mark pryme ..	2
Isable Ansell ...	1	John Savoye ...	1
Wedow Johnson	3	Wedow thornton	2
John ffowler ...	2	Thomas Cotton ...	4
Thomas Hawes ...	1		
Wedow philpott ...	3		11
	19		19
		Some sakes	30

16 At a vestry holden the xxviijth daye of Januarij A^{o} 1587 it was condesended & Agreed that m^{r} fforman shulde kepe & haue the Accompt in his hands for this year alsoe following vnto the feast of the birth ow^{r} Saviow^{r} Christ

At a vestry holden the iiijth daye of februarij A^{o} 1587 it was condesended & Agreed that m^{r} Jaques & w^{m} withnall should collect & gather A nother Collection for the mayntenance & chardg of the sute in lawe for the Lande Lying in fleet streete now in the posession of wytton

An assessemente made by the Righte Worshipfull Mr Antony Rattlyfe Alderman and Mr Henry Becher Mr Thomas Terrell & Mr William Rider for Sarten Moneye to be levyed to ffollowe a shewte depending in lawe for serten Howses lyinge in ffletstreete belonging in time past to our pishe of Sct xpofers which Sessers where chosen the iiijth of ffebruarij 1588 A vestery holden in the same pishe & the Collectors chosen & named John Jaques & William Withnall & the monney to bee Deliuered to Thomas fforman Churche Warden

Mr Alderman Rattlyfe ...	xx^{s}	Thomas Taylor ...	... vj^{s} viij^{d}
Mr Alderman Skynner ...	xx^{s}	John Whoocke ...	xvj^{d}
Mr Henry Becher	xv^{s}	Richarde Robinson ...	xvj^{d}
Mr Richarde Candler ...	v^{s}	John Jaques	x^{s}
Arnolde Richardson	... iij^{s} iiij^{d}	Thomas Smith ...	... iij^{s} iiij^{d}
John Leaues	xvj^{d}	xpofer Midleton	ij^{s}
Richard Heayes	xvj^{d}	Mr Thomas Tirrell ...	x^{s}
Henry Suker	... vj^{s} viij^{d}	Robarte Parpoynt	ij^{s}
William Wythnall ...	... iij^{s} iiij^{d}	Henry Alworth	ij^{s} vj^{d}
Thomas Addames	xvj^{d}	Mr John Bowser ...	... vj^{s} viij^{d}
Jeffery Lenarde	ij^{s} vj^{d}	Thomas Pauelye	ij^{s}
Thomas Turner	v^{s}	Humphery Street ...	x^{s}
Henry smalewod ...	... iij^{s} iiij^{d}	William Rider	x^{s}
John Heathe	... iij^{s} iiij^{d}	Raphe Bosswell	ij^{s} vj^{d}
William Towrall ...	... iij^{s} iiij^{d}	Edwarde Rider	x^{s}
Randall Knevyete	v^{s}	Richard Addams paide ...	ij^{s}
John Harrison ...	o	John Brogden ...	... vj^{s} viij^{d}
Widdowe Sprage ...	... iij^{s} iiij^{d}	Thomas Parradine	v^{s}
Nicholas Barnesly	x^{s}	Israell Owyne ...	... vj^{s} viij^{d}
Robart Harrison ...	... iij^{s} iiij^{d}	Thomas fforman ...	x^{s}

17 Att A vestry houlden at St Christofers one Sundaye the ixth of June 1588 before Mr Alderman Rattlyfe and Mr Chris Skynner and other parishioners there it is agred that Mr Edward Ryder haberdasher and William Towerold stationer shall collect a forth assessement at the rate as afore time payde towardes the accomplishing of a sute begone in law for certaine landes belonging to the parish. Theis of the parish hereafter named weare present at the same vestry and writ downe one names Mr Antoine Rattlyf Alderman Mr Thomas Skynner Shrif and Alderman John Thorp p'son Thomas Tyrrell William Ryder Thomas fforman Nicholas Barnsly Robart Cudner Humphry Streete William Towroolde Hugh Owb'y John Leaues John Heath William Wythnall

Mr Alderman Rattlyfe	xx^{s}	Henry Suker ...	... vj^{s} viij^{d}
Mr Alderman Skynner ...	xx^{s}	William Wythnall ...	... iij^{s} iiij^{d}
Mr Henry Beecher	xv^{s}	Thomas Addames	xvj^{d}
Mr Richard Candler ...	v^{s}	Jeffery Leonard	... ij^{s} viij^{d}
Arnolde Richardson	... iij^{s} iiij^{d}	Thomas Turner ...	v^{s}
John Leaues ...	xvj^{d}	Henry Smalewod	... iij^{s} iiij^{d}
Richard Hayes	xvj^{d}	John Heath ...	... iij^{s} iiij^{d}
William Towrold ...	... iij^{s} iiij^{d}	Mr Thomas Tyrrell	... vj^{s} viij^{d}
Randall Knevite	v^{s}	Robart Parpoynt ...	ij^{s} vj^{d}
John Harrison	o	Henry Alworth	ij^{s} vj^{d}
Widdow Spragg ...	... iij^{s} iiij^{d}	Mr John Bowser ...	vj^{s} viiij^{d}
Nicholas Barnsley	x^{s}	Thomas Pauely	ij^{s} vj^{d}
Robart Harison ...	... iij^{s} iiij^{d}	Humfrey Stret ...	x^{s}
Thomas Taylor ...	... vj^{s} viij^{d}	Wylliam Ryder	x^{s}
John Hooke	xvj^{d}	Raphe Bosswell	ij^{s} vj^{d}
Richard Robinson	xvj^{d}	Edward Ryder ...	... vj^{s} viij^{d}
John Jaques	x^{s}	John Brogden	xvj^{d}
Hughe Owb'ye ...	xvj^{d}	Thomas Paradyne	v^{s}
Thomas Carpenter	ij^{s} vj^{d}	Israell Owynne ...	... vj^{s} viij^{d}
Thomas Smyth ...	ij^{s}	Thomas fforman	x^{s}
xpofer Midleton ...	ij^{s} vj^{d}		

A^{o} 1588 18

At a vestry holden the xxxth daye of June ther was Chosen Collector for the poore of Christs hospitall Thomas Turner in the Rowme of John Hooke & soe to remayne towe years according vnto an order & Chardg geven ffrom the maisters of the hospitall and Edward Ryder to bee the vpper collector for this yeare following & to receave & pay all Chardges therto belonging

At a vestry holden the xxvth of August 1588 it was Agreed & condesended that wheras willm wytton did offer vnto the prishners for there right in certayne howses in ffleet streete v^{li} xiij^{s} iiij^{d} yeerly without any Chardgis for the sute or any Arearadges due for the same howses whiche offer was not lyked of by the greatest pte of the pishioners Therefore it was ordered at this vestry That Thomas fformans & Robt Cudner Churchwardens & Nichās Barnesley wth ffraunces Greeneham shall goe & geve Aunswer to him or ye attorney that the sayd prishners doe not lyke of his sayde offer These hereafter named wer p'sent at this vestry Thoms Tyrrell Willm Ryder Nichās Barnesley Homphrey Streete Thoms Addams Thoms Turner Thoms Smith John Jaques Thoms pavely John Hook willm withnall Henry Smallwood Thoms Carpinter Richard Hayes John Heath wth others & Thoms fforman Churchewarden

At a vestry the vjth of October 1588

The Seasment of A fyfteene Graunted ye Queenes Matie by Acte of Parliamente the xxix^{o} yeere of Ma^{tes} Raigne for the p'cinct of Sainct xpofers prishe in the ward of Brodstret Seased by they whose names are heere vnder Wrytten

Mr Aldermā Ratlyfe ...	xiij^{s} iiij^{d}	Arnould Richardsons backromes	xij^{d}
Mr Aldermā Skinner ...	xiij^{s} iiij^{d}	John Leaves	iiij^{d}
William Towrall	vj^{d}	Richard Ravenscroft	vj^{d}
Randall Knevett	xx^{d}	James Standley	vj^{d}
Widdow Spragge	viij^{d}	Cornelis Spering	viij^{d}
Thomas Crayford	iiij^{d}	Richard Hayes	iiij^{d}
Nicholas Bacon	o	Jerrom Suker	xij^{d}
Robart Cudner	iiij^{d}	John Bowsers backromes	iij^{s} iiij^{d}
Nicholas Barnesley	ij^{s}	Hughe Dale	ij^{d}
ffraunces Lodge ...	xviij^{d}	Willm wythnall	vj^{d}
Robart Harrison	vj^{d}	Thoms Doughty	iiij^{d}
Thomas Taylor	ij^{s}	Jeffrey Leanard	iiij^{d}
John Billingforde ...	vj^{d}	Thomas Turner ...	xviij^{d}
Mr Henry Beecher	vj^{s} viij^{d}	Henry Smalwod	vj^{d}
Richard Candler ...	xx^{d}	Henry Smalwod	vj^{d}
Widdow Bright	xvj^{d}	Ric $^{Brogden}_{Addams}$ Bakromes	vj^{d}

Thomas Parradine backromes	viij[d]	Israell Owine backrome	vj[d]
John Heath	viij[d]	Thomas fformans watercou'se	vj[d]

In the Churche yearde

Richard Robinson	iiij[d]	Widdow Thornton	o
John Whooke	vj[d]	William Martine	ij[d]
Lewys Morgan	o	Henry Smyth	ij[d]
John Strawham	iiij[d]	Willm Robarts	ij[d]

M[r] Candler
Nichas Barnesley
Robt Cudner Churchwarden
& Thomas Addames } Sessors

Willm Withnall
Henry Smalwod } Collectors

The xxvij[th] of October it was condecended and agreed by certayne of the most Aunsient of the p̄rishe being then present that the Church wardens according to their good discression shoulde paye giue or bestowe for the more expedicion of the cause nowe depending in Lawe the som̄e of five pounds or there about

At a vestry holden the xv[th] of December 1588 these p̄sons heare vnder named being present

M[r] Alderman Ratlyfe	Thomas fforman } Churche wardens	
John Thorp p̄son	Robart Cudner }	
Richard Ravenscroft	Willm Wythnall	Nicholas Barnsly
Robart Parpoynt	Raphe Boswell	Humphrey Streete
Richard Robynson	John Hooke	Jerom Suker
Henry Smalwood	John Leaves	Jeffry Leonarde
Thomas Addams	Hughe Dale	Arnolde Richardson
Thoms Turner	Izraell Owyn	

Memorandum that the day and yeeres aboue wrighten at a vestrey howlden in the p̄ishe of S[t] xpofers in London by the p̄sones aboue named It was agred that Henry Beecher, Nicholas Barnsly, William Ryder, Humphrey Streete, and Rychard Ravenscroft shall not only stand and be auditores to avdite and p'vse the accompte of the said Thomas fforman for suche somes of money as hath byne by him disburced towchinge the recou'y of those lands which lately have byne recou'd to the vse of the p̄ishe aforesayde being in S[t] Donstones in the weste but also the same p̄sones by the like consent of the sayde p̄ishoners shall indifferently assease all and all man' of the p̄ishon's of the p̄ishe aforesayde to be contribtores vnto the payment of suche money as shalbe founde by the sayde Avditors that the sayde Thomas fforman hath layde owte and disburced aboute the same seutes and recou'y more then he hath receaued After w[ch] it is likewise by the consente aforesayde ordred that Thomas Taylor and Thomas Parradyne shall collecte of the p̄ishoners aforsayde all suche money as shalbe so asseased by the p̄sones aforesayde.

Memorandū that there is xx[s] j[d] to be recouered agaynst William Wooton and xpofer by order of Courte of kynges benche giuen against him towching the foresayde recouery.

It is likewise ordred that a p̄fecte entre shalbe made in the Churche booke of all the p̄cedinges of the same sewte

It is likewise ordred that there shalbe p̄vided by the Churche wardens a Com̄one Cheste w[ch] shall haue vnto it iij keyes and iij lockes and that therein shall be put in all the goods and wrightings belonging to the saide Churche and that there shalbe ij Inventories Indented especifyinge not only all the Churche goods, but also the testem̄ of eu'y dede of there lands one of which Inventories shall continewe in the same Cheste w[th]out removing, the other p̄te to remayne w[th] the elder Church warden, and likewise the same three keyes to remayne in this sorte vidz. one key w[th] the p̄son of the same Churche, one other w[th] the Churchwardens and the thirde w[th] M[r] Alderman Ratclife

It is ordred also that in one of the dayes w[th]in Christmas being Monday before Newyeares day there shalbe tyme taken for the p̄fectinge of the p'misses.

It is likewise ordred at the same vestry that Israell Owyn shalbe Churchwarden in the Rome of Thomas fforman for the yeare ensewing

It is also ordred that Thomas Paueley & Henry Smalwood shalbe sidemen for the yeare to come

It is also ordred that the quitrents belonging to S[t] Bartholmes hospitall and the Companye of the Drapers shalbe paid by the said Churchwarden vntill furthe' order by the said p̄ishoners shalbe taken

It is likewise ordred that there shalbe a fayre table wth a frame wherin shalbe wrighten fayre in p̄chement for the better memory of the Churchewardens all suche payments as ar to be payd forth of the lands belonging to the p̄ishe of S[t] xpofers to be fixced in the Churche wth one Iron Chayne

At a vestry holden the xxix of June A° 1589 Thear was chosen Collector for the poore Thomas Smith in the rowme of Edwarde Ryder and so to remayne towe yeers according to the order expressed & Thomas Turner to bee the vpper colector for this yere following & for to receaue and paye all manne' of paymentes and chardges thearunto appertayning

The ix[th] daye of November 1589

M[d] that Thoms Tyrrell W[m] Ryder Homphrey Street & John Jaks haue made promis vnto Israell Owyn Churche warden to make payment vnto him agayne vpon his request for suche Chardges as hee shall needfully Imploy abowt or for the obtayning of all suche monie as is dewe vnto the p̄rishe by Willm Wytton & George Wytton Also to this graunt & p̄mys theis parsons hear under named more doe Affyrme the same so that the som be not above tenne pounds

Thomas terryll
Willm Ryder
homfreye Streate
Jn° Jaques
Nycholas Barnsley
Thoms fforman
Edward Ryder
Thomas Turna'
w[m] withenell
Thomas Pavelley
Robart cudrar
Raf boswell

At a vestrye holden the xj[th] daye of Januarye 1589 by m[r] Alderman Ratcliffe and other the p̄sones whose names are herevnder named. It is fullye agreed that the former vestrye holden the ix[th] of November last past and all things therein conteyned to be from hensforth voyde. And that the whole p̄ishe and p̄ishion's of the same shalbe assessed and made Contributorye for the levyenge of tenne poundes wch shalbe spent in the sute wth is nowe dependinge for the obtyninge of thexecucõn of xx^{li} or thereabouts adiudged heretofore to the p̄ishe agaynst one willm̄ wotton ; and also to be spent in a Newe sut to be begonne & followed agaynst George wotton for such arrerags as be nowe due to the p̄ishe. And that m^{r} Tirrill & m^{r} Streat for Cornhill syde and m^{r} Candeler & m^{r} Tourner for the backsyde shalbe Cessors, and m^{r} Taylor & m^{r} Paradyne shalbe collecto^{rs} wch collectors shall pay the mony collected over to the Church wardens, and to receyve an acquyttance

Israell Owen & John Leaves Churchwardens

At this vestrye

John Thorpe Parson
Thomas Tirrell
Willm Ryder
Nichãs Barnsley
Richard Candler
Humfry Streat
John Bowser
Thomas Taylor
Tho: Tourner
Robt Cudner
Richard Heys
willm wythnall
Robt wyncoll
Hugh Dale
James Stanley wch Stanley shalbe solicito^{r} for the pishe

The xviij^{o} of Octob^{r} 1589 the first fyfteene

The seasment of A fyfteene Graunted the Queenes Matie by act of Parliamẽt the xxxj^{o} yeere of her reign for the p^{r}sinct of S^{t} xpofers p̄yshe in the warde of Brod streete Seased by they whose names are heare vnder wrytten

Sessors

m^{r} Candler
nichãs Barnsley
Robt Cudne^{r} Churchwardẽ
Thoms Addams

Sr Phillip Butler	xiij^{s} iiij^{d}	Ric Rauenscroft	vj^{d}
John Howell	vj^{d}	Jams Standley	vj^{d}
Whyt	xx^{d}	Cornelis Speering	viij^{d}
John Harrison	~~ij^{d}~~	Ric Haighes	ij^{d}
Robt Cudmr	iiij^{d}	Jerom Suker	xij^{d}
Bayly	iiij^{d}	m^{r} John Bowser bakroms	iij^{s} iiij^{d}
Nich^{a}s Barnesley	ij^{s}	Hughe Dale	ij^{d}
ffrauncs Lodge	xviij^{d}	Willm Withnall	vj^{d}
Robart Stratford	viij^{d}	Thomas Cockshoote	iiij^{d}
Thoms Taylor	ij^{s}	Thomas Turner	xviij^{d}
John Billingford	vj^{d}	Henry Smalwod	vj^{d}
Henry Beecha^{r} ...	vj^{s} viij^{d}	John Brogdens bakroms ...	viij^{d}
Ric Candeler	xx^{d}	Thoms Parradins bakroms	viij^{d}
Robart wynckole	ij^{s}	John Heath	vj^{d}
m^{r} Aldermã Radclife ...	xiij^{s} 4^{d}	Israell Owins bakroms ...	vj^{d}
Arnold Richardsons Bakroms	xij^{d}	Thoms formans wate^{r}cow^{r}se	vj^{d}
John Leaves	ij^{d}	George Hunt	vj^{d}

The Alley

Thoms doughty	iiij^{d}	Samwell Dowte	ij^{d}
John lofte ...	ij^{d}	Thoms Howson	o
widdow Spragg	viij^{d}	m^{r}k Pryme	o

The Church yeard

John ffludd	ij^{d}	willm Martin	ij^{d}
Ric Robinson	ij^{d}	John Straughan	iiij^{d}
John Hooke	vj^{d}	Robart Hudson	ij^{d}
Lewys Morgan	iiij^{d}	Henry Smithe	ij^{d}
Joyse Skipper	iiij^{d}	widdow Thornton	o
willm Robartts	ij^{d}		

Jerrom Suker
ffrauncs Lodge } Colectors

At a vestry holden the vijth of December A^{o} 1589 thear was Chosen to be Churche warden for Robt Cudne^{r} John Leaves for to remayne wth Israell Owyn for this yeare following begennyng at Christms next commyng & the sayde John Leaves to remayne Churche warden the tyme of ij years According to the accustomed order of the p̄rishe

Alsoe the same tyme & at the same vestry was Chosen to be swornmen for one yeer John Jakes and James Standley

At a vestry holden the viijth of m^{r}ch A^{o} 1589 Willm yearington was admytted by the condesend & Agrement of the whole p̄rishe to Receave the weekely pencion of vj^{d} which Magdelin philpot deceased Lately hadd to be payd to him during his naturell Lyfe by the collector^{s} of the parrishe

At a vestry holden the iiijth daye of December 159 . . ther was Chosen Churchwarden In the rome of Israell Owyn Henry Allward & the same Henry Allward to remay̅e According to the Aunsient custom of ij yeers and was Omytted to be wrytten vntill his daye being the vth daye of December 1591.

An assesement graunted at a vestrey holden the xjth of January 1589 for the some of tenne pounds to be Levyed & delivered vnto the hands of Israell Owyn Church warden to follow the sewt for the obteyning Stayne Arearages dew vnto the p̄rishe by George Wytton & W^{m} wytton

Sr Phillip Bottle^{r}	xx^{s}	Willm withnall	iij^{s} iiij^{d}
Mr Aldermã Radclyf ...	xx^{s}	Jerom Suker	v^{s}
Mr Henry Beechar ...	xv^{s}	Ric Hayes	xvj^{d}
Mr Candlor	v^{s}	James standley	ij^{s} vj^{d}
Jno Billingford	xvj^{d}	John Leaves	xvj^{d}
Thom Taylor	vj^{s} viij^{d}	Jno Jakes	x^{s}
Robe^{r}t wyncoll	v^{s}	Thom Carpinter	iij^{s} iiij^{d}
ffraunes Lodge	v^{s}	Arnold Richardson ...	vj^{s} viij^{d}
Robt Stradford	ij^{s}	Thom Smith	v^{s}
Jno Hooke	xvj^{d}	xp̄ofer Mydleton	ij^{s} vj^{d}
Jno straughan	ij^{s}	Mr Tyrrell	x^{s}
Ric Robinson	xvj^{d}	Robert Parpoynt	ij^{s} vj^{d}
Nichãs Barnesley	x^{s}	Henry Aylword	ij^{s} vj^{d}
Robt Cudner	ij^{s} vj^{d}	Jno Bowser	viij^{s}
Mrs Spragg	iij^{s} iiij^{d}	Thom Paveley	ij^{s} vj^{d}
Jno whyt	iij^{s} iiij^{d}	homphry Streete	x^{s}
Isak kylborn	xvj^{d}	w^{m} Ryder	xv^{s}
Jno Howell	xvj^{d}	Raphe Boswell	ij^{s} vj^{d}
Jno Heath	iij^{s} iiij^{d}	Edward Ryder	viij^{s}
George Hunt	iij^{s} iiij^{d}	Jno Brogden	xvj^{d}
Henry Smalwod	iij^{s} iiij^{d}	Thom Paradine	v^{s}
Thom̄ Turner	vj^{s} viij^{d}	Israell Owyn	vj^{s} viij^{d}
Thom Addams	xvj^{d}	Thom fforman	x^{s}

Sessors	Thoms Tyrrell	Thomas Parradyn	Colectors
	Ric Candler	Thoms Taylor	
	homphry street	new Chosen Jerrom Suke^{r}	Collectors
	Thom Turne^{r}	1590 Thoms Paveley	

At a vestry holden the xth daye of Maye thear was Chosen for to bee the Awditors of the acompt of Robt Cudner late Churche warden Nichās Barnesley Homphrey Street Thoms fforman and Thom Addams

And at the same vestry it was condesendid and agreede that Thoms Pavelye & Jerom Suker shulde take in chardge the collecting of the resedew of that assesment which was graunted for the sute of the Arearages of willm & George Wytton, and also that the Receaue into there handes the same Monney whiche Thoms p'adyne & Thoms Taylor haue in ther handes & so to be accomtable vnto the Churchewardens for the whole som whiche they shall receave.

At a vestry holden the xth daye of Maye Anno 1590 it was condesended and Agreed that whear John Shubnall will not Asigne ou^{r} the Judgment of xx^{li} j^{d} recou'ed in the kings benche to the prishe without that the prishnors doo make Allowance owt of the same to George Wytton for his chardges in that Accion disbursed the sayd prashnors doo condesend and Agree that Alowance shalbe made acordingly to him after the rate as the prashnors shall haue for ther portion Disbursed in that accion the sayde wytton making contribusion towards such chardges as shalbe spent in obtayning of the sayd xx^{li} j^{d} or any p't therof after the rate of his portion that hee shall haue

At a vestry holden the xxviij of June 1590 Thomas Taylor was Chosen Colector for the poore in the rome of Thoms Turner & Thoms Smith still to remayne for one yer more According vnto the order in that behalfe p'voyded

At a vestry holden the xxxj of Januarij A 1590 ther was Chosen Awditors for the Accompt of Israell Owyn lat Churche warden Thoms fforman Robt Cudner John Bowser & Thoms Addams

Att the same vestry it was condescended and Agreede that Katterin Rawne nowe being maintayned at the Chardges of the parrishe by monethly collection shall nowe be deliu'ed ou^{r} vnto the Chardg and Custody of John Dickinson of the hospitall of kingsland who is the Guyder therof & hee to haue the som of fowre pounds in monney & duble Apparell with bedding and he the sayde Dickinson & Roger Spence plasterer to be bound by Obligacon in the som of xiij^{li} vj^{s} viij^{d} to mayntayner & kepe her well so long as shee shall leve & so dischardge ye prishe for eu^{r}

At the same vestry was chosen Colector with Thoms Smith, willm withnall in the rowme of Thomas Taylor

At a vestry holden the xxth of June 1591 was Chosen Colector in the rowme of Thoms Smith John Jaques and willm withnall to remayne According to order for twoe yeers space

At a vestry holden the vth daye of December A^{o} 1591 theese parsons heareafter mensioned being p'sent Mr Alderman Radclyf Mr Alderman Ryder M^{r} thorpp parson Mr Nichās Barnesley Mr Ric Candler M^{r} homphrey street Robt Cudner Edwd Ryder Thoms Turner Arnold Richardson Jerrom Suker Robt wincott James standley w^{m} withnall hughe dale Thoms Doughty & henry Allward Churche warden ther was Chosen Churchwarden in the Rome of John Leaves Richard Hayes to continew According to the Aunsient custom for ij yeares next ensuyng & m^{r} Barnesley & m^{r} standley having pmised to be ayding & assisting for the sute in lawe

At the same vestry was Chosen sydemen Jerom Suker & Thoms Carpinter

At the same vestry it was decreede that the collectors for the poore shall eu'y yeere heareafter yeeld & leev A coppy of ther Accompt reiestred in ye Church book vnder ther handes

At a vestry holden the xxv of Aprill A^{o} 1591 it was Condesended & xviij li.
Agreede that thear shuld be An other Assement and collection as a for sayd for the som of tenne pounds to be deliu'd vnto the hands of John Leaves [church] warden to follow the sute for the obtayning of S'tayne Arearages dew vnto the parishe By George wytton for those tenements houlden [by] him in fleetstreet

Mr Aldrmā Radclif	xx^{s}	Joyse	ij^{s}
Mr Thatcher	xv^{s}	Richard Hayes	xvj^{d}
Mr Henry Beeche^{r}	xv^{s}	Cornelis Spering	xx^{d}
Mr Candlor	v^{s}	James Standley	ij^{s} vj^{d}
John Billingford	ij^{s}	Richard Rauescroft	o
Robert wincoll	v^{s}	John Leaves	xvj^{d}
Robert stratford	ij^{s} vj^{d}	Mr Jaques	x^{s}
Jerrom Suker	v^{s}	Thoms Carpinter	iij^{s} iiij^{d}
ffrauncs Lodg	v^{s}	Arnold Richardson	vj^{s} viij^{d}
John Hooke	xvj^{d}	Mr Smith	vj^{s} viij^{d}
John Strachan	ij^{s}	xpofer Mydleton	iij^{s}
Lewys Morgan	xij^{d}	Maister Tirrell	xij^{s}
Nichās Barnesley	x^{s}	Robert Parpoint	ij^{s}
Robert Cudner	ij^{s} vj^{d}	Henry Aylword	ij^{s} vj^{d}
Mrs Spragg	iij^{s} iiij^{d}	Mr Bowser	viij^{s}
John whyt	iij^{s} iiij^{d}	Thoms Pavely	iij^{s} iiij^{d}
Izaak Kylborn	xx^{d}	Mr Street	x^{s}
John howell	xvj^{d}	M^{r} w^{m} Ryder	xv^{s}
John heath	o o	Raphe Boswell	ij^{s} vj^{d}
Georg hunt	iij^{s} iiij^{d}	Edward Ryder	viij^{s}
Henry Smalwod	xij^{d}	hughe Grave	iij^{s} iiij^{d}
Thoms Turner	vj^{s} viij^{d}	Thoms Paradyn	v^{s}
Thoms Addams	o o	Israell Owē	viij^{s}
Hughe Richards	xij^{d}	Mr Thoms fformā	x^{s}
willm withnall	iij^{s} iiij^{d}		

Thomas Tirrell	Sessors	Thoms Paveley &	Collectors
Nichas Barnesley		Jerom Suker	
homphrey Street			
Thoms Turner			

At A vestry holden the vth of July 1591 for A seasment of A fyftene xiiv. s.
According to A p'sept from my lord mayiore to be Imployed for her ma^{ties} p'sent S'vice

Mr Thatcher	xiij^{s} iiij^{d}	Jerrom Suker	ij^{s}
Mr Alde'mā Radclyf	xiij^{s} iiij^{d}	John Billingford	iiij^{d}
John howell	vj^{d}	M^{r} henry Beecher	vj^{s} viij^{d}
John whyt	xij^{d}	Mr Candler	xx^{d}
Izaak kilborne	viij^{d}	Robert wincoll	xvj^{d}
John Hodson	iiij^{d}	Arnold Richardson bakroms	xij^{d}
Robert Cudner	iiij^{d}	John Leaves	ij^{d}
James Bayly	ij^{d}	Ric Rauenscroft	vj^{d}
Nichas Barnesly	ij^{s}	James standley	vj^{d}
ffrauncs Lodge	xviij^{d}	Cornelis Speering	vj^{d}
Robert Stratford	vj^{d}	Ric hayes	iiij^{d}

Joyce Otkar	xij^{d}	Piers Mansprugh	iiij^{d}
John Bowsers watercowrse and Back gate	iij^{s} iiij^{d}	shoomakr	ij^{d}
		George hunt	viij^{d}
hughe dale	ij^{d}	the taylor	ij^{d}
willm̄ withnall	vj^{d}	Thoms Paradins bakroms	viij^{d}
hughe Richards	iiij^{d}	John Heath	iiij^{d}
Thoms Turner	xviij^{d}	Israell Owin bakroms	vj^{d}
Henry Smalewod	vj^{d}	Thoms fformans watercowrse	vj^{d}

The Alley

Mrs Spragg	viij^{d}	Samewell Dowle	ij^{d}
Thoms Doughty	ij^{d}	Symon Jenson	ij^{d}
John merryott	ij^{d}		

The church yerd

John Hook	vj^{d}	Lewis Morgan	ij^{d}
Ric Robinson	ij^{d}	Willm Roberts	ij^{d}
John Strachan	iiij^{d}	Johne wright	ij^{d}
w^{m} martin	ij^{d}	Robert hudson	ij^{d}
John Cuddok	ij^{d}		

Collectors

John Howell
Izaake Kylborne

To bee deliu^{r} by these colectors to m^{r} Thoms Lawrens According to ye p^{r}sept from ye L mayo^{r}

At a vestrye holden ye xxvjth of Marche 1592 yt was agreed y^{t} ye wages of Thomas nebbes sexten of ye paryshe should be augmented to ye sūme of liij^{s} fowre pence by ye yeare by ye Consent of ye paryshioners whose names followe

Mr Aldermā Radclyffe M^{r} aldermā Ryder John Thorpe ꝑson Thom Tyrrell williā Aylward Rich Candler Thom fforman Nicholas barneslye Ed ryder Israell owen John Jaques Tho paradyne Jerō suker Robt Cudner Tho Adams ffrancis Lodge Tho pauelye Williā Wignall Hugh Graues Rics Robynson Jeames Stanlye

Henry Alward
Richard heyes } Churchwardens

At a vestrye holden in ye paryshe Churche of S^{t} xpoffers ye 2^{d} daye of Julye 1592 ye paryshe Clarck being dead there were theise two Williā Robartes & Thomas Nebbes propounded for a Clarcke at wch tyme Williā Robartes was Chosen to be y^{e} ꝑryshe Clarcke by ye Consent of all theise ꝑryshioners wch follow

John Thorpe Parson	Henry Alwarde } Churche wardens	
Mr Aldermā Radclyffe	Richard heyes	
Mr Aldermā Ryder	Thomas Tyrrell	Thomas fforman
Nicholas barnesly	Williā Mylward	Humfreye Streat
Edward ryder	Thomas Turner	John hooke
Tho Carpenter	Robart Cudner	Jerō Suker
Williā Wignall	Robart Wincoll	xꝑoffer Mydleton
	George Hunt	Hugh Richardson

The same daye yt was agreed y^{t} Jerom suker was appoynted to be Collector ffor ye poore ffor two yeres to come next Insuinge

The same daye also yt was agreed y^{t} ye Parson & Churchewardens wth Mr Anthony Radclyffe alderm̄ Williā Ryder Alderm̄ Thomas Tyrrell williā mylwarde Thomas fformā Hūfry Streat Nicolas barneslye & Jeames stanly shall at any tyme apoynted or any of them to ye nomber of sixe meete to take order ffor ye lyinge out of such charges as shall serue to prosecute ye paryshe suite ffor ye arrerages of rent wthholden ffrom y^{e} ꝑryshe by george witten wch Mr Barnesly hath promysed to doe & prosecute

At a vestry holden ye xth day of december 1592 there was chosen Church warden in the rowmth of henry Alward Raphe boswell & so to Contynew Churchwarden ij yeres next Insuinge.

At ye same vestry yt was agreed by ye Consent of all ꝑryshioners then pn̄ y^{t} ye parson & Churchwardens shall pay all such somes of mony vnto Nicholas barnsely out of ye rent dew to ye paryshe as he ye sayd Nicolas barnseley shall wth ye Consent of y^{e} ꝑson & Churchwardens wth others as is ordred aboue at a vestry bearing Date ye 2^{d} day of July 1592 lay out for ye recou^{r}y of ye Arrerages dew to y^{e} ꝑrysh by george witton wch he hath promysed at ye same vestry to doe

At ye same vestry were Chosen Auditors for ye Accoumptes of henry Alwarde late Churchwarden Humfry Streat Izraell owen Nicolas barnesly Robt Cudner

At ye same tyme were chosen sydemen xpoffer mydleton & ffrancis Lodge

Willm Ryder	Richard heye
John Thorp Parson	Rſ Raphe boswell's m^{r}ke churchwarden
Thomas tyrryll	Thomas Turnā
w^{m} milward	Jerom Suker
homfreye Streete	Wm Wythnolle
Nycholas Barnsley	ffrauncis lodge
Israell owyn	Robart Carter

Memorandū y^{t} ye xxxth of september 1592 was payd vnto Thomas 95
Wyckyn draꝑ & rent gatherer of ye drapers—iij^{s} iiij^{d} to ye vse of ye poore brethren of ye Company aforesayd according to ye last will of benedict harlewyn deceased by henry Allward Churchwarden

Memorand y^{t} ye xvijth day of october 1593 was payd vnto Thomas Wickin draꝑ & rent gatherer of ye drapers—iij^{s} iiij^{d} to ye vse of ye poore brethren of ye Company afore syde according to ye last will of benedict harlewyn deceased by Richard Heyes Churchwarden.

A Booke ffor all such thinges as [are] agreed vpon at ye vestries in ye parysh of St xpoffers neare ye Royall Exchaunge begiñinge this pn'te 9th day of Decẽber 1593.

1593

Att a vestrye holden ye 9th day of december 1593 was chosen Churchwarden in ye roome of Richard Hayes Thomas Turner & so to Contynew Church[warden] two yeres followinge

At ye same vestrye were Chosen sydemen Lewis Morgan and Hugh overy

At ye samevestrye were chosen Auditors ffor Richard Hayes his accompte for one yere last past } Tho fforman, Nicolas barnesly, Israell owen, Robt Cudner

At ye same vestrye it is allso agreed y^t Edward Ryder and ffrancis Lodge together wth Tho fforman Nicolas barnesly Israell owen and Robt Cudner shall Audit ye accoumpte of William Withnall & John Jaques Collectors for ye poore and also together wth one of ye Aldermen shall ceasse them y^t are vnceassed for ye same Collection

It is also agreed at ye same vestrye y^t y^e ꝑsons aforenamed shall haue Authority to reforme ye byll for ye Clarkes wages

Surueyghors for ye pish

Hũfrye streate, Nicolas barnesly } Tho fforman, Robte Cudner } Tho Turner, Tho pauely }
Edward Ryder, Tho Adams } 9 of decẽber 1593

At a vestry holden ye 16 of december 1593 It was agreed y^t y^e Ceassors for y^e Collection for y^e poore shall ceasse y^e paryshioners of this paryshe towards y^e payment of ij^d aweeke ffor one whole yere according to y^e statute for y^e relieffe of y^e poore soldiars & also for y^e Arrerages since y^e 3^d of July last past 1593

Att a vestry holden y^e $xxiiij^{th}$ day of february 1593 yt was agreed y^t there should be a loane of so much mony as is according to y^e rate as was heretofore ceassed vpon the paryshioners of this payshe to follow y^e suite agaynste Georg witton vpon his bond and all other sutes betwene him and y^e parson & churchwardens. prouided alwayes y^t yff ye sayd George witten doe accept of ye last agreement offred vnto him to geue his assurance by bond and allso to make ye parson & Churchwardens a generall release of all sutes at or before ye feaste daye of Easter next that then this order to be of no effect

The ceassers appoynted ffor this loane } Thomas Tyrrell, Nicolas Barnesly, Israell owen, Jerome suker

The collectors } Raphe Boswell, Thomas Turner

John Thorp parson
Willm̃ Ryder
Thomas tyrryll
Israell owyn
Jerom Shuker
ꝑ me Jacobũ Stanley
Richard heye

Raphe boswell, Thomas Turner } Churchwardens
Nycholas Barnsley

1594

At a vestrye holden ye xxv^{th} daye of March 1594 was Anne [ ] widow chosen pencyoner in ye roome of williã yarington late deceased

At a vestry holden ye first daye of december 1594 was Chosen Thomas Paradyne to be churchwarden for two yeares in the roume of Raphe boswell

A the same vestry were chosen syde menn John Carpenter and Hugh Richards and in ye stead of John Carpenter who is gon away was chosen sideman Richard Mydleton.

Att a vestry holden in ye paryshe Church ye xix^{th} day of January 1594 were appoynted Auditors ffor ye Accoumpte of Raphe Boswell Churchwarden

Hũfry streate, nicholas Barnsely }
Israell Owen, Robte Cudner }

At ye same vestry these auditors aboue named are appoynted to examyn ye accompte of Jeames stanly for ye charge of ye paryshe suite

1594

At a vestry holden ye xvj^{th} day of ffebruary in ye paryshe Churche of St xpoffers it is ordered y^t ye eldest Churchewarden shall allwayes put in a sufficient suertie wth him selfe & be bounde to Aunswer all such mony goods and ornaments of ye Church as shalbe deliu'ed to ye said eldest Churchwarden and Thomas Turner now Churchwarden is to beginne accordinge to this order The vse of wch stocke and mony of ye Church is to be referred vnto ye good will and discretion of eu'y Churchwarden This order was sett downe By consent of the ꝑyshioners whose names are subscribed ye daye and yere aboue written p'uided allwayes y^t ye suertie is to be w^{th}out the paryshe

	Thomas tyrryll	Willm̃ Becher
p me Johne Thorp	Nycholas Barnsley	homfrye streate
Rectore xpofferi	Israell owyn	Raphe boswell
	Jerom Shuker	Robart codnar
	ꝑ me Jacobũ Stanly	Thomas pavelly
	hugh Dale	Thomas adams

Hugh dale his m^{ck} H M H L

Att ye same vestry y^t was agreed y^t Thomas fforman and hũfry streat Nicolas barnsely and Robt Cudner should refourme ye byll of ye Clarkes wages & ye same ꝑsons shall ceasse for ye maymed souldyers

At a vestrye holden ye xxx^{th} day of June 1594 was chosen Collector for ye poore ffrauncis Lodge to be ioyned wth Thomas paradyne and to contynew two yeres acording to ye late precept.

1595

At a vestrye holden ye vj^{th} day of July 1595 was chosen Collector for ye poore Thomas pauely in ye roome of Thomas paradyne to contynew for two yeres next followinge to remyne one yere next Insuing wth ffrancis Lodge now Collecter

At a vestrye holden ye vij^{th} day of december 1595 was chosen Williã Withnall Churchwarden in ye rowme of Thomas Turner to contynew two yeres next following

At ye same vestrye were appoynted Auditors ffor Thomas Turner his accompte vid' Israell owyn
Rich hayes
Rafe boswell
Nicolas Barnsely

At ye same vestrye were chosen swornemen Richard Smyth and George hunt

At a vestrie holden ye 27th day of June 1596 was chosen Collecter ffor ye poore in ye roome of ffrancis Lodge and to ioyne wth ye elder Collecter Thomas pauely hugh dale to Contynew two yeres next following.

ffyveth of december 1596

Att a vestrye holden the day and yere abovesaid m^{r} Edward Ryder was Chosen Churchwarden for two yere in the steede of m^{r} Paradyne and Thomas Westwraye grocer ~~and Arthur Middleton m^{r}chauntaylor were Chosen Sydemen~~ and John Thorowgood Haberdasher were Chosen Sydemen.

Att the same vestrye were chosen to audyte the accompt of m^{r} Paradyne Churchwarden nowe goinge out
Mr Streat
Mr Boswell
Mr Barnesley
Mr Heys

The xiijth of Marche 1596

Md at a vestrye holden this day yt was agreed that Mr Barnsley should kepe the bond for the Church goods wch bond he nowe receyved. Rcd by me Nycholas Barnsley

2 b. The xxvth of m'che 1597

At a vestrie holden the day and yeare abovesaid there was chosen and appoynted for a pencioner in the steede of Goodwyfe Nebbes, John Heath nowe lyenge Bethred [bed-rid] and hath bene longe sycke. And yt is further graunted and assented vnto That the next pencioner that shall fall Goodwyfe Harris shall have the next place of the same pencioner because shee hath bene often pmised yt and is nowe disapoynted thereof

Thomas tyrryll — George hunt
Nycholas Barnsley — Thomas T C Collins Marke
Jno Quarles Jun' — hugh Dale
Jerom Shuker — John Thorowgood
James Stanley — georg makereth
Thomas Carpenter

The xixth of June 1597

Att a vestry holden the day & yere above wrytten Ther was chossen and apoynted a collecter ffor the pore in the rome of Thomas pavley Thomas carpender

w^{m} withnoll } Churchwardens
Edward Ryder }
Nycholas Barnsley
homfrye Streete
Jerom Shuker
ffrauncis lodge
Thomas paveley

3 a. The xj day of december anno 1597

At a vestry holden the day & yeare above written was apoynted for ij yeares ensuyng to be churchwarden Jerome Shukar in the place of william withnall, & at the same tyme were apoynted sydemen Rychard Sandar & George mackerell

At the same vestry were apoynted auditers to receyve the accompt of william withnall churchwarden now going out m^{r} nicholas Barnesly Rychard heyes m^{r} Thomas Tyrrell m^{r} humfry Street

Andr: Arnolde — w^{m} withnall
rector eccles. — Edward Ryder

The viijth of ffebruary 1597

There was a veiwe made in the vestry howse of the dedes and wrytings concerninge o^{r} Land in ffletstreat to fynd out when m^{r} wyttons lease began And we fynd that the lease of ffortye yeres did begyn the vjth of August 1585 as yt doth appeare by the copye of the speciall verdyct and by a lre of Attorney and a note fixed to the same remayninge in the Chest. wytnesses we whose names are here vnder wrytten

Edward Ryder } Cherche
Jerom Shuker } wardens
Nycholas Barnsley
James Stanley

It was also agreed by a gen'all vestrye That forasmuch as the said witton at Sondry Tymes hath much abvsed the pishe even to their faces making his Comparisons wth them and that as knaves he founde them so knaves he would leave them and wth many other Lewd speeches wch the pishioners have taken to hart. And therefore have agreed and desire the same at their Successors hands That the said witton may never have nor any of his s[uccessors] have any new lease of the said messuags But that the same howses may remayne vnleased vntill the lease in possession shalbe ended. And then the most to be made for the pishe that wilbe geven for the same.

Att a vestreye holden in o^{r} pishe of St Crestophers this p^{r}sent 2d of July 1598 was Chosen Collector for the poore in the Roome of hene dale Thomas Westwraye for thys ij yeres folowyng 3 b.

	Andr: Arnolde parson
Edward Ryder } Church	Nycholas Barnsley
Jerom Shuker } wardens	homfrye Streate
Humphrey milward	w^{m} wythnoll
John fewilliams	Richard heye
By me Anthonye Clowes	Thomas pavelly
By me Edw. Erby	Thomas Carpenter
By me william Salway	m^{r} collins T C marke
By me John Bell	John thorowgood

Att a vestrye holden the xxixth of October 1598 was chosen in the place of m^{r} Mackareth that went out of the pishe afore the yere ended beinge for that yere Chosen a Syde man Willm Newbye was newly Chosen Sydeman to be sworne on the monday following afore the ordynary for the tyme to come and the yere to Come

A. Arnolde parson
Edward Ryder } Church warden
Jerom Shuker }

At a vestrie holden in this parrishe the 19th of November 1598. It was agreed by a whole consent to be suters to Christs hospitall for the obteyninge of a childe to be taken into the hospitall wch was misbegotten by John Spragge in this parrishe wch childes name is Alice and Christened in this parrish the 17 daie of this said moneth of November 1598.

Andrew Arnolde parson
Jerom Shuker Cherchwarden

Sonday the 3 of December 1598

Att a vestry holden the day and yere above said was Chosen in the place of Edward Ryder Churchwarden nowe goinge out: James Stanley Churchwarden to Joyne wth Jerome Suker Cheif Churchwarden And the said James to s've for two yeres from xpmăs next as a Churchwarden

Also more the day and yere abovesaid Chosen for sydemen for one yere from xpmăs next Willm Nuby and Hughe Goddard.

Audytors for the accompt of m^{r} Ryder Churchwarden goinge out were Chosen

Mr Tho: Tyrrell
Mr Humphr Streat
Mr Nichlas Barnsly
Mr Wm Withnall

Sonday the second of December 1599 accordinge to auncyent Custome vsed in this pishe the next Sondaie after St Andrewes day alwayes vsed was Chosen in the place of Jerom Suker Churchwarden nowe going out, Att this vestry nowe holden ffrauncs Lodge to Joyne wth James Stanley thelder Churchwarden And they both to s've for one hole yere from xpmaš next as Churchwardens.

This day also were Chosen Sydemen Thomas Alport and Henry Levett to serve this yere

Audytors Chosen to Audytt m^{r} Sukers accompt

Mr Barnesly
Mr Streat
Mr Ryder
Mr Withnall

xxvj^{o} die Octobris 1600

At a Vestrey holden the xxvjth daie of October A^{o} dñi 1600 by the whole consente of all the Parrishioners then pn'te were nõiated and chosen to ioyne wth James Stanley and ffrauncs Lodge Churchwardens for to make an assessem^{t} for the releife of Maymed Souldiers accordinge to the Statute made in A^{o} Regni Elizabethe xxxix^{o} these psons whose names heereafter ffollowe viz

Nicholas Barnesley
Humfrey Streate
Thomas Paueley
Thomas Westwraye
Humfrye Myllwarde
Thomas Carpenter

At that Vestry also were nomynated and appointed for newe Pentioners to have the releife that Wyddowe ffowler and Isabell Ansell had the wch are nowe dead viz The Children of Robts the Clarke and the Children of Guyons.

The vijth of decembe^{r} 1600

At this Vestry was chosen in the place of James Stanley Elder Churchwarden nowe to goe out John Jakes to serve for Two yeeres as the Custome is and Edwarde Erbye and Thomas Collins for the Two sydemen

Awdito^{rs} for James Stanleyes accompt

Mr Streat	Auditors	A: Arnolde	Antho: Radclyffe
Mr Barnesley		John Quarles	Tho: Paueley
M^{r} fforman		Hum: Streate	Tho: Alporte
Mr Suker		Jerom: Suker	Hum: Myllwarde
		Willm: Withnall	John: Thorowgoode
		Richarde: Smyth	Hughe: Dale
		Nichos: Barnesley	Rich: Heyes
			Thomas: Westward

A note of the most pte of the goodes and ymplemts belonginge to the Parrishe of S^{t} xpõfers neere ye Stocks by James Stanley Churchewarden afore his goinge out viz in Decemb^{r} 1600

Itm j large Byble
Itm 2 service Bookes
Itm ij bookes called the Paraphrases of Erasmus
Itm iij olde Psalters
Itm j Surplis
Itm quarte and a pottle pott
Itm j Velure Table Cloth
Itm j olde Velvet Table Cloth
Itm j hearse Cloth
Itm j Pulpytt Cloth
Itm ij Lynnen Table Cloths one of wch is of Diap the other of Callico
Itm j napkin of diap
Itm j olde Turkey Carpett Cloth
Itm j Cheste in the Vestrey wth a Counter
Itm j Presse and a little olde Cheste
Itm xj fformes
Itm ij olde Coffins
Itm xxiiij^{o} Bucketts
Itm vj Belles wth newe Ropes
Itm vij Printed and wrytten Tables
Itm 4 Ladders
Itm ij shovells j spade and j pickaxe
Itm ij paire of Tressells
Itm j howreglasse
Itm the Cōmunion Cupp wth a silver Cover
Itm a silver plate for the Cōmunion breade
Itm of Readye Monye ... ... xxxv^{li} xv^{s} iij^{d}
delyu'ed m^{r} Lodge 2 m'ch 1600
All theis mony and goods were delyu'd m^{r} Lodg

xxvj^{o} die Decembris 1600

A Cessem^{t} and Taxacõn made vppon eu'y Inhabitant able to paie wthin the pishe of S^{t} xpõfer nigh the Stocks in London for the releife of Maymed Soldiers and Marryners accordinge to the Statute in such case pvyded by Nicholas Barnesley Humfrye Streate James Stanley Thomas Paveley and Humfrye Myllwarde Chosen for that purpose by consent of the whole Parrishioners at a Vestrye the xxvjth of October 1600.

Wyddowe Jarvis	vj^{d}	Richarde Saunders	iiij^{d}
John Quarles	xvj^{d}	Raphe Robinson	vj^{d}
Thomas Westwraye	x^{d}	Richarde Buishopp	ij^{d}
John ffeewilliams	iiij^{d}	Charles Walmesley	ij^{d}
John Keelinge	viij^{d}	John Jaques an empty howse	viij^{d}
John Laramore	ij^{d}	Hughe Dale	ij^{d}
Nicholas Barnesley	xiiij^{d}	William Withnall	viij^{d}
Richarde Neale	ij^{d}	Phillipp Sparke	viij^{d}
ffrauncs Lodge	x^{d}	Hughe Richardes	ij^{d}
Mathewe Smith	ij^{d}	Henrye Levett	vj^{d}
Jerom Suker	x^{d}	Thomas Collins	vj^{d}
Rice Webb	vj^{d}	Anthonye Clowes	viij^{d}
Richarde Haies	iiij^{d}	Hughe Goddarde	viij^{d}
Peeter Tryan	ij^{s}	Thomas fforman ...	xiiij^{d}
Humfrye Myllwarde	x^{d}	William ffinche	viij^{d}
Mr Anthonye Radclyffe ...	ij^{s}	ffrauncs Needeham ...	x^{d}
Cornelius Speeringe	viij^{d}	Xpõfer Monke	vj^{d}
Edmonde Hynton	vj^{d}	John Thorowgood	viij^{d}

Thomas Carpenter ...	x^{d}	[5 b.] Richarde Smyth	x^{d}
Leonarde Harwood	vj^{d}	Thomas Tirrell	viij^{d}
Thomas Alporte	x^{d}	Thomas Pavior	vj^{d}
Humfrye Streate ...	xiiij^{d}	James Stanley	x^{d}
Thomas Paveley	vj^{d}	William Neweby	viij^{d}
Rowlande Backehowse a shutt in	xviij^{d}	John Jaques a howse shutt in	x^{d}
Mason	vj^{d}	John Jaques	xij^{d}
		Edward Erbye	vj^{d}

Sonday the 6 day of December Anno dñi 1601

At a vestrie holden the day and yeare above written was chosen in the place of ffrancs Lodge churchwarden now going out, Hugh Dale to ioyne wth John Jacques now chief churchwarden and to serve for ij yeares from xm̃as next as churchwarden.

the sayd day and yeare were chosen sidemen for this yeare francis needham and Humphry milward.

Auditors for the accompt of m^{r} ffrancis Lodge were then chosen

M^{r} fforman
Mr Street
Mr Barnesley
M^{r} withnall

[6 a.] Sondaie beinge the vth daie of December Ao Dom. 1602

At a vesterey holden the daie and yeare aboue written was Chosen in the place of John Jaques Churchwarden now going Thomas Carpenter to Joyne wth Hughe Daile Cheif Churche warden and the said Tho. Carpenter to serve for two yeares from xp̃mas next as a Churchwarden

And also were the daie and yeare abouesaid Chosen for one yeare from xpmas next Leonard Harwood and Anthony Clowes Sydmen

Auditors for the Accompt of John Jaques

M^{r} forman
Mr Strete
M^{r} hayes
Mr Lodge

Sunday being the xxvijth of november Anno dñi 1603

At a vestry holden the day and yeare above written was chosen in the place of Hugh Dale churchwarden now going out Thomas westrow to be ioyned with Thomas Carpenter now chief churchwarden and the sayd Thomas westrow to serve for ij yeares to come from xm̃as next

The same day were chosen for this yeare to come from Christmas next william fynch and Raph Robinson sidemen

Auditors for the accompt of Hugh Dale

m^{r} forman m^{r} Street
m^{r} Hayes m^{r} Lodge

[6 b.] At a vestrie holden the 31 of march the yeare of our lord 1605 were chosen churchwardens for the yeare following Thomas westrow and Richard Smyth and for sydemen to assist the churchwardens the same yeare were chosen William Lee and Rice Webb

Itm the same day were appoynted Auditors of Thomas Carpenters accompt m^{r} Humphrey Street and m^{r} Thomas forman m^{r} ffrancis Lodge and m^{r} Hugh Dale

Itm the same day were chosen overseers for the poore to assist the churchwardens, Thomas pavier and Henrie Jackson John nevill and william Swan.

1606

At a vestrie holden the 13 of April anno 1606 were chosen churchwardens for the yeare following Richard Smyth and Humphrey milward and for sidemen to assist the churchwardens the same yeare were chosen Thomas pavier & John nevill and for Auditors of Thomas westrowes accompt m^{r} Humphrey Street m^{r} Thomas forman m^{r} Thomas Carpenter m^{r} John Quarles m^{r} francis Lodge and m^{r} Thomas moulson or any 4 of them the day of the accompt to be god willing the 6 of may next ensuing

Anno dñi 1607

At a vestrie holden the 5 of Aprill were chosen Churchwardens for the yeare folowing, Humphrey milward and Thomas Alport: for sidemen to assist the Churchwardens were chosen the same day Henrie Jackson and Humphrey waterson: and for Auditors of Richard Smith his accompt, m^{r} Humphrey Street m^{r} Thomas fforman m^{r} francis Lodge m^{r} Thomas moulson m^{r} Thomas Carpenter and m^{r} Thomas westrow or any foure of them, the day to be wthin one moneth after Easter. The same day were chosen overseers for the poore or sessors for the yeare following John nevill, Thomas pavier, Robart Heyes, Rice webb.

At a vestrie holden the 27 of march 1608 were chosen Churchwardens for the yeare following Mr Thomas Alport and Mr Rice webb, for sydemen m^{r} Thomas Saxebie, and m^{r} John keasor, and for Auditors of m^{r} milward his accompt, m^{r} humphrey Street, m^{r} Thomas forman m^{r} Richard Smyth, m^{r} francis Lodge, m^{r} Thomas westrow, m^{r} Thomas Moulson, or any foure of them.

The same day were chosen overseers or sessors for the poore m^{r} Antonie Elowes, m^{r} Ruben Boorne m^{r} Denham m^{r} william Swan

At a vestrie holden the 4 of Aprill 1613 was chosen for elder churchwarden m^{r} George Low, and for the other churchwarden m^{r} Laurence Norcot, & for sidemen henrie Ashton and John browne, & for Auditors of m^{r} william lees accompt m^{r} humphrey streat, m^{r} Richard Smyth and m^{r} Thomas Alport m^{r} francis Lodge, m^{r} Thomas westrow m^{r} Thomas Moulson or any foure of them, the day to be the 4 of may next ensuing.

At a vestry houlden the 24 of Aprill 1614 were chosen m^{r} Lawrence Norcott fo^{r} Elder Churchwarden and m^{r} Henry denham fo^{r} thother churchwarden & fo^{r} Sydemen m^{r} Richard Doleman and m^{r} Thomas fforman, & fo^{r} Auditors fo^{r} George Lowes accompte m^{r} Humfry Streete m^{r} Thomas Alporte m^{r} ffrancis Needeham m^{r} Thomas Westrowe m^{r} Thomas Moulson and m^{r} ffrancis Lodge or any foure of them the day to be the 17 of may next 1614.

At a Vestry holden the 16th Aprill 1615 were chosen

Mr Henrie Denham ye elder } Churchwardens
Mr Richard Byarde ye younger }
Mr Phillip Harrison } Sidmen
Mr Thomas Dringe }

Auditors for m^{r} Lawrence Norcotts accompts

Mr Humfrey Street
Mr Thomas Westrowe
Mr Thomas Moulson
Mr Francis Lodge
Mr Thomas Alport
Mr Francis Needham
Mr John Neuill
Mr William Finch
Mr Rice Webb

or any foure of them vppon such a day as the churchwarden shall appoint, wth his best conveniency; being now sick.

Att a vestrie houlden the 22[tie] of June 1615 it was there concluded that a colleckcyon should mee made for the releife of m[rs] Arnold the widdo of m[r] Andrew Arnold o[r] late parson towards the w[ch] those hervnder written gaue as ffolloweth vide[r]

S[r] Samewell Tryon	...	...	xl[s] — oo
M[r] Thom[s] Mowlson	...	...	xl[s] — oo
M[r] Thom[s] westroe	...	...	xl[s] — oo
M[r] Georg Loe ...	...	...	xl[s] — oo
M[r] John Nevill ...	...	...	xxx[s] — o
M[r] Humphrie Street	...	...	xx[s] —
M[r] ffrauncis Lodg	...	...	x[s] —
M[r] William Chapman	...	...	x[s] —
M[r] William ffintch	...	...	x[s] —
M[r] ffrauncs Needham	...	...	x[s] —
M[r] Thom[s] Alportt	...	...	x[s] —
M[r] Richard Downes	...	...	x[s] — o
M[r] Georg Harwood	...	...	x[s] — o
M[r] Ant[o] Clowes ...	...	...	xx[s] — o
M[r] Richard Lee ...	...	...	v[s] —
M[r] Lawrence Norcott	...	...	v[s] — o
M[r] Isack Seward	...	...	xviij[d]
Hen Denham	...	...	v[s] — o

The whole sum w[ch] is collleckted and delivered to hir amounteth to ... ... } xv[li] xvj[s] vj[d]

p mee Henry Denham

the 12th of November 1615

M[d] that at a vestry holden the day and yere abovewritten it was then and there agreed by the said pishion's that on thursday next w[ch] shalbe the sixteenth daie of this instant moneth of November, are appoynted M[r] Docto[r] Peirse pson M[r] Denham and M[r] Byard churchwardens M[r] Humfry Street M[r] Thomas westrawe M[r] Thomas Molson M[r] George Lowe and M[r] Thom[s] Alportt together wth M[r] Woodward Sen[r] to meete at the pish Church of S[t] Christofers and there to conferr together concerning the lands of the said pish

It is likewise agreed at this vestrie that for the leckt[r] one Sunday in the afternoone w[ch] is now concluded vppon there shall bee allowed thirtie three pounds six shillings eight pence to bee raysed vppon the pishe rateably according to each mans assessm[t] to the poore but if ~~fortie pounds may bee raysed~~ somutch may bee raysed over and above the said assessm[t] as will make the said sum to amount to ffortie pounds then the same to contynew during the pleasure of the parson and pishoners.

Note that the first qrt[r] what wanteth of x[li] is to bee made vpp out of the churchstock.

It is likewise concluded att this vestrey that a mason shall bee agreed with for p[r]sent ~~mending~~ repacyon and mending of the fower windoes in the steeple and likewise to haue a Carpenter to vew the church wall whether there may convenyent sheds bee made agaynst the same if not then forthw[th] to haue a fayre bentch there sett vpp for the p[r]venting of soyle and filth w[ch] is contynewallie there laid

b. March xxxj[tie] 1616

Att a vestrie houlden the day and yeere abouewritten there is chosen for the elder churchwarden m[r] Richard Byward and for the othe churchwarden m[r] Thomas Foreman and for sidemen m[r] Robertt parcell and m[r] John Helms There is likewise chosen for Auditors for the account of Henry Denham late churchwarden m[r] Humphrie Street m[r] Ant[o] Clowes m[r] willim ffintch m[r] Thom[s] westrow m[r] ffrauncis Lodg and m[r] ~~william Chapman~~ Jn[o] Nevill

The 20th of Aprill 1617 beinge Easter day

At a vestry houlden in S[t] Christophers Parish Church it is agreed that there are chosen for churchwardens m[r] Thom[s] forman for the elder churchwarden and m[r] Richard Downes for the yonger churchwarden and for sidemen m[r] Isack Seward and m[r] Thomas Jackson

Thomas Foreman, Richard Downes } Churchwardens

Isaack Seward, Thomas Jackson } Sidemen

Likewise there are chosen for the Auditing of the acc[o] of m[r] Richard Byard late churchwarden these whose names are heervnder written

M[r] Humphrie street
M[r] Ant[o] Clowes
M[r] W[m] Fintch
M[r] Thomas westroe
M[r] John Neuill
M[r] Henry Denham

The Audite day is appoynted to bee one the Thursday next beefore Whitt sunday

The sixth of July 1617

At a vestrey houlden the day and yeare abovewritten in the parish Church of S[t] cristopher yt was agreed by generall consent that yf the lands in fleet streete can be let fo[r] 150[li] fine and fourscore pownds p anno that yt shall be let fo[r] 31 yeares in reversion after the expiracon of the lease now in beinge

William Peirs

Thomas forman, Richard Downes } Churchwardens

The 3th of Auguste 1617

At a Vestry holden this morninge it was condescended and agreed by the most and better sort of the parishioners of S[t] Christophers then ther presente, that ther shold be ffower score and Ten ponds Allowed to doctor Pearce, towards the newe buildinge of the one pte of his house In the Church yeard, the w[ch] said some before mentioned is the full agremente wth the Carpender, Bricklayer, and Plaisterer, for ther seuerall works, the w[ch] ffowerskore and Ten ponds is to be deducted out of the Hundreth and ffifteye ponds w[ch] is to be Receaued from the Tennants In ffleatstreat for ffynes for ther houses vppon leaces In reuertion, In witnes wherof we the parishioners whose names are hervnder written doe set to our hands as a ffurther ratefying and full Consent therto.

The 2 of november 1617

At a vestry holden this day yt was agreed that the title in question betuene the parish and m[r] Israell Owen concerning m[r] ffinches house shall be referd to m[r] Solicitor generall to the kinge on our behalfe and m[r] Owen to Chuse another at his discretion vnto which two we are all content to refer both the hearinge and determinacon of the title in question yf they both accorde to yelde the title to eyther pty of both vnder both their hands otherwise to take such other Course as shall be thought fit by the parish

William Peirs
Thomas Mowlson
Thomas westrow
homffrye streete
Anthonye Clowes
Thomas Buckner
John Nevell
Henry Denham
Laurence norcott
T C
George Harwood
Hughe Moorar
John Helmes
Thomas Jackson
Isack Seward
Thomas forman } Churchwardens
Richard Downes }

The 17th of december 1617

At a vestry holden this present day yt was agreed that the matter in question betwene m^r^ owen and the parish is referred to the docto^r^ and the churchwardens to prepare themselues agaynst the next terme and in the meane to advise themselues as fully as they may eyther for the reference to m^r^ solicito^r^ and m^r^ overbury o^r^ for the prosecuting of the suite yf the reference be not pformed

William Peirs
Thomas Moulson
Thomas westrow
John Nevell
Thomas Buckner
w^m^ Chapman
Laurence norcott
George Harwod
Nicholas Bourne
John Helmes
Thomas Jackson
Thomas forman } Churichwardens
Richard Downes }

Md that the xxviij^th^ day of Marche anno dñi 1618 Thomas fforman and Richard Downes Churchwardens receyved of Thomas Parks and John keasar Executo^rs^ of the last will and testam^t^ of Margery keeling widow decessed the Sumne of tenne pounds of lawfull Englishe money wch the said Margery in and by her said last will and testam^t^ gave and bequeathed to the Churchwardens of this Parishe Church of S^t^ xpofers and to their Successors to the intent that the same should be a stocke here and that the pfitt thereof should be disposed by them to the poore of the same parishe yerely at xpemmas for eu^r^ } x^li^

Thomas Forman
Richard Downes

At a vestry holden the 5th of Aprill 1618 there was Chosen Churchwardens and sidemen these whose names are vnderwritten

Richard Downes & } Churchwardens
William Chapman }
Mr Ken & } Sidemen
Mr Hooke }

There are also nominated for the auditing of the accompt of m^r^ Thomas fforman

Mr Street
M^r^ ffynch
Mr Norcott
Mr Mowlson
Mr Nevill
Mr Buckner or any foure of them

The audite day is appoynted on the 20th day of Aprill nextt cominge in the foornoone

Md att a vestrie houlden the 17 day of Aprill 1620 was chosen ^11^ George Harwod for the elder churchwarden and John Helnes for ye younger and for sidmen william Vicker and Auerie Gaskin

George Harwood } Churchwardens
John Helmes }
William Vickers } Sidemen
Auerie Gaskin }

Md that itt was agreed vppon att a vestrie houlden the 1th of June 1620 that Steuen Lasey is to pay three poundes towardes the bying of a comunion Cupp wch he lost, out of his wages by xx^s^ a yeare

md allso it was aggred that the churchwardens should pay to Reynold Trip three poundes yearely so long as he contineweth in the parish.

Att a Vestrye houlden the ffirst of Aprill 1621 there was chosen ^11^ churchwarden and sidmen these whose names are here vnderwritten

John Hellmes } Churchwaden
Isack Seward }
William Perkins } Sidemen
John Risley }

There was allso nomiated for the auditing of the account of George Harwod

m^r^ Streett	m^r^ Moulson
m^r^ norcott	m^r^ Neuill
m^r^ Downes	m^r^ Buckner
	m^r^ Chapman

The auditt Day is appointed on the 17th of Aprill next Coming in the fornoone

memorandum a vestrie houlden the 14th may 1621 it was then and there agreed by the said pishioners that the Churchwardens should take vp ffiftie Poundes at viij^s^ the hundred to wardes the payment of the monyes m^r^ George Harwood layd out in the tyme of his Churchwardenshipe and it is ffurther concluded and agreed the p^r^ishioners shall see the Churchwardens saued harmles

Immanuel Bourne
John Nevell
homfrye strete
Thomas Mowlson
Thomas Buckner
w^m^ Chapman
Thomas Forman
T C
Thomas Jackson
Thomas Carleton

memorandum a vestrie houlden the 24th June 1621 & ther was apoynted a vew day to be one the tenth of July nex Cominge and ther is apoynted to be vewers mr Borne mr Nevell mr Moulson mr Buckner mr Chapman mr fforman mr norcott mr Harward and the Churchwardens or any fouer of them to vew the Landes in ffleetstreat belonginge to this parishe

b. at a vestery houlden the 14th of July 1621 and there it was concluded and agreed by the parisheners of this parrishe that the Church should be new whitted and painted

At a vestrey houlden one sundaye the xiijth day of January 1621 whereas there is by the assent and Conssent of all the parishioners of this parrishe of St Cristoffors a lease made and sealed by mr docter peirce Rector of this parishe church and John Helmes and Isacke Shewerd gardians of the same parishe Church two one thomas fforman of this parishe and in like manner by the advise of the learned Counsell in the Lawe of the saide parishe there is a lease made by the saide thomas fforeman to one Laurence norcott all wch leases are made for the tryall of the Right of the saide parishe to a house in Cornhill in London Called the goulden Hinde some tymes in the tenner of one will Ramsie and late in the tenure and Occupacion of one Isarell Owyne or his assignee or assignes the benifitt whereof is to Redowne and accrue to the generall good and Proffit of the saide Church and parisheners Of this parishe Itt is therefore this daye wth the free assente and Conssente of all the parisheners (by Reasone the afore named persons are but vsed in trust for the good of the saide parishe publiquely and generally) agreed vnto that aswell the saide docter peirce John Helmes and Isacke Shewerd and Thomas fforeman: their leasee as alsoe the saide lawrance norcott leasee to the said Thomas fforeman shalbe from tyme to tyme and at all tymes hereafter saved and kepte harmles and indempnified or Recompensed by the parishioners of this parishe of for and Consarninge all shutes expences execucions and damages whatsoeuer wch shall heareafter arise grow or Come against them or any of them there or any of thire goodes Chattells landes and teniments by Reasone of the leases aforesaid or any of them or Cōmensinge any shute or deffendinge any shute in lawe towchinge or any way Consarninge them or the tytell of the foresaide house or any entery made by them or any of them threin two and that all mony and Charges whatsoeuer wch shalbe disbursed and laide out in and about the ꝑsecusion or defendinge of any shute or shutes or other expences and Charges whatsoeuer any growinge dew for or by Reason of the said house in whose name and against whomsoeuer the same shalbe Comensed and ꝑsecuted or brought shalbe from tyme to tyme laide out expended and disbursed by the now Churchwardens and hereafter by the then Churchwardens for the tyme beinge whereby none of the afforesaide parties may or shalbe any way dampnified and that all such mony and expences shalbe allowed and paide to them againe by the said parishoners vppon theire accoumts. wittnes our handes heare vnto Subscribed the day and yeare aboue written

John Nevell	T C	ffredericke Goodsonne
homffrye streete	John Helmes	Mathew fforster
Thomas Mowlson	Isack Seward	Tho drayton
Thomas Buckner	Thomas Jackson	John Rathband
wm Chapman	Thomas Carleton	
Thomas forman	Geo Haughton	

Laurence norcott	Humfry strete
Jno Kendricke	John Rushton
Richard Downes	
George Harwod	

A vestrie houlden the 17th of march 1621 and there it was Concluded and agreaed by the greater parte of the parishinoers of this parrishe that mr Blackwell the elder and mr Hord should be in tertayned for lecterors for one qurter of a yeare and at the qurters end to be at the pleasuer of the parrishe wheather one of them or both shall continue any longer and they are to begine at our ladie day next and soe to Continue vntell midsomer next

Immanuel Bourne	John Nevell
T C	Thomas Mowlson
Hughe Mooris	Israell owyn
John Roberts	homffrye streite
John Rushton	Jno Kendricke
John Helmes	wm Chapman
Isack Seward	Richard Downes
	Thomas forman
	George Harwod
	Thomas Jackson
	Anthony Hurst
	Humfry Castell
	Geo. Haughton
	Thomas Carleton

a vestrie houlden the 21th of Aprill 1622 and then and there it was concluded and agreed by the most and greatest part of the parishinors of this parrishe that mr John Kendricke should for the some of fortie poundes freely to be geven by him to the saide parrishe in consideracions of the freeing of him of ffive severall offeces ved' scauenger side man Quest man Constable and Churchwarden that is to say he shall never be Questned for any of them or Chosen by any of the foresaid parishinors

a vestrie houlden the 21th of Aprill 1622 and there was Chossen for vpper Churchwarden mr Isacke Seward and mr Thomas Jackson vnder churchwarden and side men mr Joanas Hopkings and mr william Barffild

and for the audditinge of John Helmes now Churchwarden his account is apoynted to be the seauenth of may beinge tewesday and ther is apoynted to be avditers mr Strete mr moulson mr nevell mr Bucknr mr Kendricke mr Chapman mr norcot mr Downes or any foure of them

A vestrie houlden the 13th of Aprill 1623 there was chosen for vppchurchwarden mr Thomas Jackson and mr Thomas Carleton vnderchurchwarden and sidmen mr Thomas Drayton and Jhon Rathborne

A vestry the 20th of Aprill 1623 weare apoynted for audittinge of the accompt of Isack Seward mr Jhon Nevill mr Hamphery streete mr Thomas moulson mr Thomas Buckner mr Lawrence Norcot mr George Harwood mr Chapm mr Richard Downes

At A Vestrey houlden the 13th of Jullye 1623 there was St Jeames his daye the 25th of this Instant month Appoynted ffor A vewe daye of our Landes in ffleete streete And there was Appoynted to veiwe them mr John Hellmes mr Isaack Seward mr Jonas Hopkins mr Bareffeild and the Churche-wardens and sidemen that now Are

A Vestrey houlden the 28th of marche 1624 there was chosen mr Thomas Carleton vpper Churche Warden and mr Thomas Buckener vnder Churche Warden and mr George Haughten and mr John Robartts sidemen ffor the yere ensuinge

A Vestrey houlden the 4th daye of Aprill 1624 were Apoynted ffor the Audyting of Thomas Jackson his Accounte mr John nevyll mr John Kendryck mr william Chapman mr Thomas fforman mr Humphrye Streete mr Lawrence norcott mr Richard dounes mr George Harwood or Any ffowre of them & The daye to bee teusdaye the 13th of Aprill next

At a vestery houlden the 18th day of Aprill 1624 it was then and ther agreed by the parrishinors that the Church wardens should tak vp mor ffyfte pounds to mak that some oweing to mr Lawrence wch is 150li two hundred pounds and That mr Thomas Jacksone should be payd his monyes layd out in is Churchwardenship and it was further concluded and agreed vppon yt a wrytyng should be made and sett doune in this vestrey book where vnto the sayd pishinors are to sett to their hands and that the Churchwardens are by them saued harmeles frome tyme to tyme

A vestery holden the 2th of may 1624 it was ther agreed that Edward Gyles wth hath the nurssing of Robert wilcockes should haue the keeping of hime tell mydsomer quarter next coming and then to bryng him vp and put in securety to ye parishe in dischardging them of him all wayes provided it may be to the lyking of the parishinors and the good of the Chyld

At a vestery houlden the 14th of July 1624 ther was Appoyntted for vewers of our land in fleetstreet mr Chapman mr Helmes mr Sayward mr Jacksone mr Hautton mr Roberts and the Churchwardens then being And there vew daye was one the 29 day of this Instant mounth aboue wryt

Memorand that whearas at a vestry houlden on sonday the 18th daie of Aprill 1624 it was agreed by the parishioners of this parishe of St Christofers nere the Royall exchange in london That Thomas Carlton and Thomas Buckner Churchwardens of the same pishe for the yeare insuinge should take vp two hundred pounds at eight in the hundred of mr Adam lawrens for the service of the parishe now this writing wytnesseth that we the parishiones of the said whose names are heare vnder written do promisse to and with the said Thomas Carlton and Thomas Buckner that if ony losse should happen to be ether for the principall mony of 200l or the interest therof at 8 p. cent that every of vs shall beare his pte therof and that the said Churchwardens Thomas Carlton and Thomas Buckner shall not be charged saue wth their owne proportion therof (althoughe they alone haue giuen their bonds for the same) according to the true meaninge of these p'sents. Wyttnes our hands geven this second daie of may 1624

Thomas Mowlson
John Nevell
homfrye streete
Jno Kendricke
wm Chapman
George Harwood
John Helmes
Thomas Jackson
Geo. Haughton
John Rushton
John Larymer
Humfrey Castell
Thomas Carleton

Memorand that at a Vestry held September 23th 1633 There was giuen to the Tenants of the pish in Fleetstreet towards the making of a new fünell of lead for a vault the sume of three pounds to be payd when the worke is finished and not otherwise

John Macarnesse
Tho Mowlson
George Harwood
Thomas Carleton
John Larymer
John Rushton
Humfry Castell

A vestery holden the 17th day of Aprill 1625 ther was chossen ffor vpper Churchwarden mr Thomas Buckner and ffor vnder Churchwarden mr Alvery Gascoigne and for sydmen mr mathew foster for Cornehyll syd and mr william williamson for brod street syd

At a vestry holden the 27th day of Aprill 1625 it was agreed vpon and concluded that frtr Thomas Buckner elected formerly churchwarden agayne for the second yeere should be dispensed withall for this office vpon payment of 5li in the name of fine to the parishe to be payd into the handes of the churchwarden

At the same Vestry frtr Thomas Foreman was elected vpperchurchwarden for this yeere followinge and to hold this office only for this yeere

At the same Vestry it was concluded that frtr Thomas Carletons the vpper churchwardens accompt for the yeere past should be Audited the 19th of may next

Auditors named frtr Nevill
frtr Streete
frtr Norcott
frtr Harewood
frtr Buckner
frtr Downes
frtr Chapman
frtr Elmes
frtr Jackson or any six of these

mdnmdum that about the end of mr ffomans yea' theare was a vestrey Called to expresse thea' pleasewre concerning mr Blackwells Contiuance whea' he was againe newly elected and Chosen lecturer there being p'sent doctor Perce Alderman Moulson mr Humphry Street and mr Israell Owen wth many others

Receaued this 19th of maye 1625 of mr Thomas Buckner the some of ffiue pounds beinge in full payment of his ffyne for his Churchwardenship accordinge to the order aboue mentioned

Tho Forman Churchwarden

Receaued this 19th of maye 1625 of mr Thomas Buckner late Churchwarden the some Thertene Shillinges and Seauen pence beinge the foale of his accompte, and the Surplusage of his accompt more then he hath paied this yeare to the poore I saye Rd — 00li — 13s — 07d

Tho forman Churchwarden

At a vestry holden this 9th of Aprill 1626 ther was Chossen for vpper Churchwarden mr Aluery Gascoyne and for vnder Churchwarden mr John Larremer and for sid men mr Anthony Hurst for Cornhill sid and mr Humphre Castell for broad street side

At the same Vestrey it was Concluded that Thomas fforman accompt for the yeare past shuld be audited one the 9th of maye next 1626

Awditors named
M^r^ nevill
Mr Chapman
Mr Jackson
Mr Bucknar
Mr Downes
Mr Streat
Mr Narcot
Mr Harwood
Mr Lee
Mr Helmes or any Sixe of them or ffower

It is ordered this 9th of Aprill 1626 that the vpper Churchwarden shall gather m^r^ blackwell his Lecter monye and paye him quarterly accordinge to Auncient Custome

At a Vestry holden this 25th of march 1627 ther was Chossen for vpper Churchwarden m^r^ John Larremer and for vnder Churchwarden m^r^ Jonas Hopkins And for sid men m^r^ George Webb and m^r^ Nathaniell fflacke

At the same Vestry it was Concluded that m^r^ Aluery Gascoyne his accompt for the yeare past shuld be Audited one the 17th daye Aprill next Cominge 1627

Auditors named
Mr Alderman molson
Mr John neauell
Mr Willeam Chapman
— Thomas fforman
Mr Georg Harwood
Mr Isack Seward
Mr Richard Downes
Mr John Helmes
Mr Thomas Jackson
Or Any Sixe or ffower of them

At a Vestrey holden this 13th of Aprill 1628 ther was chossen for vpper Churchwarden m^r^ Jonas Hoppkins and m^r^ John Rvshton for vnder Churchwarden And for Sid men m^r^ Willeam Bolton And m^r^ Toby maydwell

At the same Vestry it was Concluded that m^r^ John Larremer his Accompt for the yeare past shall be audited one the 29th of Aprill 1628 beinge Tuesdaye

	Auditors named
Thomas Mowlson	Mr Alderman Molson
Andrew Blackwell Curat	Mr John Neavell
John Nevell	Mr Thomas Bucknar
Thomas Buckner	Mr John Helmes
Richard Downes	Thomas fforman
Tho forman	Mr Richard Downes
George Harwood	Mr George Harwood
John Helmes	Mr Isack Seward
Isack Seward	Mr Thomas Carlton
Thomas Jackson	Mr Aluery Gascoyne
Thomas Carleton	Mr Thomas Jackson
John Larymer } Churchwards	Or Any Seauen or ffiue [of] them
Jonas Hopkins }	

At the same Vestrye it was Concluded and Agreed that m^r^ Jonas Hopkins vpper Churchwarden for the yeare ensewinge shall giue in his owne Securety for the some of ffifteye pounds for the Church stock

And at the same Vestry it was Concluded that from hence forth each Churchwarden that shall succead in that office shall put in Securety for soe much as the parish shall think ffitinge according to the stocke of the Churche

At a vestrey holden this 16th of Aprill 1628 Ther was Chossen for Sid man m^r^ Sammuell Lenicar in the place of m^r^ William Bolton who was despenced wth all for a certeyne ffyne

Att a Vestry holden this 27th of Aprill 1628 ther was graunted to Rebecca Madox widdowe Twelue pence A weake duringe the goodwill of the Parrishioners and not otherwise.

Att a Vestrey Houlden the 19th of Octobr 1628 thear was Chossen wth full consent of the Pearreshenrs of this Parresh m^r^ Andrew Blackwell for the Afternones lecttor one the Sabooth daie for the year Inshuinge by full consent of the Parreshnors of St Christophers Church

Att a Vestrey houlden this 5th of Aprill 1629 ther was Chossen wth full consent of the parrishioners of this parish m^r^ John Ruston and m^r^ John Robbards Churchwardens m^r^ William Watkins and m^r^ Andrew Glascote Sidmen

And at the same Vestrey it was Concluded that m^r^ John Ruston vpper Churchwarden shall giue In securety for one hondreth pounds to m^r^ Alderman molson to the parishes vse and the sid men to seae the saied bound Sealed

At the same Vestrey it was Concluded that m^r^ Jonas Hopkins his accompt for the yeare past shall be Audited one the 21th of Aprill 1627 being Tuesday by thes

m^r^ Alderman Molson
m^r^ John Neavell
m^r^ Thomas Bucknar
m^r^ John Helmes
m^r^ Richard Downes
m^r^ George Harwood
m^r^ Isack Seward
— Thomas fforman
m^r^ Thomas Carlton
m^r^ Thomas Jackson
m^r^ Aluery Gascoyne
Or Aney Seauen or ffiue of them

Thomas Mowlson	Isack Seward
John Nevell	John Helmes
Thomas Buckner	Thomas Jackson
Richard Downes	Thomas Carleton
John Heath	Aluerry Gascoigne
Thomas fforman	Jonas Hopkins
George Harwood	John Rushton

1629

At a generall vestrye houlden vpon sunday the 28th of ffebruarye it was graunted to m^r^ Blackwell vppon his request made, that hee should haue a reader to help him ffor six months tyme accoumpting ffrome ou^r^ Lady day next and the parrish to allow the sayd reader ffor the sayd tyme the some of Three pounds and that to bee payd out of the rent of the Lands in ffleet street which was graunted by a full Consent of the parishishioners by reason of his wiues Long signesse and his owne extraordenarye weaknesse and infirmetie

At a vestry houlden the 28th of March 1630 theare was Chosen wth ffull Consent of the porishioners of this parish that John Roberts and Humphrye Castle shall bee churchwardens ffor the yea' insewing and william Lea and Edward Ridlye shall bee sydemen

And it was concluded at the sayd vestrye that John Roberts shall giue seevritie or some ~~other~~ satisfaction by bond or otherways to the sayd parishioners Concerning the Charge which hee shall bee possest wthin the ye'e insewing belonging to the parrish

At the same vestrye it was Concluded that m' John Rushton his accompt ffor the ye'e past shall bee Audited the 29th of Aprill next 1630

m' Alderman Moulson
m' John Neuell
m' Thomas Buckner
m' John Helmes
m' Richard Downes
m' George Harwood
m' Isaack Seward
m' Thomas fforman
m' Thomas Carlton
m' Thomas Jackson
m' Jonas Hopkins

Or any Seauen or fiue of them appoynted Auditors for the sayd accompt

At a vestry holden this 31th of August 1630 it was Agreed that ffower Searchers for the Sicknes shuld be Apointed whose names are

Goodwiff Robinson
Goodwiff Perkins
Goodwiff Jenkins
Goodwiff Madox

The wch ffower are to be Sworne according to Custome

Item at the same vestry it was agred that the Chanlg laied out by m' Willeam Willeamson in the Shut against Andrewe Slad shuld be repaied him againe by the vpper Churchwarden m' John Robarts beinge the some of ffower Pounds Twelue Shillinges and towe pence

Wm Lee Sydeman
John Roberts } Churchwardens
Humfry Castell }

William Watkin — Thomas Buckner
Mathew fferne — Tho: forman
Rich: Abbott — John Helmes
George Goodday — Roger Garland
George Webbe — Nathanell fflack

At a vestry houlden the 6th day of October 1630 theare was chosen by a ffull Consent of the parishioners of this parish M' Andrew Blackwell ffor the after noones Lecture one the sabath days ffor the yee' ensewing by full Consent of the parishioners afforesayd and hee to haue for his paynes the beneuolence of the sayd parishioners as accustomed

John Lorym' — Thomas Mowlson
John Rushton — John Nevell
Rich: Abbott — Thomas Buckner
William Williamson — Tho forman
Toby Maydwell — Richard Downes
Andrew Glascock — Edmund Vnderwood
Heriot Washebourne — John Helmes
Mathew fferne — Isack Seward
Andrew Hodges — Thomas Carleton
Peter Eldred — Wm Bolton
John Roberts — Joseph vaughan

Humfry Castell — William Blundell
Edward Ridley

It was allso agreed by all the parties aboue written that the table ffor parish duties shall bee reformed by those whose names are vnderwritten and the sayd table afterwards to bee ratefied by another vestrye written the day and yea' aboue

M' John Neuell
M' Thomas Buckner
M' Thomas forman
M' Richard Downes
M' George Harwood
M' John Helmes
M' Thomas Jackson
M' Tho Carelton
John Roberts
Humphrye Castell

These or any six of them are to vew and reforme the table abouesayd and to p'pare it ffor a vestry as abouesayd

At a vestry houlden the twenteth day of October 1630 the table ffor duties aboue spesified (being reformed by the p'ties abouesayd) it was ratefied and Confirmed of which table thea' is allso a Coppy written in a parchmt Roule, to which all thea' hands are putt which wea' p'sent, which Roule is to remaine in the chest vnder the saffe custodie of the church wardens and the table to hang in some Conuenient place in the church

At a vestrye houlden the 10th of Aprill 1631 thea' was Chosen by a full consent of the parishioners of the parish of S' Christophers M' Humphry Castell to bee vpper churchwarden and M' William Boulton ffor vnderchurchwarden and for sidemen M' Richard Abbott and m' william Blundell:

Att the same vestrye it was allso concluded that the accompt of John Roberts ffor the yea' past; shall bee audited vpon the 28th of this month of Aprill: 1631 being Thu'sday

Auditors appoynted for this accompt:

M' Alderman Moulson — Thomas Mowlson
M' John Neuell — John Nevell
M' John Helmes — Israell owyn
M' Tho: fforman — Richard Downes
M' Richard Downes — Thomas Forman
M' George Harwood — Edmund vnderwood
M' Tho Carlton — Thomas Carleton
M' Averye Gaskoyne — Jonas Hopkins
M' Jonas Hopkins — John Rushton
M' John Rushton — John Roberts

or any ffiue or seauen of them

At a vestry holden the 9th July 1631 it was agreed that the parishioners should haue libertie to make Choise of a lecturer and that they should Consider to nominate some fit men that might stand in election for that place such as may be p'pounded by the parishe and Conformable to the government of the Church of England m' Macarness our parson did consent hear vnto

At A Vestery holden the 22th of July 1631 ther was the election of a lecturer to preach once euery Saboth for on yeare, when the parishioners did make chose of m' Dell, to be lectrur for one yeare insuing;

William Williamson — Thomas Mowlson
Andrew Glascock — John Nevell

George Webbe
Joseph Vaghan
John Parker
George Goodday
Mathew fferne
Michaell sisson

Richard Downes
George Harwood
Thomas Carleton
John larymer
John Rushton
John Roberts
humfry Castell } Church
w^m Bolton } wardens

At a vestery aforesaied it was concluded p the parishioners that the lecture mony should be colected p the Churchwarden for the last quarter past for m^r maconesse and that the parishioners whould give to m^r maconesse twenty pounds out of the Church stock teward the repaireing of his house and other charges that he hath bine at

At a vestry the 14th of dec: 1631 it was Concluded that m^r fforman m^r dowes and the Churchwardens should confer and make an end wth m^r Hopkins for his ingagement toward the Chargees of his maides Child

allso that m^r dell should be paid one quarters salery till michellmas and take the benevolence of the parishe as the Churchwardens can gaither it

Tho: molson Alderman
m^r maconesse — m^r Rustan
m^r fforman — m^r Roberts
m^r downes — m^r Carleton
m^r Harwood — wth the Churchwardens } Humfry Castell
m^r Helmes — and many other parisheniers } w^m Bolton
Churchwards

At a Vestry holden this ffirste of Aprill 1632 ther was chossen by a full Consent of the Parishioners of S^t xpoffers m^r Willeam Boulton for vpper churchwarden and m^r Willeam Willeamson for vnder Churchwarden and for Sid men m^r Gilbert morwood and m^r mathewe fferne

Tho Mowlson
Pieter Rychaut
Tho: forman
Richard Downes
George Harwood
Thomas Carleton
Alvery Gascoigne
John Larymer
John Rushton
John Roberts

At the same Vestrye it was also concluded that the Accompt of m^r Humphrey Castell for the yeare past shall be Audited vppon the last daye of Aprill next ensewinge being mondaye. Auditors apointed for this Accompt

Mr Alderman Moulson
Mr John neuell
Mr Richard downes
Mr Georg Harwood
Mr Thomas Carlton
Thomas fforman
Mr John Ruston

Mr John Robbarts
Mr John Helmes
Mr Aluery Gascoyne

Or any ffiue or seauen of them

At the same vestry it was also concluded that m^r Jonas hopkins and Ambrose Goodart the Supposed ffather of Rebeca Goddart shall be saued and kept harmles from any molestation concerninge the parish In Considderation of the some of Twelue pounds pd by the saied Jonas hopkins vnto Edward Lewys of mitcham husbandman

At a vestry holden the 6th of Novemb^r 1632 It being propounded and the parishioners mette for the Choise of a lecturer ther was chosen wth a free Election m^r Rogers for on yeare from Christmas next and to be paid by the Churchwardens for his paines till Christmas

Allso it is was concluded and agreed that m^r Hocke should haue paid him by the Churchwardens 7^li 10^s for some paines he had taken and not till now satisfied

Likewise it was ordered that the Churchwardens should colect for m^r Maconesse the money that was vnpaid to him for midsomer and michellmas quarters and what could not be gaitherd that it should paid out of stock

More over the parishioners did conclude to give m^r maconesse ten pounds for on yeare as a gratuitie of thir loue and m^r maconesse did pmise to be asisting in the establishing of m^r Samuell Rogers to be our lecturer as aforesaid m^r maconesse being psent

Tho Mowlson
John Nevell
Richard Downes
Tho: forman
George Harwood
John Helmes
Thomas Carleton
John Larymer
Jonas Hopkins
John Rushton
John Roberts
Humfry Castell
Andrew Glascock
Peter Eldred

March 19th 1631

Memorand that having rec^d a Certificate from Docto^r Wilson Physician that m^r William Bolton w^thout great danger of his health could not feed vpon Lenten Fish dyet, I did giue him my lycence to feed vpon flesh. And finding that the weaknes of his body was such at the space specifyed in the Statute giues way to was not able to endure after according to the Statute I haue registred it the day and yeere aboue written

Joannes Macarnesse Rector Ecclia: s^ti x^pferi

At a vestrey Howlden the 21th of Aprill 1633 There was Chosen by a full Consent of the Parrishoners of St Christophers William Williamson for vper Chirchwarden m^r Georg Webb for vnder Churchwarden and for Sydmen m^r John Parker and m^r Roger Garland

Att the same vestrie it was Concluded that the ACompt of m^r William Boulton shalbe Audiated the fourteenth of May being Tewsday Auditors apointed for this acompte

Mr Alderm Moulson
Mr John Nevell
Mr Richard Downes
Mr Georg Harwood
Mr John Helmes
Mr Thomas Carleton

Tho Mowlson
John Nevell
Richard Downes
Tho: forman
George Harwood
John Helmes
Thomas Carleton

Mr Thomas fforman	Jonas Hopkins
Mr John Rushton	John Rushton
Mr Homfrey Castle	John Roberts
Mr John Robts	Humfry Castell
Mr Jonas Hobkins or any five of them	

At a vestrey howlden the 31th of October 1633 yt is ordered by them first that the Church shalbe suffitiently repayred with all Convenyent speed to wch end the twoe Churchwardens for the tyme beinge together with the Assistance of mr Thomas fforman and mr John Helmes and mr Homfrey Castle and mr Tobias Maidwell for this sid of the parish: for Cornewell [Cornhill] side mr Richard Downes mr Harwood mr Roberts mr Willm Boulton mr Gilbert Moorewood who are Intreated by the said parish to Take Care for the performeance of all things therein requisit both for Masons Worke Timber worke plumers worke Glasiors Worke Plaisterers worke Painters worke or any other worke that shalbe Needful to be done in and touchinge the repayeringe and Bewtifyinge of the said Church. And for the Charg that it shall amount vnto we doe Promise and bind our selues and the whole Parish whose names are herevnder written to see all the costs of the said Church dischardged what eu' shalbe concluded by any six or more of them of the boue names and Mr Mathewe ffearne alsoe to be an Assistant for this side, and alsoe wee whose names are vnderwritten to not only Bind our selues but the whole parish for the pform' of ye said Costs and Chargis. In Wittnes whereof we haue sett to our hands the day and yeare aboue written. And furth' agreed 15th Aprill 1635 That Mr Wm Williamson and Mr Joseph Vaughan shalbe Assistants as above and Mr Abraham Chambers in Mr Downes his place

Churchwardens	Willm Williamson	Tho Mowlson
	George Webbe	John Nevell
	p me Mathew fferne	Richard Downes
	Richard Abbott	Thomas forman
	Andrew Glascock	George Harwood
	George Goodday	John Helmes
	Henry Baynbrigg	Thomas Carleton
	Peter Eldred	John Larymer
	Roger Hunt	John Rushton
	Isaack Knight	John Roberts
	Blackwell	Humfry Castell
	the marke of Mathew Strangim	Gilbert Morewood
		Nathaniell fflacke
		Toby Maydwell
		Edmund Vnderwood

At a vestry holden the 19th day of decembr 1633 yt was agreed that mr Samuell Rogers should be our Lecturer for one yeare beginig at the aboue said tyme to read sirvice and preach every Saboth daie in ye afternoone and is to haue for his paines thirty pounds to be paid him by the Church Wardens

And mr Mackarnis is to haue tenn pounds for The said yeare for giving way to be his lecturer

Att the same vestrie it was agreed that ye comitie wch are vnderwritten or any 3 of them wthe the Churchwardens shall advise wth mr Mackarnis concerning duties and other bussines in the pish and to conclude fullie thereof

mr Thomas fforman
mr George Harwood
mr Richard Downes
mr William Bowlton
mr Thomas Carleton
mr John Roberts

Att the same vestrie was alsoe fullie concluded and agreed that whereas the parish Church of St Christophers is to be repaired and great som of monies to be disbursed to the raising of which monies the parishionen whose names are vnderwritten haue promised ffreelie to Lend the seuerall somes heareafter menciond And the vestrie hath concluded the said monies shalbe Repaied out of there Rents in ffleet street At two or three yeares by the Churchwardens that shall then be: viz halfe of the said somes at one three years end And the other halfe at six yeares End to the pties menciond which shall Lend the said somes or to there Exector' or Assignes And for pformeance hereof the said pish haue Jointly and seuerally Ingadged them selues for pformance thereof

Monies promised to be Lent to the repayreing of the Church of St Christophers

1	Mr Alderman Mowlson ...	050. 00. 00
2	Mr John Nevill twenty pounds ...	020. 00. 00
4	Mr Thomas fforman	005. 00. 00
3	Mr Petter Ricaut	025. 00. 00
5	Mr Georg Harwood tenn pounds	010. 00. 00
	Mr Richard Downes tenn pounds	010. 00. 00
7	Mr John Helmes six pounds thirten shill iiijd	006. 13. 04
24	Mr Thomas Carleton three pounds	003. 00. 00
36	Mr John Rushton fforty shill	002. 00. 00
6	Mr William Bowlton tenn pounds	010. 00. 00
8	Mr John Roberts six pounds thirteen shill iiijd	06. 13. 04
11	Mr Tobyas Meadwell five pound	05. 00. 00
12	Mr Edmond Vnderwood ffive pound ...	05. 00. 00
13	Mr Kyng five pound	05. 00. 00
14	Mr William Lea fiv pound	05. 00. 00
19	Mr Georg Goodaye foure pound ...	04. 00. 00
15	Mr Homfrey Castle five pound ...	05. 00. 00
26	Mr Andrew Glascocke three pound ...	03. 00. 00
20	Mr Petter Eldred foure pound ...	04. 00. 00
21	Mr Richard Abbott foure pounds ...	04. 00. 00
16	Mr Henry Benbricke five pounds ...	05. 00. 00
27	Mr Joseph Vaughan Three pounds ...	03. 00. 00
22	Mr Mathew ffearne foure pounds ...	04. 00. 00
25	Mr Nathaniell fflacke Three pounds ...	03. 00. 00
28	Mr John Parcker Three pounds ...	03. 00. 00
29	Mr Joseph Blackwell Three pounds	03. 00. 00
37	Mr Hamer twoe pound	02. 00. 00
	Mr ~~Michell Cassen twoe pounds ... ...~~	~~02. 00. 00~~
23	William Williamson foure pounds ...	04. 00. 00
30	Mr Georg Webb three pounds	03. 00. 00
	Mr ~~Jonas Hopkins fyve pounds ... ...~~	~~05. 00. 00~~
9	Mr Gilbert Moorewood	
	~~Mr Harrisone eight~~	
10	Mr Chambers	10. 00. 0
31	Mr Hobbs three pounds	03. 00. 0
17	Mr Hewitt Leate	05. 00. 00
32	Mr Alvery Gascoigne ...	03. 00. 00
33	Mr Jonas Hopkins ...	03. 00. 00
38	Mr John Lorymer	02. 00. 0
	Mr Samuell Lynaker ...	
	Mr John Chancey ...	

39	Mr Skynner ...	02. 00. 00
40	Mr John Thorpe	2. 00. 00
42	Mr Mathew Stangrum	1. 00. 00
41	Mr Hunt	1. 10. 00
	Mr Charles	
34	Mr Thomas Bolton ...	03. 00. 00
43	Martyn Dallison	1. 10. 00
35	Widow Jackson	03. 00. 00
	Widow Garland	
	Mr Hill	
18	Mr Bowden	05. 00. 00
	Mr Knight	
	Mr Thomas Snart	
	Mr Robert Holden	
	Mr Ridley	

At a vestrye howlden the 11th of Aprill 1634 there was Chosen by a ffull consent of a vestrie by the parishoners of St Christophers for the yeare Insveinge mr George webb for vper Churchwarden and mr Nathanell fflacke for vnder Churchwarden and for sydemen mr Georg Gooday and mr Joseph Vaughan And the accompt of William Williamson to be Audiated the ffirst of May being Thursday. Auditors apointed for his accompte

mr John Nevell
mr Richard Downes
mr Thomas fforman
mr Harwood
mr Helmes
mr Castle
mr Roberts
mr Wm Boulton
mr Laramore
mr Carleton
} or any five of them

Tho Mowlson Maior

John Nevell	Wm King
George Harwod	Hu Paveley
John Helmes	Thomas Hobs
Thomas Carleton	John Thorpe
John Roberts	Isaack Knight
John larymer	Jno Chauncy
Humfry Castell	Henry Emsworth
Gilbert Morewood	John Rushton
John Saintlowe	Humfrey Wattsonn
Andrew Glascock	mathewe + stangram
John parker	Joseph Blackwell
Richard Abbott	mr Eldred aproued of chirch . . .
Mathew fferne	William Williamson } Churchwardens
Abraham Chambers	George Webbe }
Henry Baynbrigg	

Att a vestrie howlden the iith of Aprill 1634 by the parishoners of St Christophers and there was Chosen by full Consent of the said vestrie for sexton for a yeare next Ensweing Nathaniell Jermond m. alsoe Mr John Saintlowe being Chosen for sideman and haveinge served it elsewheere 17 yeares agoe doeth freelie give forty shillings to the parish for the benefit of the Church wch the pish doe accept of for the said office and soe quit him for that. alsoe these things weare agreed vpon by those whose names names are vndrwritt on the Contray side the daie and yeare abouewritt

Att a Vestrey holden the xxvijth of December 1634 it was concluded and agreed That Mr Samuell Rogers should be or Lecturer for one yere begyning at the abovesaid tyme to read service and preach every Saboth day in the Afternoone And is to have for his paines Thirty Pownds to be paid him by the Churchwardens And Ten pownds more which form'ly was given to Mr Makarnesse

Att a vestrey houlden the 27th of January 1635 it was concluded and agreed that mr Samuell Rogers should be or Lecterer for one yeare begging at the aboue said tyme to Rede Saruise and prech euery Saboth day in the after noone and is two ha e for his paynes thirtie poundes to be paid him by the Churchwardens and ten pounds more wch formarly was geuen vnto mr makarnes

Tho Mowlson	Huett Leatt
Thomas forman	John Saintlowe
George Harwood	Richd Abbott
John Helmes	Mathew fferne
Wm Bolton	Henry Baynbrigg
Humfry Castell	John Parker
Willm Williamson	Joseph Vaghan
Toby Maydwell	John Thorpe
Gilbert Marwood	Roger Hunt

Att a Vestry holden On Easter day being the Nyne and Twentith Day of March 1635 there was chosen by a full consent of the said Vestry for Vpperchurchwarden Mr Nathaniell fflack and Mr Andrew Glascock for Vnder Churchwarden of this Parish And for Sidemen John Thorpe and Joseph Vaughan

And the Audite for Mr George Webb his accompt is appointed to be vpon Thursday the ~~Nyne and twentith~~ last day of Aprill next by the Auditors chosen whose names are herevnder written

Mr Thomas fforman
Mr George Harwood
Mr John Helme
Mr William Bolton
Mr Thomas Carleton
Mr John Roberts
Mr John Rushton
Mr Avery Gascoigne
Or any ffower of them

Att a Vestrie holden the ffifteenth Day of Aprill Ao dni 1635 It was ordered and agreed by the Parson and the Major part of the Parish then p'sent That from henceforth no Vestrie shalbe called or held in the Parish vpon the Saboth Day And that the choosing of Churchwardens and other Officers for the Parish shall every yere be vpon Easter Munday

John Macarnesse Rector	Tho Mowlson
Wm Lee	Thomas forman
Nathaniell fflacke	George Harwood
Andrew Glascock	John Helmes
Mathew fferne	Thomas Carleton
	Humfry Castell
	Willm Williamson
	Gilbert Morewood
	John Saintlowe
	Joseph Vaghan
	Peter Eldred
	Tho: Hamor

Joseph Blackwell
John Thorpe
Hu Paveley
Abraham Chambers
Martyn Dallison

27 a. Whereas there is now remayning in the Registry of the Arches Court in London the some of One hundred Pownds of lawfull mony of England which was given and bequeathed by S[r] Peter le Maier Knight late of the City of London deceased in his will and Testam[t] to the Poore of the Parish of S[t] Christofer in London to be setled as a stock for them by his Executo[rs] of his last will and Testam[t] Now we whose names are vnderwritten being of the Vestry of the said Parish are contented and do desire that the said Hundred Pownds be delivered vpon bond to George Webb late Churchwarden of o[r] said parish to the vse of o[r] said poore to be setled for them as aforesaid Nathaniell fflack and Andrew Glascock o[r] now Churchwardens of the same parish and John Thorpe Sydeman ioyning with him in the said bond In witnes whereof we have subscribed o[r] names this Last day of Aprill 1635

which note was dd to the said Churchwardens to carry into the Court of Arches wth these names subscribed viz[t]

John Makarnesse Rector
Thomas fforman
George Harwood
John Helmes
William Bolton
Thomas Carleton
John Rushton
John Roberts
Humfrey Castell
Peter Eldred
Henry Baynebrick
Mathew ffearne
Toby Maydwell
Abraham Chambers
John Lorymer
William Lee
Richard Abbott

27 b. Whereas Nathaniell fflack and Andrew Glascock now Churchwardens of the Parish of S[t] Christofer in London, and John Thorpe one of the Sydemen of the same parish (according to a note or agreem[t] made the Last Day of Aprill now last pas[t] as appeares on th'other side) have entred into an obligac̃on of the penalty of 200[li] the Copy whereof is entred into this booke towching the receipt of One hundred Pownds out of the Registry of the Arches Court in London which was there deposited by S[r] ffrancis Crane Knight Executo[r] of the last will & Testament of S[r] Peter le Maier Knight deceased in full paym[t] of all legacies given to the poore of the said Parish by the said S[r] Peter Le Maier in & by his last will & Testament And for that the said Nathaniell fflack & Andrew Glascock have received the said One hundred Pownds for the vse of the poore of the said parish Now we the Parishioners of the said Parish whose names are herevnder subscribed are contented & agreed & do hereby promise for vs and the hole parishe and o[r] Successors parishioners of the same parish for the tyme being That the said Nathaniell fflack Andrew Glascock & John Thorpe their executo[rs] & admistrato[rs] shalbe from tyme to tyme saved & kept harmeles by the Parishioners of the same parish for the tyme being of & from all sutes Costs charges execuc̃ons & damages to arise or happen to them the sd Nathaniell fflack Andrew Glascock & John Thorpe their executo[rs] or admistrato[rs] or any of them or their or any of their goods Chattells lands or Tenements towching or concerning their entring into the obligac̃on aboue mencc̃oned in any manner of wise And it is further ordered & agreed That when it shall happen any of them the said Nathaniell fflack Andrew Glascock & John Thorpe to depart this life or decay in estate and that warning shalbe given for procuring of new surety or sureties to enter into the like bond or obligac̃on of Two hundred Pownds with such like Condic̃on as the said Nathaniell fflack Andrew Glascock & John Thorpe are bound vnto That then in such case the Churchwarden or Churchwardens of the said parish for the tyme being shall enter into the like obligac̃on and Condic̃on as is afore menc̃oned, order being taken for his or their indempnity & saving harmeles from the same as aforeherein is expressed. In witnes whereof we have herevnto subscribed o[r] names the Anno dñi 1635

Thomas forman
John helmes
Thomas Carleton
John Roberts
Gilbert Morewood
Toby Maydwell
Mathew fferne
w[m] Bolton
W[m] Lee
Peter Eldred
Richd Abbott
John Larrymor
Henry Baynbrigg
Humfry Castell

Ex Regro Curie de Arcubus London extract[t].

Noverint vniversi p̃ p'ntes nos Nathanielem fflack parochie S[ti] Christoferi prope le stocks London Civem et Grocer London Andrew Glascock eiusdem parochie Civem et Haberdasher London et Johannem Thorpe parochie pred Civem et Carpenter London teneri et firmiter obligari Venerabili et egregio viro domino Johanni Lambe militi et legum doctori alme Curie Cant de Arcubus London Officiali principali in Ducents libris bone et legalis monete Anglie solvend' eidem domino Johanni Lambe aut suo certo attornato executoribus admistrator' vel assignatis suis Ad quamquidem soluc̃onem bene et fidel̃r faciend obligamus nos et quemlibet nostrũ per se pro toto et in solid heredes executores et admistr' nros firmiter per p'ntes Sigillis nostris sigillat Dat Nono Die Mensis Maii Anno regni domini nostri Caroli dei gratia Anglie Scotie ffrancie et Hibernie Regis fidei defensoris &c Vndecimo Annoque dñi 1635.

The Condition of this obligac̃on is such That whereas Sr Peter Le Maier Knight late of the City of London deceased in & by his last will & Testament gave and bequeathed to the poore of St Christofers in London the soñe of One hundred Pownds in this forme of words following or the like in effect vizt (And my body to be buryed in the Church of St Christofers in London, and I give to the poore of that parish the soñe of One hundred

Pownds to be setled as a stock for them by my Executors of this my last will and Testament) And whereas after sute comenced in the said Court of Arches by George Webb & Nathaniell ffack Churchwardens of the said parish church against Sr ffrancis Crane Knight Executor of the last will & Testamt of the said deceased the some of One hundred Pownds of lawfull mony was tendred & left in the Registry of the said Court of Arches on the part of the said Sr ffrancis Crane in full payment of all legacies given to the said poore of the said Parish And wherealso the said Nathaniell ffack and Andrew Glascock the now Churchwardens of the said Parish of St Christofer have accepted the said One hundred pownds in full payment of all legacies given to the said poore in the said will & by the decree of the right worll Sr John Lambe Principall Officiall of the said Court & by the deliu'y of Matthew Thwaits Deputy Register of the same Court have had and received the same to be setled as a stock for the vse of the said Poore. If therefore the said Hundred Pownds shalbe setled as a stock for the poore of the said Parish of St Christofers according to the true intent & meaning of the will of the said Testator and shalbe so from tyme to tyme contynued wthout wasting or dyminishing of the said Hundred Pownds And also if the said Nathaniell ffack Andrew Glascock & John Thorpe their heirs executors and admistrators do and shall at all tymes hereafter & from tyme to tyme save defend or otherwise sufficiently keep harmeles as well the said Sr ffrancis Crane his executors and administrators as also the said Sr John Lambe and the said Matthew Thwaits and all other the Officers and Mynisters of the said Court of Arches their severall executors & admistrators from and against all and every other person and persons having or pretending to have any right title or interest in or to the said Hundred Pownds or to any part thereof and from and against all sutes, troubles Controversies damages expenses and incombrances whatsoever which shall or may any way happen to them or to any of them for or by reason of the said Hundred Pownds or any part thereof And lastly if the said Nathaniell ffack Andrew Glascock & John Thorpe or any of them shall happen to depart this life or to decay in estate Then if they or any of them or any of their executors or admistrators shall within One Monethes space next after warning given to them or any of them procure one or more sufficient surety or sureties by the Officiall principall of the said Court of Arches to be approved & allowed to enter into the like bond or obligacon of Two hundred Pownds with such like Conditions for the surety or sureties to performe as are above recyted to be performed by the said parties bound in this obligacon Then this obligacon shalbe void and of none effect, or ells the same shall stand & be in full strength and vertue.

Sealed and delivered in the presence of	Nath: ffacke.
Matt: Thwaits.	Andrew Glascocke.
Wm Durham.	Jo. Thorpe.
Edm. Arnold.	

a Vestry holden On Easter Monday being the Eighteenth Day of Aprill Anno dñi 1636 there was chosen by a full consent of the said Vestry for ~~Vpper~~ Churchwardens Mr Andrew Glascock ~~And for Vnder Churchwarden~~ & Mr Toby Maidwell And for Sydemen Mr Peter Eldred and Mr Abraham Chambers

And the Audite for Mr Nathaniell ffack his accompt is appointed to be Vpon the Seaventeenth Day of May next by the Auditors chosen whose names are herevnder written

Mr Thomas fforman
Mr George Harwood
Mr John Helme
Mr William Bolton
Mr Thomas Carleton
Mr John Roberts
Mr John Rushton
Mr Alvery Gascoigne
Mr Humfrey Castle
Mr William Williamson
Mr George Webb
Or any ffower of them

John Macarnesse
Thomas forman
George Harwood
Thomas Carleton
John Rushton
Humfry Castell
William Williamson
George Webbe
John Saintlowe
Peter Eldred
Abraham Chambers
Henry Baynbrigg
Tho: Bolton
John Thorpe
Roger Hunt
Nathaniell ffacke

At a Vestry holden one Easter monday beinge the 10th Aprill Anno domine 1637 ther was chosen by ffull consent of the saied Vestry for churchwardens mr Toby maydwell and mr Willeam Leigh. And for Sydmen mr Willeam King and mr Thomas Boulton

1° a. The parson was absent this yeare.

And the Audit for mr Andrew Glascocke his Accompt is appointed to be One tuesdaye the 9th daye of maye 1637 by the Auditors chossen, whose names are hervnder written by ffiue or six of them

Wm Bolton
Thomas forman
Thomas Carleton
John Robbarts
Georg Harwood
Nathaniell ffack
humphrey Castell
Willeam Williamson
George web
John Ruston
Aluery Gaskoyne

Thomas forman
Wm Bolton
Thomas Carleton
John Rushton
George Webbe
Nathaniell ffacke
John Saintlowe
Andrew Glascocke
Edmund Vnderwood
George Goodday

Att A vestrie holden one Easter Mundaye beeinge the 26th day March 1638 ther was Chosen by full Consente att the saide Vestrie by mr Backer our pa'sone and the parishioners for Churchwardenes mr William Lee and mr Mathew fferne and for Sidesmen mr Thomas Hobes and mr Joseph Blackewell

And the Auditt for Toby Maydwell his accompte is apoyented to bee vpon Tuesdaye beeinge the 24th daye of Aprill 1637 by the auditurs chosen whose names are heare vnder written by 5 or six of theme

Thomas forman

Sa: Baker Parson
John Nevell
Thomas forman
George Webbe
Nathaniell ffacke
John Saintlowe
George Goodday
Peter Eldred
Henry Baynbrigg

Nathaniell ffacke
fo' auditors 1638
John Nevell
Tho: forman
m' Carlton
m' will: Bolton
m' J^{no} Roberts
m' Williamsone
m' ffacke
m' Webb
m' Gaskine
m' Rushton

Tho. Bolton
Wm King
Tho: Hamor
Huett Leatt
Edmund Vnderwood
Thomas Cullinge

10 b. Att a Vestry holden the fifteenth day of Aprill A° dñi 1639 was M' Mathew fferne elected Vpper Churchwarden for the yere ensuing ending att Easter 1640. And M' Gilbert Morewood was chosen Vnderchurchwarden; but att his owne request (as by the Letter affixed appereth) he was wth consent of this Vestry remitted, for the said place of Churchwarden, and for the place of vpper-churchwardenshipp wch would fall vpon him the next yere. The said M' Morewood paying for his ffyne Twenty pounds to be laid out for plate for the Lords Table, and in his the said M' Morewoods sted was chosen for Vnderchurchwarden M' Edmond Vnderwood, and M' Thomas Hamore and M' Hugh Souden were then by the like consent chosen Sidesmen

And the Auditt for M' William Lee his accompt is appointed to be vpon the ffouerteenth day of May next by the Audito^{rs} chosen whose names are herevnder written or any Six ffyve or fower of them
Thomas fforman
Thomas Carleton
John J. Rushton
John Roberts
William Williamson
George Webb
Nathaniell ffack
Toby Maidwell

Sa: Baker Parson
Thomas forman
Thomas Carleton
John Rushton
John Roberts
William Williamson
George Webbe
Toby Maydwell
Peter Eldred
John Saintlowe
Tho: Bolton
Thomas Hamor
Tho: Peapes
Georg Bromhall
William Somerfeilde

11 a. The ffive & Twentith Day of August A° dñi 1639

Att a Vestry holden by the Parishioners of this Parish there was chosen for Lecturer to preach on Saboth dayes in the afternoone M' Edmond Brome for the space of one whole yere from Michas next ensuing there being the number of Thirty & ffive persons giving their names for the election of the said M' Brome being the greater number of the whole Parishioners of the said parish, the rest being but Thirteene in number for the election of Three others then in nomynacōn giving their consent to pay him whome the major part should choose.

11 b. At a vestrey the 8th day of Aprill 1640 was Ellected M' Edmond vnderwood for vperchurchwarden and M' Georg Gooday for vnder Churchwarden for the yeare Insving And M' Henry Benbricke and M' Martin dallison for sidemen

And the Audyt of M' Mathew ffearnes acompte is apointed to be vpon the seventh day of may next following. Audito^{rs} Chosen whose names are vnder wrytten
M' fforman
M' Carleton
M' Robts
M' Rushton
Willm Williamson
Nathaniell ffacke
Georg Webb
M' Moorwood
M' Maidwell or any five of them

Thomas forman
Thomas Carleton
John Roberts
John Rushton
Willm Williamson
George Webbe
Nathaniell ffacke
Wm Lee
John Saintlowe
Hu Sowdon
Joseph Vaghan
Tho: Hamor
Tho: Snart

The ffirst Day of ffebruary 1640.

Att a Vestry holden by the Parishion^{rs} of this parish there was chosen for Lecturer to preach on Saboth dayes in the afternoones M' Christofer Cartwright for the space of one whole yere from the tyme he cometh to reside wth them there being the number of Thirty Seaven p'sent whereof Thirty & ffive gave their consents & subscribed for the choice of M' Cartwright the other two, one of them gave their hands for one M' Nelson, and the other for one M' Randall who were putt in nomynacōn wth M' Cartwright. And there was agreed to be given M' Cartwright Ten pownds for his charges of his Journeyes: Also its agreed that M' Cartwright shall preach Monethly a p'paracōn sermon before the Sacrament on Thursday or ffriday at his election ffor wch weekly Lecture & for the p'paracōn sermons the parish agreed to give ffifty pownds this yere at the least.

Wm Myddelton
Pieter Rychaut
Jo^{n} Roberts
Wm Williamson
George Webbe
Nathaniell ffacke
Tho. Cullinge
Toby Maydwell
Stephen Bolton
Martyn Dallison
Henry H W Ward
Wm Lee
Christop English

Thomas formā
John Rushton
Gilbert Morwood
John Saintlowe
Joseph Vaghan
Henry Hardcastle
Thomas Hobs
Henry Baynbrigg
Roger Hunt
John Hawes
Tho. Snart
John Brett
Stephen Joy
Georg Goodday

Memorand That this Last day of March A° dni 1641 there was chosen for Clarke of this parish of S' Christofer William Mercer an Inhabitant in this parish there being in nomynation wth him John Roch & Nathaniell German also inhabitants in this parish And there being then p'sent in the Vestrey Thirty of the Parishioners Two & twenty of them gave their voice & choice for the said William Mercer and Two for John Roch and Sixe for Nathaniell German.

Att a Vestrey the 16th Day of Aprill 1641 was elected M' George Goodday for Vpperchurchwarden and M' John Saintlowe for Vnderchurchwarden for the yere ensuing and M' Henry Eynsworth and M' Roger Hunt for Sidemen

And the Auditt of M' Edmond Vnderwoods accompt is appointed to be vpon the Twelveth Day of May next

Thomas forman
John Roberts
John Rushton
Willm Williamson

Auditors chosen whose names are herevnder written vizt
Mr Thomas fforman
Mr John Roberts
Mr John Rushton
Mr William Williamson
Mr Nathaniell fflack
Mr George Webb
Mr Gilbert Morewood
Mr Toby Maidwell or any five of them

George Webbe
Wm Lee
Tho Bolton
Joseph Blackwell
Henry Baynbrigg
Tho. Hamor
Joseph Vaghan
Tho Peapes
John Hawes
Stephen Gey
Richard williames
Martyn Dallison
Tho. Cullinge
Stephen Bolton
John Brett
Peter Eldred

b. At a vestrey howlden the 8th day of Septbr 1641 There was Chosen
a. for our Lecturer Mr James Cranford for one whole yeare to preach twise euery Lords day And a preparation Sermon euery monthe and to Begin at the feast of St michell next pvided he be free from other pastoral Charge or Cure

John Hansley Rector
Thomas forman
John Rushton
Willm Williamson
George Webbe
Lady Mowlson
Wm Lee
Peter Eldred
Will: Sheward
Henry Emsworth
Roger Hunt
Henry Baynbrigg
Tho: Peapes
Stephen Gey
John Hawes
Tho. Snart
William Walker
Edmond Balye
ffrancis Burton
John Lammas
Ricd Elkin
George Goodday
John Saintlove
William Mercer Parrish Clarke

b. At a vestrey houlden the 17th december 1641 the names of vs vnderwritt of the parish of St Christophers in the precinct of St Christop in Brodstreet ward haue acepted of eight pounds from mr henry Benbrick & it is for Constable & questman and for euer acquiting ye same mr Benbrick of the sd offices for the said money in the sd precinct, wittnes our hands day & year aboue

Thomas forman
John Rushton
Willm Williamson
Peter Eldred
John Hawes

Att a vestrey howlden the iith day of februrij 1641 There was Chosen to be Auditors of Mr Georg Gooday deceased being vper Churchwarden for his acompt dureing the tyme he Continved in the place these whose names are vnderwritten & to be Audiated the 17 of this Instant being thursday

Mr Thomas fforman
Mr John Roberts
Mr Moorewood
Mr Maidwell
Mr fflacke
Mr Lea
Mr Webb
Willm Williamson
Mr vnderwood or Any five of them

At a vestrey houlden iith of Aprill 1642 There was Chosen By full consent of a vestrie Mr John Sainctloe for vper Churchwarden and Mr Richard Abbott for vnderchurchwarden and for Sydmen mr Thomas Peeps And mr Stephen Gey. a.

Thomas forman
John Roberts
John Rushton
Willm Williamson
George Webbe
Nathaniell fflacke
Wm Lee
Joseph Vaghan
Henry Baynbrigg
Tho: Hamor
Tho: Cullinge
John Hawes
Tho: Snart
William Withers
Robt Coker

At a Vestrey houlden the 3 of Aprill 1643 the names of vs the pishioners of Christophers here vnder written it was agred one as ffolloweth viz b.

That Mr Cranford for his ffirst quarter next insuing to Midsummer for the pay for his Lecture he is Content to stand to the ffree will of the parishioners.

That mr Cranford hath declared his willingnes to stay with vs though he hath benn offered greater preferment.

That the parsonidge house wherin mr ffranckline now liueth shalbe repared at the cost & Charge of the parrish

At the same vestrey was Chosen for vpper Churchwarden for the year Insuing mr Richard Abbot and for vnder Churwarden Captin Joseph vaughan and for Sydesmen Captin John Brett & mr henry ward

James Cranford rector
Wm Myddelton
Thomas forman
John Roberts
Willm Williamson
John Rushton
George Webbe
Nathaniell fflacke
Wm Lee
John Saintlowe
Tho. Cullinge

And the acompte of mr John Sainclowe to be Audiated vpon the 9th of may being tuesday & Auditors
mr James Cranford
mr fforman
mr Maidwell
mr John Roberts
mr John Rushton
mr Georg webb
mr Willm Lee

Stephen Gey
Henry Emsworth
Tho: Peapes
John Hinde
John Hawe
William Withers

m Nathaniell ffiack
Willm Williamson
or Any 4 of or 5 of them

*Att a vestry howlden the 13th of ~~Aprill~~ ffebruarij 1643 we the parishoners whose names are vnderwrytten of St Christophers for the Incoriging of m^r Cranford for his great paines that he takes wth vs shall have *for his Lecture euerey Lords day* in the after noone & monthly before the sacremt yearely the *Some of Threescore pownds* and it is desired the Churchwardens shall Indeuor to gather it of the pishioners and what shall fall short the *shall pay out of the Church Stock.* By the Churchwarden

Wm Williamson
John Rushton
Nathaniell ffacke
John Saintlowe
Ri: Abbott
John Brett
Will: Sheward
Stephen Gey
William Withers
John Hinde
John Hawe
Jno Sordell
William Bird
ffrancis Burton
William Walker
Tho: Cullinge

The Order aboue was Reversed by a vestry held the first of may 1644.

Att A vestrey houlden this 22th Aprill 1644 of the whole Parishoners of this Parish it is Agreed vppon Captine Joseph Vaughan for ye vpp Church warden for ye yeare ffollowinge & for ye vnd^r Church warden for ye yeare ffollowing Mr Hugh Sowden & for Sidmen for ye yeare ffollowinge Mr Thomas Cullen & Mr Humphrey Blundell & wee here p'sent haue vnd^r written our hands

John Roberts
Gilbert Morewood
John Rushton
Henry Emsworth
Joseph Blackwell
Wm Marsh
Henrey H W Ward his marke
Peter Cole
John Saintlowe
Ri: Abbott
Will: Sheward
William Withers

Itt is Agreed vppon at this vestrey houlden this 22th Aprill 1644 that for the Auditting of Mr Richard Abbott Churchwardens Accountt shall bee 15th of May next followinge & the Auditors to be mr James Cranford m^r John Robart mr Wm Williamson mr Tobias Meadwell mr Gilbert Morewood mr John Rushton mr Georg Webb mr Nathaniell ffiacke mr John Santloe

* This minute is crossed through with the pen, and the italicized words are further obliterated and almost illegible.

Itt is Agreed vppon att this Vestrey houlden this 22th Julij 1644 That mr Humphrey Blunden is to Take Anne Christoph^r to searue him After the maner of Apprentize duringe the Tearme of ffive yeares duringe wch Tearme shee shall Carey & behave her selfe as a App'ntize ought to doe both honnestly & justly ffor wch wee Ingage ou^r selves & wee Towards byinge nesecareys of Cloths Convenient for her wee pmise to give him Three pownds

James Cranford pson
Wm Williamson
Gilbert Morewood
John Rushton
Toby Maydwell
Ri Abbott
Nathaniell ffacke
Stephen Bolton
Tho: Cullinge
Joseph Vaghan } Churchwardens
Hu: Sowdon }
John Saintlowe
John Brett
Stephen Gey
John Hawe
William Walker
Hum Blunden

* The ffirst of Awgust 1644

Att a Vestrie then held John Christofer one of the parish children was by consent placed p'ntice to William Sweby Citizen & Clothworker of London & Gloũ[er] by profession for nyne yeres from Midsomer last and Three pounds money was agreed to be giuen when he is bound att Clothworkers Hall according to custome and the M^r ~~att the end of the terme~~ is to enter the boy in the howse of Bridewell to the end that when he cometh forth of his time he may be capable of ffive pounds giuen to poore boyes in like kynd

The ffirst of Awgust 1644

Att a Vestrie then held John Christofer one of the parish children was by consent placed appñtice to John Reynolds of the parish of St Dunstan in the west Taylor ffor eight yeres from Midsomer last and ffower pounds money was agreed to be paid when he is bound att Drapers Hall to George Young of this parish Taylor and free of the Drapers and John Reynolds is to cause George Young to make the said John Christofer free of the said Company att the end of his terme

John Roberts
Wm Williamson
John Rushton
Nathaniell ffacke
George Webbe
John Saintlowe
Richrd Abbott
Tho: Hamor
ffrancis Burton
Ge: Nieren
Tho: Cullinge
William Withers
Wilt. Sheward

* This entry is crossed with the pen in the original.

Att a Vestrey holden the 15th August 1644 its agreed that the Churchwardens shall rayse the Roufe of mr James Cranfords house at the Charge of the parrish and the monye to be raysed in ꝑportion as men are Rated for the poore

Wm Myddelton
Wm Williamson
John Rushton
Gilbert Morewood
Toby Maydwell
Wil̃ Sheward
John Hawe
Robert Coker
Stephen Bolton
Edward Ridley
William Stratford
John Roberts
John Saintlowe
Gerha: Nieren
Ri: Abbott
Joseph Vaghan
John Brett

1644

Att a Vestery holden the 22 of Septemƀ its agreed that what mony shalbe payd by the parisherners to the repare of mr Cranfords house shalbe repayed them agayne out of the Chvrch stocke if it be ffound it may be disposed of to that end

Wm Williamson
John Rushton
George Webbe
Toby Maydwell
Richard Abbott
Tho: Cullinge
Tho: Bolton
John Hawe
William Bird
Joseph Vaghan
ffrancis Burton
Edward Ridley
William Walker

Att a vestrey houlden ye 16th of december 1644 whereas John Reynolds Taylor of the ꝑish of St Dunstons in ye west hath taken to prentise John Christopher one of this parish Children for his aprentice for eight years and his tyme to begin at Midsomr last for the tearme of 8 yeares and the said Renolds is to haue foure pounds wth the said John Christop this vestrey orders that mr Reynolds shall haue three pounds paid him in pt of the some and the other 20s when the said John Christopher shalbe made free of this Citty or in a Capasity of being made free of this Citty

Ja: Cranford
Wm Williamson
Gilbert Morewood
John Rushton
John Saintlowe
Ri. Abbott
Tho: Bolton
Stephen Bolton
Henry Emsworth

William Withers
the marke H W of Henery Ward
William Bird
Richard Williams
John Hawes

The 16th January 1644 39 a

At a vestry then held it is Concluded yt Humfrey Stockwell be discharged by the Churchwarden for his Arrerages of Rent vpon payment of Twenty foure pounds The lease being deliu'ed vp & quyett possession yeelded And also yt the house be surrendred vnto Henrye Sharpe who is to be entertayned Tenant for this yeare ensueing beginning the 25th day of december 1644 at Twenty pounds for the yeare, paying it by fyve pounds quarterly

Ja: Cranford Rector
Wm Williamson
Gilbert Morewood
John Rushton
Nathaniell ffacke
Richard Abbott
William Sheward
Stephen Bolton
John Hawe
William Walker
Christop English
Richard Ryman
Joseph Vaghan
Hu: Sowdon

At a vestrey Houlden 28th of march 1645 It is orderd that Mr John 39 b
Saintlowe shall pay ffifty pounds due to Hills twoe Childr to ye hands of Maior Joseph Vaughan Nowe Church Warden of the sd parish and he shall disburse the same for the parishes vse and be acomptable to the ꝑish for the same and vpon Audiating of the acomptes the Childr shall haue alloweance for the same, out of wch mony Recd he is to pay the workem for Repairinge Mr Cranfords howse and this vestrie doeth further order that the said parishoners that have disbursed money to that end shalbe reimbursed of there monies out of the parish stock

Wm Williamson
Toby Maydwell
John Rushton
Richard Abbott
Nathaniell ffacke
Wil̃: Sheward
Tho: Cullinge
John Brett
John Hawe
Roger Hunt
Peter Cole
William Bird
Thõ Ashton
Edmond Balye

Att a vestery Houlden this 11 Aprill 1645 of the whole ꝑishion of 40 a
this ꝑish it is agreed vpon that mr Hugh Souden for the vpper Churchwarden and for the vnder Churchwarden mr Thomas Boulton and for sidesmen for the yeere ffollowing mr William Walker and mr William Shewarde and we here p'sent haue vnto set our hands

Ja: Cranford ꝑson
John Roberts
Wm Williamson
Gilbert Morewood
John Rushton
John Saintlowe
Richard Abbott
Joseph Vaghan
John Brett
Tho: Cullinge
Stephen Gey
Toby Maydwell
Will: Sheward
John Hawe
Ge Nieren

Its agreed vpon at a vestery houlden the day aboue sayd that for the Audidings of Joseph Vaghans Account the 13 may 1645 shalbe Audito^rs^ m^r^ James Cranford m^r^ John Roberts m^r^ Williamson m^r^ Toby Meadwell m^r^ Gilbert Moorewoodd m^r^ John Sayntlo m^r^ Richard Abbott and that widow Snart shall haue the money paid her that her husband did lend to ye repayre of this Church

John Roberts
Wm Williamson
John Saintlowe
Ri: Abbott
Toby Maydwell
Tho: Cullinge

Att a vestrey holden the 30th of Ma'ch 1646 of the whole parrish itt is agreed vpon that m^r^ Henrey Benbrige is Chosen fo^r^ Vnder Churchwa'den and m^r^ Thomas Bouelton fo^r^ vpper Chu'chwa'den and fo^r^ Sidesmen fo^r^ the yeare ffollowing m^r^ Steephen Bouelton fo^r^ Cornewell [Cornhill] side and fo^r^ ou^r^e side m^r^ William Witheres and wee thatt wer p'esent att this ellectione haue heare vnder sett ou^r^ hands ye daye and yeare aboue written

Att this p'esent vestrey itt is ordered the daye and yeare aboue saide that the Auditinge of Toby Maydwells accompt shall bee vpon the twentith eight of Ap'ill beeing friday and the Auditors are toe bee m^r^ Will Williamson m^r^ John Roberts m^r^ Richard Abbutt m^r^ George Webb m^r^ John Rustone and m^r^ Nathaniell ffacke and m^r^ Gilbert Morewood & Maior Vawhone or ancy fiue of them

p me John Roberts
Wm Williamson
John Rushton
George Webbe
Nathaniell fflacke
Tho. Cullinge
Joseph Blackwll
Toby Maydwell
John Brett
Will: Sheward
John Hawe
William Walker
Tho: Coleclough
Richard Williams

att A Vestry holden the 30th of Apill 1647 we whoss names are vnder writt have Chosen m^r^ Henry Bainberg for the year insueing to scarve the plac of vper Churchwarden & m^r^ Josep Blackwell for vnder Churchwarden and m^r^ wm Streattford & m^r^ John Haw for Sidmen

John Rushton
Nathaniell fflacke
Toby Maydwell
Tho: Cullinge

John Brett
Stephen Bolton
William Walker
Garrard Dickins
Thomas Chubbe
ffrancis Burton
ffrancis Maye
Thomas Lowe
Richard Ryman
Tho Bolton

Att This presentt vestry itt is Apointed The Auditt day of Tho Bolton is to be vpon Tewsday the first of Junne next and the Auditors to be is

m^r^ wmson
m^r^ Robertts
m^r^ morwood
m^r^ maydwell
m^r^ vaughan
m^r^ fflack
~~m^r^ webb~~
m^r^ Rustian
m^r^ Abott

ore any fiue of them

At a vestery houlden the prime of m'ch 1647 it was agreed as ffolloweth—that if John Roach tayler being a poore man of this ꝑishe hauing six small chilldren shuld gett his Sonne Joseph being about three yeares & a halfe ould to be receiued into the Maintenance & keeping of St Bartholmewes Hospitall; that then the ꝑishioners of this ꝑishe shuld ffree the said Hospitall of the charge of the said childe when he came to the age of ffifteene yeares. witnesse our handes as ffoll

William Walker

Ja: Cranford rector
Gilbert Morwood
John Roberts
John Rushton
George Webbe
Richard Abbott
Tho. Bolton
Tho Culling
Stephen Bolton
ffrancis Burton
henry Troughton
Thomas Lowe
Henry Baynbrigg } Churchwardens
Joseph Blackwell }
Richard Ryman

At a Vestery houlden the 3^d^ of Aprill 1648 m^r^ Joseph Blackwell was Chosen Senior Churchwarden and m^r^ Thomas Cullen Junior; and m^r^ Thomas Chub and m^r^ ffrancis Mao Sidemen for this yeare ensuinge and it is appointed at the same vestry that m^r^ Henry Baynbrigge his Audite day bee vpon wednesday the third of may, the Auditors to bee ye mjnist^r^, m^r^ williamson, m^r^ Roberts, m^r^ Morewood, m^r^ majdwel, m^r^ fflacke, m^r^ Abbot, m^r^ webb, m^r^ Rushtjan, m^r^ vaghan, m^r^ Bolton, or any five of them

Richard Ryman

Ja: Cranford
Gilbert Morwood
John Roberts
John Rushton
George Webbe

Richard Abbott
Toby Maydwell
Tho. Bolton
Henry Baynbrigge
Stephen Bolton
John Brett
Christo: Jenner
ffrancis Burton
Henry Troughton
William Walker
Thomas Lowe

a. Att a vesterye the 26 March 1649 it was agreed that m^{r} Thomas Cullinge Chosen Senior & L^{t}. Col: John Brett Junior Churchwardens, and Mr Thomas Aston and m^{r} Peter Cole sidesmen for this yeere Ensuing and that the Acc^{o} of m^{r} Joseph Blackewell shalbe Audited the third of may 1649 the Auditors m^{r} Cranford m^{r} Roberts m^{r} Ruston m^{r} Morewood m^{r} Williamson m^{r} Thomas Boulton m^{r} Vaghan or any ffiue of them

Ja: Cranford
John Roberts
John Rushton
Gilbert Morwood
Joseph Vaghan
Tho: Bolton
Henry Baynbrigg
Joseph Blackwell
Stephen Gey
John Hawe
Garrard Dickins
Ben Oldfeild
Richard Ryman

b. Att A vestrey Houlden this 23th of Aprill An^{o} 1650 there was Chossen officers for this Parish for the yeare ensuinge Both for vpp & vndr Churchwardens & sidmen Accordinge to the vote of the vestrey & the Parishon^{rs} whoes names are here vnder written. The officers for the Church are these Maigo^{r} John Breet for the vpp^{r} Churchwarden for the yeare ensinge & for the vnd^{r} Church warden is mr Stephen Gey for the yeare ensuinge & for sidemen mr Richard Williams ffor Threedneled Precincte & mr Wm Marsh for Cornhill side

And the Audiett day is Appoynted the 15th day of may next & the Audito^{rs} for mr Thomas Cullen Accountt are these followinge m^{r} Cranford mr Morewood mr Robarts mr Williamson Corn^{ll}s Vaughan mr Meadwell mr fflacke mr Thomas Boulton mr Banbricke & mr Blackwell or ancy ffive of them

Ja: Cranford ꝑson
John Roberts
Wm Williamson
Nathaniell fflacke
Joseph Vaghan
Henry Baynbrigg
Joseph Blackwell
Tho Bolton
William Sheward
John Hawe
William Walker
Tho Culling
Tho Ashton

Richard Raymond
Henry Troughton
William Bird
Stephen Parker
James Berblok

Att a Vestery holden the 19 Nouē 1650 it is ordred that (whereas by Acc^{o} seuerall yeeres past there was due to Jō Hill & Sarah Hill Children of Thomas Hill who was a pensioner to ye parish sixty nyne povnds ffower shillings & nyne pence) there shall be paied to them for ye same 80^{l} to bee equally djvjded y^{t} is to say fforty povnds to Jo & fforty pounds to the said Sarah, and the Bonnd due from Tailor is to be deliuered vnto the said Jō Hill and what one the bond is receiueed is equally to be deuided betwixt the sayd Jō and Sarah. thirty pounds of this mony the Churchwarden is to paye and shalbe alowed one Acc^{o} the other ffifty pounds Mr Henry Banbricke lendeth and is to haue bond from the Churchwardens by order of this Vestery for which we are to paye 53^{li} to m^{r} Banbricke the ffirst Jany 1651 the 80^{li} is to be payd the sayd Children the ffirst Jan: 1650 and the vestry and parish is to safe ye Churchwardens harmelesse from their bond 41 a.

Att the same vestery and the day & yeere aboue sayd Richard knight was Chosen (during his good behauior) Sexton of this parish and to receiue the pay of the same accordingly

Ja: Cranford parson
Wm Williamson
Nathaniell fflacke
Joseph Vaghan
Henry Baynbrigg
Joseph Blackwell
Tho Culling
John Brett } Churchwardens
Stephen Gey }
John Hawe
Garrard Dickins
Richard Richardson
Jno Sordell
Thō Ashton
Richard Reymond

The iith of ffebrarij 1650 41 b.

At a vestry houlden the day abouesaid Mr Cranford did proffer and desire to Catechize those yonge people of this parish euery Lords day begining the 23th of this Instant in ye afternoone that haue not yett Receud the Sacram^{t} the wch ye vestrey did Willingly and thanckfully Accept of and Doe promise to send there Children accordingly and doe hope the whole parish Willbe redy to Submitt to this order

Ja: Cranford parson
Wm Williamson
Joseph Vaghan
Henry Baynbrigge
Tho Culling
John Brett
Stephen Gey
John Hawe
Peter Cole
Garrard Dickins
Christo: Jenney
Richard Williams
Thomas Hinde
Richmond Reymond
Edward Moore

The 9^{e} of Aprill 1651 41 a.

At a Vestry helde the day aboue sd theire weare Chose for officers for the parish the ꝑtyes vnderneath exprest by the ꝑtyes whose names are vnder subscribed viz for Church Wardens stephen Jey the Seanior Churchwarden and Humph Blundell for the Junior and Rich Raymond and Jno Hynde for Sydemen And the Auditt day for the perusall of the Churchwardens Accompt is appwinted the 13th day of May next, the officers aboue exprest are for the yeare insuinge and the Auditors for Jno Bretts Accompt for the last year of Accompt are Mr James Cranford Rector Mr Jno Roberts, Mr Wm Williamson, Mr Natha ffiack, Coll Josep Vaughan Mr Hen Bainebrigg Mr Tho. Bolton Mr Josep Blackwell and Mr Tho Culline or any 5 of them

Ja: Cranford parson
John Roberts
Nathaniell ffiacke
Joseph Vaghan
Henry Baynbrigg
Joseph Blackwell
Tho Culling
Stephen Bolton
John Adrian
Richard Richardson
Garrard Dickins
Richard Williams
John Robinson
Christop English
John Brett

4 b. The 19 Aprill 1652

Att the day and yeere aboue sayd ther weare Chose officers for the parish for the yeere insueing for vpper Church Warden & vnder Churchwarden & sids men according to the vote of the vestery by the parishioners whose names are here vnder written vpper Churchwarden Mr Humphery Blunden vnder Churchwarden Maior Richard ffinch sidsmen Mr Thomas Colcloth and mr ffrancis Burton

And the Audit day is oppoynted the 13th may next and the Auditors for Mr Steuen Gey acco are these that follow, mr Cranford mr Williamson mr ffiacke mr Henry Banbricke mr Thomas Bolton mr Joseph Blackewell Mr Thomas Cullin Maior Jō Breett & Joseph Vaghan or any fiue of them

Ja: Cranford
Henry Baynbrigg
Joseph Vaghan
Joseph Blackwell
Tho Bolton
Nathaniell ffiacke
Tho Culling
Richard Richardson
Garrard Dickins
Thō Ashton
Peter Cole
Richard Reymond
John Punter
William Walker
William Pope
Stephen Gey

The 18th of Aprill 1653

Att a Vesterey holden the day & yeare abouesaid, there was Chosen Churchwardens & Sydemen for this pishe for the yeare Insuing as ffoll: mr Richard ffinch, Senior Churchwarden, mr Wm Stradford Junior Churchwarden, mr Garrard Dickins, & mr Nathniell Brookes Sydemen. And the 4th of May next Apoynted for the Auditt of mr Humphry Blunden his accoumpt, Mr Cranford, mr Cullen, mr Williamson, mr Vaughan, mr ffiack, mr Boulton, mr Blackwell, mr Brett and Mr Baynbrigg or Any ffive of Them are Apoynted Auditors. Allso it is Orderred that the Senior Churchwarden shall giue bond of Two hundred poundes by himself and a Suffitien Suerty, for the rendring a Just & true Accoumpt for the trust reposed in him

Ja: Cranford
Henry Baynbrigg
Tho. Bolton
Nathaniell ffiacke
Joseph Blackwell
H. Blunden
John Hawe
ffrancis Burton
Richard Reymond
Tho Ashton
Tho Lowe
will Bird
Stephen Parker
Garrard Dickins
Nathaniel Brookes

The 4th of Aprill 1654

At a vestry Houlden the day and yeare aboue said There was Chosen Churchwardens and Sydmen for this parish for the yeare Insueing as ffolloweth Mr William Stratfford Senior Churchwarden Mr John Hawe Junior Churchwarden and Mr Thomas Lowe and Mr William Simpson Sydemen, and for the Audiat of Maior ffinches Accompt wee apoynt the 9th day of May next and for the Audiat of the said Accompt wee doe Apoint Mr Cranford Mr Cullen William Williamson Mr Vaughan Mr ffiack Mr Boulton Mr Blackwell Mr Brett Mr Baynebrig Mr Blunden or any five of them Apoynted Auditors and mr Geij

Alsoe it is ordered that the senior Churchwarden shall give Bond of twoe hundred pownds by himselfe and a suffitient Suerty for the rendring a Just and true acompt of the trust reposed in him

Ja: Cranford parson
Wm Williamson
Henry Baynbrigg
Nathaniell ffiacke
Joseph Blackwell
Will Stratford
John Hawe
Tho: Colclough
William Walker
Richard Reymond
Richard Williams
Tho: Lowe
William Bird
Nath Brooke
Stephen Parker
John Punter
Robert Watkins
Peter Aylworth
Jerimie Gregory

The 28 of Aprell 1652.

sueance of A warrant from the right hono^{rable} the Lord Maio^{r} dated the 25th of this present Aprell grounded apone an ordinance of his highnes ye lord p'otector of England et^{c} of y^{r} 12 of this month for Chooseing of Surveÿors and Scavenger^{rs} for amending Clengesinge of high waÿes and streetts et^{c} wee of the parish of Christoph in the waurde of Broad streett London haue Chosen and doe present Thomas Loue and Willÿam Pope to Bee Surveÿors or Scavengers ffor the precinct of Christopher London for ye yeare ensueinge accordinge to ye purposs and intent of the sd ordinance:

Nathaniell ffacke	Tho Culling
John Haue	Wm Williamson
Thō Ashton	Richard ffinch
William Bird	Richard Richardson
Stephen Parker	Peter Aylworth
William Moore	John Punter
	Henry Sutton

August 17: 1654

a very full vestry in ye Parish of Christophers London, It was agreed by the Minister & the Major part of the Parishion^{rs} That Thomas Marten should be the Clerke of that parish putting in sufficient securety to the Churchwardens for to make good all such Monies & plate & all other things belonging to the Church or Parish, that the said Clerke shalbe trusted withall, or shall come, into his hands & to be accomptable from time to time as he shalbe called therevnto: And shall continue in the sd Place no longer then he shall faithfully discharge his office & performe this agreem^{t}. And in case he come into ye Parish to inhabite there, to secure the parish from his charge of wife and children

Ja: Cranford Rector
Will Stratford } Churchwardens
John Hawe }

In this vestree were p'sent
m^{r} Culling
m^{r} Bainbrigge
m^{r} Williamson
m^{r} Vaghan
m^{r} Blackwel
m^{r} Bolton
m^{r} Brette
m^{r} Blunden
m^{r} Guy m^{r} ffinch
m^{r} Webbe
m^{r} Nuttall
m^{r} Brookes
m^{r} Bird
m^{r} Astill
m^{r} Skiñer
m^{r} Dickens
m^{r} Burton

The 2: feb. 1654

[The Tenants in ffleetestreete appearing and desiring that their Leases might be renewed. It was thought fitt to appoint & nominate m^{r} Stratford Colonell Vaughan Majer Brett m^{r} Blackewell & Mr Bolton for Cornhill side, & Mr Haw m^{r} Culling m^{r} Bambridge major ffinch & m^{r} fflacke for the other side to be a Comittee to view the houses in ffleetestreete & to treate wth the Tenants and report to a vestry how they find the same.

March 16th 1654°

At a vestry holden the day and yeare aboue written. It is upon the Peticons of the Tenants in ffleetestreete, & full Consideration thereof, thought fitt & ordered That the sd Tenants surrendring up their old leases shalbe tenants to ye Parish for their seu'all tenem^{ts} at & vnder ye Condicōns following. vizt James Vade paying seauenty pounds fine at ye sealing of his lease and ye yearely rent of 30^{li} to be made q'terly shall hold ye same for 31 yeares, the rent to be brought home to the Churchwardens. That Wm Smith paying 28^{li} fine & 16 rent p añ shall have a lease upon the like tearmes. That Henry Sharpe paying 28^{li} fine & 24^{li} rent p anñ shall also haue a lease on the same tearmes. And that Richard Scrivener paying 20^{li} fine & 14^{li} rent p Anñ shall haue a lease granted him as ye rest. And that ye seu'all fines be paid by the tenants upon sealing of their Leases, and the Leases to Comēnce from Lady day next.

At ye same vestry it was also ordered That from & after the 25 day of this insta..t March John Roach shalbe Sexton of this p̄ish to execute the same during his good behavio^{r}. And that 4^{s} weekely shalbe paid to W^{m} knight the p'sent Sexton for his weekely pencōn

Ja: Cranford Rector
Henry Baynbrigg
Nathaniell fflacke
Tho Bolton
John Brett
Richard ffinch
Tho: Colclough
William Walker
William Moore
John Webb
John Robinson
John Punter
Thō Ashton
Chr: Marsham
Edward Moore
Nath Brooke
Garrard Dickins
Thomas Hinde
James Nuthall
Jerimie Gregory
John Cumberland
Will Stratford } Churchwardens
John Hawe }

The 24th of Aprill 1655

At a vestry holden ye day & yeare abouesd, there were chosen Churchwardens & Sidesmen for this parish for the yeere ensuing as followeth Mr John Haw Senior Churchwarden mr Thomas Colecloth Junior Churchwarden mr Stephen Parker & mr Edward Barriffe Sydesmen. And the 22th of May next is appointed for the Auditt of mr Wm Stratford his Accompt And mr James Cranford mr Tho. Culling mr Henry Baynbrigg mr Wm Williamson mr Thomas Bolton, mr Joseph Blackwell mr John Brett mr Richard ffinch mr Joseph Vaughan mr Nath^{ll} fflacke or any fiue of them are appointed audito^{rs}. Also it is ordered that ye Senio^{r} Churchwarden shall giue bond of 200^{li} by himselfe as a sufficient suerty for ye rendring a just & a true Accompt for ye trust reposed in him.

At the same vestry it is also further Ordered that at ye costs & charges of the p̄ish the Church shalbe forthwth whited & the pillars done in oyle as form'ly: & that ye Ten Comandem^{ts} the Lords

Ja: Cranford Rector
Henry Baynbrigg
Wm Williamson
Tho Bolton
Joseph Blackwell

Prayer & the Creed shalbe decently sett vp & painted at ye east end of the Church or Chancell. And whereas at a vestry holden the 16th of m'ch last Richard knight was displaced from being sexton & John Roach appointed to execute that place & it was ordered that Knight should haue his pencōn made up iiij^s weekely. It is now thought fitt & ordered that ye sd Act in relacōn to Roach & Knight shalbe & is hereby made null and voyd. And it is further ordered (upon the peticōn of the sd John Roach) that he shall have vj^d weekely added to his pencōn from this p̄ish.

John Brett
Nathaniell ffacke
Richard ffinch
Garrard Dickins
James Nuthall
Peter Aylworth
Nath Brookes
Edward Moore
Richard Reymond
Henry Sutton
Richard Richardson

May the 24th 1655

At a vestry holden the day & yeare abouesd for auditing the Accompts of the Churchwarden for the last yeare. It is Ordered that m^rs Herseman wid shall haue given her by the Churchwardens the sume of thirty shillings eight pence as a Gift from the p̄ish: and that Richard knight haue paid him fiue shillings for cleansing the leads of the Church & for ringing the 5 of Novemb the last yeare; Both wch sumes are to be paid by mr Haw the p^rsent Churchwarden

Ja: Cranford Rector
Wm Williamson
Nathaniell ffacke
Richard ffinch
Joseph Blackwell
John Brett
Will. Stratford
Tho Colclough

August 25. 1655

At a vestry holden ye day and yeare above sd it was ordered that Edward Pejrce his bill for his worke done in the church should bee discharged and the church-warden to pay it, being 28 pound, and y^t ye church-wardens agree with, and pay of the other workemen who have brought in thejr bills for thejr worke about the church. It was likewise ordered that John Christopher bee placed as an apprentjce for thirteene yeares with Robert Lewen, and the sajd Robert Lewen give in securjty to save the parish harmeles from him for ever, and to bring him vp in his trade and bind him in the glovers hal, and make him a free man of ye citty of London, and that the churchwardens vpon this consideratjon pay vnto ye said Robert ten pounds. and ffurther ordined Mr Cranfords house in wch he now dwelleth shalbe repared at the Charge of this parish

Ja: Cranford Rector
Will Stratford
John Hawe
Tho Colclough
Richard Richardson
Garrard Dickins
William Moore
John Brett
Tho Ashton
Richard Williams

Richard Reymond
Jerimie Gregory
Henry Sutton
Thomas Hooton
Richard Kingey
Tho: Lowe
Robert Watkins

7 Aprill 1656

At a vestry holden the day & yeere abouesayd, there were chosen Churchwardens & Sidesmen for the yeare ensuing as followeth m^r Thomas Coleclaugh Senior Churchwarden m^r ffrancis Mayoh Junior Churchwarden, m^r Stephen Skinner & m^r Cave Bury Sydesmen. And the 6th of May next is appointed for the auditing of m^r John Hawes Accompt. And mr James Cranford mr Thomas Cullen mr Henry Bainbrig mr Wm Stratford mr Joseph Blackwell mr Richard ffinch mr Thomas Bolton mr Nath^ll ffacke mr John Brett mr Joseph Vaughan & mr Stephen Jey or any fiue of them are appointed Audito^rs Also it is ordered that ye Senior Churchwarden shall giue bond of 200^li by himselfe as a sufficient securety for ye rendring a just & true accompt for ye trust reposed in him.

Ja: Cranford Rector
Tho Culling
Tho Bolton
Henry Baynbrigg
John Brett
Stephen Gey
Richard ffinch
Will Stratford
Thomas Hinde
Robert Watkins
John Webb
John Punter
Steph: Skynner
Garrard Dickins
Tho: Lowe
Joseph Wright
Thomas Hooton
William Moore

The 1st of Aprill 1657

At a vestry holden the day & yeare abovesayd there were chosen Churchwardens & Sidesmen for the yeare ensuing as followeth mr ffrancis Mayo Senior Churchwarden mr Wm Walker Junior Churchwarden mr John Potter and mr Robert watkins Sidesmen. And the 2^d of June next is appointed for the auditing of mr Thomas Colclaughs accompt and mr James Cranford mr Thomas Cullen mr Henry Bainbrigg mr Nath^ll ffack major John Brett mr Wm Stratford mr Joseph Blackwell mr Thomas Bolton major Richard ffinch & mr Stephen Jey or any five of them are appointed Audito^rs. And it is ordered that ye Senior Churchwarden shall give bond of 200^li as a sufficient securety for rendring a just & true Accompt for the trust reposed in him

Nathaniell ffacke
Tho: Bolton
Henry Baynbrigg
Joseph Blackwell
John Brett
Tho: Colclough

Stephen Gey
John Robinson
Thō Ashton
Richard Reymond
Tho: Lowe
Nath: Brooke
Joseph Wright
John Punter
Richard Kinsey
Jerimie Gregory
Henry Sutton
Peter Aylworth
John Elliott

At a vestry holden the 10th of sepber 1657 doc[r] Prior was chosen Lecturer to Preach on the Lords day in the afternoone for on whole yeare beginning at Michalmas next ensuing.

Henry Baynbrigg
Nathaniell ffacke
Joseph Blackwell
John Brett
Thō Ashton
Nath: Brookes
Garrard Dickins
Richard Reymond
Stephen Skynner
Joseph Wright
Caue Bury
Chr: Marsham
Robert Watkins
Richard Poulton
Tho: Hooton
Richard Kinsey
Thomas Hinde
John Punter
Richard Williams
ffrancis Mayo Churchwarden

At a Vestry houlden the 12th of Aprill 1658 their was Chosen for church Officers for this ꝑishe for the yeare Ensueing as ffolloweth M[r] William Walker Senior Churchwarden, and M[r] Thomas Ashton Junior Churchwarden, M[r] Thomas Lambe & M[r] Christop[r] Masham Sydemen. The Auditt day is Apoynted to be the 6th day of May next. And the Auditors of m[r] Mayo his acc[o] are M[r] Cullen, M[r] Blackwell m[r] ffack m[r] Boulton M[r] Baynbrigg m[r] Stratford, M[r] Gey & M[r] Colcloth or any fower of them. The Senior Churchwarden is to giue bond & Security in 200[li] for a Just Acc[o] for all goodes & moneyes that shall come to his Custody.

James Cranford	Henry Baynbrigg
Tho Culling	Joseph Blackwell
Tho: Bolton	Stephen Gey
Tho: Colclough	ffrancis Mayo
Richard Reymond	Garrard Dickins
Tho: Long	Chr: Marsham
steph: skynner	Tho. hooton
Joseph Wright	John Punter
Peter Aylworth	Henry Sutton
	Jerimie Gregory

Att a vestry houlden the 30th of Aprill 1658 vppon the motion and request of m[r] william Hawkes for leaue to make a leaden pipe to convay the Rayne water from the gutter between m[r] Henery Banbriggs & m[r] Stephen Geyes House downe into the Church Ally to run from thence into the Com̄on shore, it was freely granted him according to his request soe farr as it conserns the Parish

Nathaniell ffacke	Henry Baynbrigg	Tho Culling
Stephen Gey	ffrancis Mayo	Garrard Dickins
Thomas Lowe	Nath. Brookes	
Richard Reymond	Jerimie Gregory	
Stephen Parker	Henry Sutton	
Robert Watkins	William Walker Churchwarden	
John Punter		

The first of October 1658

At a vestry holden the day & yeare aboversayd: It was thought fitt & ordered, That m[r] Adrian LittleJohn (who hath bin form'ly Curate to this parish and is now dismissed) shall haue for & towards his maintenance & livelihood the sum̄e of twenty shillings payd unto him q'terly by the Churchwardens for the tyme being during the pleasure of the parish and he is to haue xx[s] payd him for the q'ter ending at Michals last past

Further y[t] y[e] Churchwardens shall ꝑvide at y[e] charge of the Parish a blacke cloath for y[e] covering of the dead y[t] shalbe buryed within the Church or Churchyard

Also ordered That no Stranger shalbe buryed either in y[e] Church or Churchyard w[th]out y[e] consent of the Churchwardens together w[th] those of the parish that haue borne y[e] office of overseer for the poore or any 5 of them; first had & obteyned.

Jam: Cranford Rector
Henry Baynbrigg
Nathaniell ffacke
Joseph Blackwell
Stephen Gey
ffrancis Mayo
Richard Reymond
Peter Cole
Nath: Brooke
Peter Aylworth
Christop English
Tho: Aylward
John Rous
William Walker
Thō Ashton

At a vestry holden the 8th of ffebruary 1658 It was thought fitt and ordered that William Mathewes shalbe Sexton to the parish and continue in the sayd office of sexton for and during his good behavio[r] and the pleasure of the ꝑishe and no longer, the sayd place being now voyd vpon the decease of Richard Knight

James Cranford Rector
Tho Culling
Henry Baynbrigg
Tho: Bolton
Nathaniell ffacke
Joseph Blackwell
John Brett
Tho: Colclough
Richard Reymond

Tho: Lowe
Stephen Parker
Garrard Dickins
John Potter
Ste: Skynner
Chr: Marsham
John Punter
Peter Aylworth
Nath Brooke
William Walker

The 4th of Aprill 1659

At a vestry holden the day & yeare abovesayd, there were chosen Churchwardens and Sidesmen for the yeare ensuing as followeth mr Thomas Ashton Senior Churchwarden mr Peter Cole Junior Churchwarden, mr Thomas Hooton & mr Richard Keinsey sidesmen. And the 5th of May next is appointed for the auditing of mr Wm Walkers accompt and mr James Cranford, mr Thomas Culling mr Henry Bainbrig mr Nathanll ffIack mr Joseph Blackwell mr Thomas Bolton, major John Brett mr Thomas Colclaugh mr Stephen Jey or any 5 of them are appointed auditors. And it is ordered that the senior Churchwarden shall give bond of 200li for rendring a just & true accompt of the trust reposed in him. And it is further ordered, that the Churchyard be kept decent & cleane & the doores thereof kept shut & none permitted to dry cloathes therein or to make use thereof, but that it be reserved for the use of the parish only.

	James Cranford Rector
Joseph Blackwell	Tho Culling
Henry Baynbrigg	Tho Bolton
Nathaniell ffIacke	Tho Colclough
Stephen Gey	ffrancis Mayo
Richard Williams	Nath: Brooke
Richard Reymond	Peter Aylworth
Stephen Parker	Willm: Clarke
Tho hooton	Rowland Price
Samuell Powell	Tho: Chebsey

It was Concluded by the [entry unfinished]

At a vestry holden Thursday the 14th of Aprill 1659 it appearing that John Roch late a penconer and inhabitant of this parrish being deceased and the lease of his house and goods falling to the care of the pishoners of this parrish to be held and disposed of for the paying of his debts and good and maintenance of his children It was at the said vestry holden agreed that Mr Thomas Culling paying fforty pounds shall haue the whole interest of the lease Roch had of his house being 19 yeares & a halfe to come at or Lady day last And likewise it is ordered the Churchwardens make sale of what goods hee left and to receive the said 40li of Mr Culling and thereout to pay Roches debts and the rest remayne for the good of his children.

	James Cranford Rector
Richard Richardson	Tho Culling
Tho: Lowe	Henry Baynbrigg
Garrard Dickins	John Adrian
Peter Aylworth	Tho Bolton
Richard Remond	Nathaniell ffIacke
Henry Sutton	Tho: Colclough
John Robinson	Sam: Harwar
	John Punter
	Chr: Marsham

At a vestry holden the 19th of Aprill 1659 by St Christofers precinct John Robinson Scr was chosen Constable for this p'cinct as also Quest man for the Remaynder of this present yeare the late constable Joseph Wright being removed out of the Ward and John Punter of this p'cinct was chosen Skavenger for the Remaynder of this present yeare

James Cranford Rector	Tho. Culling
ffra: Clifford	Henry Baynbrigg
William Horsey	John Adrian
Christop English	Nathaniell ffIacke
Henry Sutton	Richard Williams
	Richard Reymond
	Steph: Skynner
	Garrard Dickins
	Tho: clayton

Att a Vestry holden on Thursday the 23th of June 1659 it was ordered and agreed that the Churchwardens shall forthwth goe and take the Advise of Councell what is requisite to be done in relation to the disposall of the Lease & estate of John Roch deceased a late Pensioner to this parish, and concerning his Children. Also it was then ordered and agreed by the Vestrey that Thomas drake be admitted to the place of Parish Clerke to officiate therein during the pleasure of the parish

Tho: Bolton	James Cranford Rector
Nathaniell ffIacke	Tho Culling
John Webb	Joseph Blackwell
James Hakes	Henry Baynbrigg
James Speght	John Adrian
Jerimie Gregory	Richard Richardson
Williã Gosnell	William Walker
	Peter Cole

At a Vestery holden the 15th of Septembr 1659 The pishoners knoweing That Mr Cranford their Minnister hath bine longe sicke & weake, Thay did Agree to giue him ffifteene poundes for his Comfort in the said Sicknesse, and hereby authorice the Churchwardens to pay the same

John Adrian	Tho Culling
Joseph Blackwell	Henry Baynbrigg
Nathaniell ffIacke	Tho: Bolton
Richard Richardson	Tho Colclough
Sam: Harwar	John Webb
Richard Reymond	ffrancis Mayo
James Hakes	William Walker
Jerimie Gregory	
Henry Sutton	

Att a vestry holden on Monday the Third day of october 1659 in respect mr James Cranford the Parson being dead they went to a choyce for a new mynister and Mr John Pearson was chosen and a peticon subscribed by the vestry directed to the Lords Commissioners of the great seale for graunting him the presentacõn to the said Church by the severall psons heereafter named

Thomas Bolton	Henry Bainbrigg	Thomas Culling
John Brett	Thomas Colclough	Joseph Blackwell
John Robinson	Peter Aylworth	Nathaniell ffIack
Christofer Marshom	John Rous	ffrancis Mayo
Gerrard Dickens	Willm Thorrogood	Richard Kelsey
James Waldegraue	William Clarke	Robert Karington

Stephen Skynner, Thomas Clayton, Nathaniell Brookes
Thomas Lowe, Thomas Chepsey, William Rutland
Thomas Horton, William Drope, Richard Raymond
Thomas Ashton, Christofer English, William Walker
Robert Watkins

Att a vestry holden on ffriday the Sixtenth day of March 1659 in respect Mr Peirsons the Recto[rs] house and garden is much out of repaire and being put to the vote whether the pish would repaire it or allow any thing towards it it was agreed that out of the Stock of the pish mr Peirson shall haue Twenty and ffive pounds towards the repaires thereof

Caue Bury, Jerimie Gregory, Tho Culling
Richard Reymond, Tho Aylward, Henry Baynbrigg
John Punter, Will[m] Clark, Tho: Bolton
steph: skynner, Tho: Harper, Joseph Blackwell
Tho: hooton, John Brett
William Rutland, Thō Ashton } Church-, Stephen Gey
Will Gosnell, Peter Cole } wardens, Tho Colclough
John Elliott, William Walker
Nath. Brooke
John Robinson

Aprill the 23[d] 1660

Att a vestry holden the Day & yeare abouesayd there weare Chosen Churchwardens Mr Peeter Cole Senior Church-warden Mr Richard Raymond Junior Churchwarden Sidesmen Mr Jeremye Grigory and Mr John Robinson for the yeare ensuing

And the Audite of mr Thomas Ashtons Accoumpt for Churchwarden the yeare past, is Apoynted the 24th of May next. And it is Ordered that the Senior Churchwarden shall giue bond with Security in the some of 200[li] for giueing a Just & true Accoumpt of all moneyes, plate, and gooddes as shall come to his Custodie by his said office of Churchwarden.

John Pearson Rector, Tho: Bolton
Henry Baynbrigg, Joseph Blackwell
Nathaniell ffacke, Tho Colclough
Henry Sutton, Stephen Gey
Peter Aylworth, ffrancis Mayo
Tho: hooton, William Walker
Edw: Buckerfeild, Chr: Marsham
W. Thorowgood, James Speght
William Rutland, John Punter
Christop English, steph: skynner
Tho: Lowe

Att a vestry holden the 27th day of June 1660 in respect the Parsonage house was much out of repaire and now being put into good repaire aswell in the ffoundacōn and all other things in doing w[ch] there hath been expended fforty and six pounds nine shillings as appeares by the workemens bylls and formerly at a vestry onely Twenty ffive pounds was allowed to mr Peirson for the doing thereof and being now put to the vote whether the residue of the money disbursed should bee allowed out of the pish stock It was agreed that the said residue of money beinge Twenty one pounds nine shillings shalbe paid out of the said pish stock

Henry Baynbrigg
Joseph Blackwell
Peter Cole } Church, Nathaniell ffacke
Richard Reymond } Wardens, Tho: Colclough
John Brett
Thō Ashton
Step: skynner
Chr: Marsham
John Robinson
John Punter
Robert Watkins
Henry Sutton
ffra: Clifford
William Rutland
John Elliott

The 26th of July 1660

Att a Vestery houlden the day & yeare aboue written Mr Stephen Skinner was Chosen Junior Churchwarden for the remaynder of this yeare, by reason mr Ramond is deceased & buried

Henry Baynbrigg, John Adrian
Tho: Bolton, Nathaniell ffacke
Joseph Blackwell, Tho: Colclough
Thō Ashton, Stephen Gey
Peter Cole, Caue Bury
John Elliott, Chr: Marsham
Tho: hooton
James Hakes

At a vestry holden the 15th of Aprill 1661 mr Stephen Skynner was Chosen Seinor Churchwarden & mr Nathaniell Brookes Junior Churchwarden for the yeare ensuing and
Mr John Punter and } Sidemen
Mr William Thorowgood }

The Senior Churchwarden is to give bond and security of the some of Two hundred pounds to deliver vp a just & true accompt of all moneys plate and goods that shall come to his Custody by reason of the said Office, when he shall be required by the Audito[rs] for the parish.

The Auditt day for the auditing of Mr Peter Coles Accompt, and also for the setling of all matters concerning the Accompts of Mr William Walker & Mr Thomas Ashton late Churchwardens, to be the 30th of May next. Mr Henry Baynbrigg Mr Thomas Culling Mr Nathaniell ffack Mr Joseph Blackwell, Mr Thomas Bolton Mr Thomas Colclough, Mr Stephen Gey & Mr ffrancis Mayo or any ffoure or ffive of them are appoynted to be Audito[rs] of the said Accompts

John Pearson Rector
Henry Baynbrigg
Nathaniell ffacke
Tho: Colclough
William Walker
Thō Ashton
Chr: Marsham
Richard Kinsey
Tho: hooton
John Punter
Tho Pratt
W: Thorowgood
Peter Aylworth
Will[m] Clarke
William Bigg
Peter Bell

Att a Vestry holden the 27th of March 1662: were chosen for the yeare ensuing

Mr Nathaniell Brookes, senior Churchwarden
and
Mr John Potter . . . , junior Churchwarden

But the said Mr Potter alledging that he was going out of the parish it was ordered that he should pay Eight pounds for a ffine, w[ch] he submitted to, But the same is ordered not to be brought into president for the future; After w[ch] was chosen in the roome of Mr Potter

Mr Christopher Marsham . junior Churchwarden

Also there were chosen

Mr Thomas Pratt
&
Mr Lodowick Lloyd } Sydemen

The senior Churchwarden is to give bond & security of the some of Two hundred pounds to deliver vp a just & true accompt of all moneys plate & goods that shall come to his Custody by reason of the said Office when he shalbe required by the Auditors for the parish

The Auditt day for the auditting of Mr Stephen Skynners Accompt and also for the setling of Mr Peter Coles and all other the late Churchwardens Accompts yet vnperfected to be wednesday the 14th of May next.

Henry Baynbrigg Esq' Thomas Culling Alderman Mr Nathaniell ffiack, Mr Thomas Bolton Mr Thomas Colclough Mr Stephen Gey & Mr ffrancis Mayo or any ffoure of them are appoynted to be Auditors of the said Accompts.

stephen skynner
John Adrian
Nathaniell ffiacke
Tho: Colclough
Peter Cole
John Webb
William Walker
Thō Ashton
Robert Watkins
John Punter
Tho pratt
Henry Sutton
Charles Innes
Peter Aylworth
Peter Bell

b. At a vestrey houlden the 10th of Aprill 1662 vpon a motion that Mrs Cranford the widdow of Mr James Cranford Deceased (their late Minnister) was but in a lowe Condition for worldly eastate, thay voted and ordered the pnte Churchwarden mr Brookes to pay and giue vnto hir the some of ffifteene pounds, provided that shee remooue all the remainder of hir gooddes out of the parsonage house.

John Pearson Rector — Tho Culling
Henry Baynbrigg — Tho Bolton
John Adrian — Nathaniell ffiacke
John webb — Stephen Gey
Peter Aylworth — Henry Sutton
John Punter — John Cockeram
John Elliott — W: Thorowgood
William Horsey — Daniell Hills

At a vestry houlden the 9th of May 1662 It being Certified vnto the pishioners That Mr Christop' Marsham Junior Churchwarden was remoouing out of the pishe & also for other Satisfactory reasons ~~was fallen to decay in his Estate~~ thay Chose mr Thomas Hooton in his roome for the remaynder of the yeare ensueing.

Henry Baynbrigg — Tho Culling — Thō Ashton
Tho Bolton — Tho: Colclough — Step: Skynner
Natha ffiacke — ffrancis Mayo — John Punter
Stephen Gey — William Walker — Tho Pratt
Henry Sutton — John Elliott — John webb
Peter Aylworth — Will Rutland — Peter Bell
Tho: Clayton — Tho: Russell
Nath Brooke

Att a Vestry holden the ffirst of August 1662 these persons following 58 were nominated to be ffeoffees in trust touching the parish Lands Mr Nathaniell ffiack being only surviving of the old ffeoffees viz: Henry Baynbrigg Esq', Thomas Culling Esq' Thomas Colclough, Thomas Bolton Stephen Skynner, Jeremy Gregory, Peter Ayleworth, Thomas Lamb & the two present Churchwardens Nathaniell Brooke & Thomas Hooton

Also these persons ffollowing were nominated & appoynted to be a Comittee for viewing of the wrytings and prosecuting the rights of the parish viz the said Henry Baynbrigg Esq' Thomas Culling Esquire Thomas Colclough Thomas Bolton Stephen Skynner Nathaniell Brooke, Thomas Hooton Nathaniell ffiack John Webb Jeremy Gregory & William Walker or any ffive of them.

Also it was referred to the said Churchwardens to repaire the Church where it is defective.

Nathaniell ffiacke — W[m] Thorowgood
Tho Colclough — John Rous
William Walker — Will Horsey
stephen skynner — W[m] Drope
Robert Watkins — Peter Bell
Henry Sutton — Tobias Davis
Peter Aylworth — Henry Beke
John Elliott

Att a Vestry holden the Nynth day of January 1662: It was ordered 58 That Abigaell Short one of the Children at the charge of this parish shalbe placed forth by and at the discretion of Mr Nathaniell Brooke and Mr Thomas Hooton the present Churchwardens whereby the parish may be freed from further charge about the said Child And that the Churchwardens shall give any some for so placing forth the said Child not exceeding Seaven pounds.

Also it was ordered at the same Vestry that the Churchwardens be desired to goe to the severall parishioners to collect such moneys as they shall freely contribute to docto' Hackett now Recto' of the said parish for and in respect of his extraordinary paines as well for the quarter now past as for the future.

Also it was ordered that the said Churchwardens shall at the parish charge repaire y[e] Chimneys that are defective in the Tenement now in the occupacon of Mr William Kensey belonging to the Glebe of this parish.

Henry Baynbrigg — Tho Pratt
Stephen Gey — John Elliott
Tho: Colclough — Will Horsey
Peter Cole — Will Thompson
John Punter — Peter Bell
George ffrancklin

William Kinsey
Nathaniel Brooke } Churchwardens
Tho: Hooton }

a. Att a Vestry holden the Three & twentith day of Aprill 1663 Mr Thomas Hooton was chosen Senior Churchwarden & Mr John Webb was chosen Junior Churchwarden for the yeare ensuing, and Mr Henry Sutton & Mr John Rous were chosen Sidesmen for the yeare ensuing. And it is ordered that the said Senior Churchwarden shall enter into bond of 200li penalty wth Two sufficient sureties for giving a just and true Accompt of what moneys goods plate vtensill & things shall come to his hands belonging to this parish as hath beene formerly accustomed when he shall be required by the Auditors. The Auditt day for the auditting of Mr Nathaniell Brookes accompt & also for the setling Peter Coles Accompt formerly Churchwarden yet vnperfected to be Thursday the xxjth of May next.

Henry Baynbrigg & Thomas Culling Esqrs Mr John Adrian Mr Nathaniell ffack Mr Thomas Bolton Mr Thomas Colclough Mr Stephen Gey & Mr Stephen Skynner or any ffoure of them are appoynted to be Auditors of the said Accompt.

Also it was ordered that all such brasses sculptures & inscripcons belonging to the monuments of the dead as have beene heretofore taken away & are remayning in the Vestry house of this parish Church shall as neare as may be forthwith be restored & affixed in their right places, and that the above named Churchwardens shall see the same done wth the advice & assistance of such of the parishioners as they shall thinke fitt.

Also it is ordered that the said Churchwardens shall cause one deed bearing date the 18th day of this instant Aprill made betweene Nathaniell Brooke & Thomas Hooton then Churchwardens of th'one pt and John Vincent Esqr of th'other pt touching an Annuity or Rent charge of ffive pounds p Ann given to this parish by Mr Thomas fforman Merchant deceased to be enrolled in the Court of Chancery & registred & engrossed in some booke of this parish appoynted for the like purpose.

Also it is ordered that the Churchwardens Constables & Sydemen for the tyme being do enquire what Inmates are or shalbe entertayned into any house or houses in this parish & take care that the parish may be saved harmeles from any charge by reason of such Inmates.

Henry Baynbrigg	Tho: Hackett Rector
Tho Bolton	Tho Culling
Tho Colclough	John Adrian
William Walker	Natha ffacke
Steph. Skynner	Jerimie Gregory
Tho Pratt	Rich Kinsey
Henry Sutton	Nath: Ruckly
John Elliott	Tho: Clayton
Peter Bell	Stephen Gey

b. Att a Vestry holden the Six and twentith day of October 1663 it is ordered that forasmuch as Dr Ralph Harrison now Rector of this parish hath expended & is like to expend a very considerable some of money in & about the necessary repaires of his dwelling house the same being at his first entrance; Therefore as a testimony of their respect to the said Dr Harrison he shall be allowed the some of ffifty pounds by the p'sent Churchwarden Mr Thomas Hooton out of the parish stock

Also it is ordered that whereas there are severall peices of old brasse formerly belonging to old Tombstones wch are broken & vnusefull they shall be disposed of by the Churchwarden towards the Charge of providing a new brasse Branch for lights in the Chancell when need shall require.

	Henry Baynbrigg
John Elliott	Tho Culling
Tho: Blagraue	Tho Bolton
Peter Bell	Tho: Colclough
Samll Harwar	William Walker
Tho Hooton	Steph Skynner
	Nath: Brooke
	Tho Pratt
	Henry Sutton
	Peter Aylworth
	Charles Innes
	John Robinson
	Tobias Davis

Att a Vestry holden the Eleaventh day of Aprill 1664: the parishioners of this parish out of their love and respects have excused Mr Christopher Marsham from being Churchwarden.

And at the same Vestry were chosen for the yeare ensuing Mr John Webb senior Churchwarden & Mr John Robinson Junior Churchwarden

Mr Robert Kerrington } Sidesmen
Mr Peter Ayleworth }

And it is ordered that the senior Churchwarden shall enter into bond of CCli penalty wth Two sufficient sureties for giving a just & true Accompt of what moneys goods plate vtensills & things shall come to his hands belonging to this parish as hath beene formerly accustomed when he shall be required by the Auditors.

The Auditt day for the auditing of Mr Thomas Hootons Accompt the late vpper Churchwarden to be Thursday the 5th of May next.

Henry Baynbrigg & Thomas Culling Esqrs Mr John Adrian Mr Thomas Bolton Mr Thomas Colclough Mr Stephen Gey Mr William Walker Mr Stephen Skynner & Mr Nathaniell Brooke or any ffoure of them are appoynted to be Auditors of the said Accompt.

Also it was ordered that Mr Thomas Drake shall be continued Clarke of this parish for the yeare ensuing.

Also William Bate was chosen Sexton of the parish during their good pleasure.

Also it is referred to the said Auditors or any ffoure of them to settle the Clerkes wages & other duties. And William Mathewes the late Sexton is ordered xxs for his keys

	Ralph Harison Rector
Samuel Powell	Henry Baynbrigg
ffracis Taylor	John Adrian
Will. Thompson	Tho: Colclough
Peter Bell	William Walker
	Nath: Brooke
	Tho: Pratt
	Peter Aylworth
	Samll Harwar
	Tho: Russell
	Rob. Kerington
	Tho: Hooton Churchwarden

Att a Vestry holden the 13th day of June 1664 M[r] Thomas Pratt was chosen Junior Churchwarden (in the roome and stead of M[r] John Robinson deceased) for the residue of this yeare ensuing

Henry Baynbrigg
Stephen Gey
Thō Ashton
Peter Aylworth
Nath: Brooke
Edw: Buckerfeild
Peter Bell
Tho Culling
Steph: Skynner
Tho. Hooton
Sam[ll] Harwar
John Elliott
Thomas Seawell
Richard Gasley
Tho: Bolton
William Walker
Chr: Marsham
Will Horsey
Tho: Blagraue
Nath: Ruckly

Att a Vestry holden the 27th of March 1665: were chosen for the yeare ensuing M[r] Thomas Pratt senior Churchwarden & M[r] Robert Watkins junior Churchwarden M[r] John Elliott and M[r] Robert Briquett Sydesmen. And it is ordered that the senior Churchwarden shall enter into bond of CC[li] penalty wth Two sufficient sureties for giving a just & true accompt of what moneys plate vtensills & things shall come to his hands belonging to this parish as hath beene formerly accustomed when he shall be required by the Audito[rs]. The Auditt day for the auditing of M[r] John Webbs Accompt the late vpper Churchwarden to be Thursday the 27th of Aprill next. And D[r] Ralph Harrison Parson, Henry Baynbrigg & Thomas Culling Esq[rs] M[r] John Adrian M[r] Thomas Bolton M[r] Thomas Colclough M[r] Stephen Gey M[r] William Walker M[r] Stephen Skynner M[r] Nathaniell Brooke & M[r] Thomas Hooton or any ffive of them are appoynted to be Audito[rs] of the said Accompt

Ralph Harison Rector
John Adrian
Tho: Hooton
Jerimie Gregory
Peter Aylworth
Rob Kerington
W[m] Droper
Edw Buckerfeild
William Horsey
Henry Baynbrigg
Tho: Colclough
Stephen Gey
William Walker
Steph: Skynner
Tho: Blagraue
John Elliott
Peter Bell

61a Att a Vestrey holden the xxviij[th] day of July 1665: it was agreed and ordered that forasmuch as it is now a tyme of pestilence, and that there is a great concourse of people to this Church especially in the afternoones many of w[ch] are knowne or believed to resort hither from places infected That therefore there shalbe a suspension of the Afternoone Sermon during the tyme of this Contagion or vntill further order, and that in the interim there shalbe only Divine Service or Comon Prayer in the afternoones on the Lords dayes.

Henry Baynbrigg
Tho: Bolton
Peter Aylworth
Rob: Kerington
W[m] Drope
Peter Bell
Tho Culling
Tho Colclough
Nath: Brooke
John Elliott
Edw: Poultney
Daniell Lingard
Tho Pratt
Robert Watkins

Att a Vestry holden the xxiij[th] of August 1665: It was ordered and agreed that forasmuch as Thomas Drake the present Clerke of the parish is intended to relinquish his said place, That therefore William Bate the present Sexton shall supply the place of Parish clerke in the roome and stead of the said Thomas Drake during his good behavio[r].

Ralph Harison Rector
Henry Baynbrigg
Tho: Colclough
Steph: Skynner
Chr: Marsham
Tho: Hooton
ffrancis Taylor
Henry Sutton
Robert Gay
Joseph ffrancklin
Peter Bell
Rob[t]: Mickell
Thomas Pratt

At a Vestry holden September the 19th 1665 by virtue of an order from the Lord Mayor Daniell Linger was chosen Constable (in the Roome & stead of Villain ~~Henry~~ Horsey who absented himselfe) for the residue of the yeare ensuing

Henry Baynbrigg
Tho Culling
Thō Ashton
Thomas Pratt
Chr: Marsham
John Elliott
John Lansdell
Joseph ffrancklin
Rob[t]: Mickell
Steph: Skynner
John Quarrington

At a Vestry holden the 20th of September 1665 that forasmuch as Daniell Langer was chosen in the Roome and stead of William Horsey, who absented himselfe (by virtue of an Order from the Lord Maior) and the said Daniell Langer being not capable of the same place. It was Ordered that Joseph ffrancklin should hold Constable in the Roome & stead of the sd Daniell Langer for the residue of the yeare ensueing and should bee discharged from serving of Constable at any time heereafter in this Precinct of S[t] Christophers

steph skynner
Chr: Marsham
John Elliott
John Lansdell
Daniell Lingard
Rob[t]. Mickell
Tho Pratt

S[t] Christophers December y[e] 20th 1665

At a vestry holden the said day were chosen for the yeare ensueing Thomas Clayton Constable and Questman and William Horsey Questman and Thomas Browne Scauinger And at y[e] same tyme William Horsey did request of y[e] said Vestry that they would be pleased to excuse him from seruing as Constable for y[e] yeare ensueing in Consideracōn of what fformer seruice he had done in the same Office. And thereupon he was willing to allow to the poore of y[e] said Parish y[e] sum of fforty shillings to excuse him from y[e] said Office And at y[e] same tyme William Drope did request of y[e] said Vestry that they would be pleased to excuse him from seruing as Constable and Questman for y[e] yeare ensueinge in consideracōn of his earnest businesse in the Countryes And thereupon he was willing to allow to the Poore of the said Parish the sum̄ of ten poundes Ster̄ to excuse him from the said Offices And at y[e] same tyme Samuell Powell did request of y[e] said Vestry that they would be pleased to excuse him from seruing as Scavinger Constable and Questman for ye yeare ensueing in Consideracōn of the weaknesse and ill disposicōn of his body And therupon he was willing to allow to the poore of the said Parish the sum of Twelue poundes Sterling to excuse him from ye said Offices In witnesse whereunto wee then of ye said Vestry haue hereunto sett Our hands the day and yeare aboue written.

	Tho Culling
Joseph ffrancklin	steph: skynner
Miles Temple Jn^r^	Thomas Pratt
	Peter Aylworth
	Tho: Hooton
	Tho: Blagraue
	William Horsey
	Samuel Powel
	ffowlke Jones
	Will Barker

1 b. St Christophers Aprill ye 12th 1666

That whereas William Drope amongst other parishoners did upon (p^r^tence of uery extraordinary businesse & going into ye Countrey) referre themselues to seuerall persons that held a Vestry on the 20th day of December last to ffine for seuerall Offices that they were then in Election to hold Whereupon the said William Drope was fined the sum of ten poundes ster. the which sum he hath euer since refused to pay Therefore it is thought fitt that euery person from henceforth shall (after he hath soe referred himselfe and is fined) pay euery such sum of money so fined before any other person or persons shall be put in Election Whereto we haue herevnto sett our handes the day and yeare abouewritten

Chr: Marsham	Tho Culling
ffowlke Jones	steph: skynner
Sam^ll^ Harwar	Tho. Pratt
	Tho. Hooton
	Stephen Gey
	Peter Aylworth
	Richard Joanes
	Will Barker
	Miles Temple Jn^r^
	John West

1669: Memorandum That the sd Wm Drope payde the sd: Tenn pounds above mentioned vpon the acc^o^: aforesd, the which Mony was Employed in the Repayres of S^t^. Christop^rs^ Church: this present yeare 1669 Wm: Horsey being then Churchwarden Witnes Peter Aylworth

Aprill ye 17th 1666

At A vestry holden then there was chosen for ye yeare ensueinge Mr Robert Watkins Senio^r^ Churchwarden and Mr Peter Ayleworth Junior Churchwarden and Mr Wm Horsey and Mr Nathan Rutley sidesmen And it is Ord^rd^ y^t^ ye said Senior Churchwarden shall enter into bond of CC^li^ penalty with two sufficient sureties for giuing a just and true Accompt of w^t^ monyes plate utensills &c: belonging to ye Parish when he shall be thereunto required. And ye Auditt day for auditing of Mr Thomas Prats Accompt is appointed ye 30th day of Maye next & Mr Hall Rector Thomas Culling Esqr Mr Stephen Skynner Mr John Adrian Mr Thomas Bolton Mr Tho: Colclough Mr Stephen Gey Mr William Walker Mr Nathaniell Brookes Mr Thomas Hooton Mr Jno Webb or any fiue of them are Appointed Auditors of ye said Accompt

Joh. Hall Recto^r^	Tho Culling	Tho: Colclough
Tho Bolton	step: skynner	Stephen Gey
Wm Baynbrigg	Tho: Hooton	William Walker
Tho Pratt	Sam^ll^ Harwar	John Webb
Chr: Marsham	Miles Temple Jn^r^	
ffowlke Jones		

St Christophers Aprill ye 17th 1666 61 a.

Att A vestry holden then It is though[t] fitt and Ordered that from henceforth noe Churchwarden shall admitt or suffer any pson to erect or build any Monument either in Church or Churchyard without a Consent of a full vestry first had and Obteyned

Joh Hall Recto^r^	Tho Culling	Tho: Colclough
Tho: Bolton	steph skynner	Stephen Gey
Wm Baynbrigg	Sam^ll^ Harwar	William Walker
Tho Pratt	ffowlke Jones	John Webb
Chr: Marsham		Miles Temple

St Christophers Aprill 12. 1667 61 b.

Att a meeting as a vestry then holden, there was chosen for ye yeare ensueing Mr Peter Ailworth Senio^r^ Churchwarden Thomas Lamb Junior Churchwarden Thomas Kemble & Wm Drope Sidesmen And it is ordered that Mr Ailworth senior Churchwarden shall enter into bond of CC^li^ with two sufficient suerties for giueing a iust & true accompt of what plate monies vtensills &c belonging to the pish when hee shalbe therevnto required, and the auditt day for auditing of Mr Robt Watkins accompt is appointed the xvj^th^ day of May being assencōn day next ensueing and Thomas Culling Thomas Colclough esq^r^ Mr Stephen Skynnier Mr John Adrian Mr Nathaniel Brookes Mr Stephen Gee & Mr Wm Walker & Mr John Webb or any fiue of them are appointed Audito^rs^ of the said Accompt

	Tho Culling
Tho Pratt	Tho: Colclough
Jerimie Gregory	John Adrian
Tho: Blagraue	Stephen Gey
William Horsey	William Walker
Will Thompson	Steph: Skynner
James Taylor	Nath: Brooke
John West	John Webb
	Robert Watkins
	Peter Aylworth

St Christophers November the first 1667 64 a.

Att A meeting as a Vestry then holden, these severall perticulers following were taken into Consideration by the Parrishioners then present, whoe then & there agreed to the Conclusions following

first An acc^o^ being given of the Disposall of the Parish Children and of Monny to be Red from the Chamber London for the farther support of the sayd Children, it is ordered that the sayd business shall be farther prossecuted by the Churchwardens with the assistance of som of the Committy after named

2 The Lead belonging to the sayd Church, was then sould to Joseph ffrancklin Plumer at 14^s^ 6^d^ p^e^ he giveing his bond with his ffatherinlaw William Jones Bricklayer for security for payment of the monny that the sayd Lead shall amount vnto, at six monthes, from this Day, with intrest for the sayd monny after the Rate of 6^li^ p^e^ p Anñ:

3. It is farther ordered that the Parish Tennants in ffleete Street shall be Treated & Dealt with for Rebuilding of theyr howses, by the sd Committy now appoynted

4. An Estemate of the Charge of Repayring the sayd Church being presented at ye sayd meeting; what Course should be taken for the Repayres of the same, was allsoe Referd to ye sayd Comty

5. Lastly it is Ordered & agreed that Tho Culling Esqr Mr John Adrian Mr Tho: Colclough, Mr Wm Baynbrigg Mr Stephen Skinner Mr Natha: Brookes Mr John Webb Mr Tho Hooton Mr Robert Watkins Mr Jerime Gregory shall be a Committy to assist the Churchwardens in Carrying on the affayres of the sayd Parrish and that thay or any fouer of them with one of the Churchwardens shall act as a Committe in behalfe of the sd Parrish, the heads of these Conclusions being Drawne vp in a paper were subscribed by the Persons then Present

	Tho: Culling
Robert Watkins	John Adrian
Samuel Powell	Tho: Colclough
Wm: Horsey	John Webb
Will: Thompson	Nath. Brooke
Joseph ffrancklin	Tho Hooton
	Tho. Pratt
	Tho. Russell

Peter Aylworth }
Tho: Lambe } Churchwardens

Decembr 21th 1667

At a meeting for the Precinckt of St Christophers in the ward of Broadstreete, were presented offisers for the yeare Ensewing

Peter Aylworth }
Mr Wm Baynbrigg } for ye Choyse of a Comon Counsellman
Tho: Blagrave }
Edw: Buckerfield } Quest men
Tho: Blagrave Constable
Edw: Buckerfield Scavinger

Decembr 21. 1668

At A Meeting for the presinckt of St Christopr in the ward of Broadstreete were presented offisers for the yeare Ensewing

Peter Aylworth }
Wm: Baynbrigg } for ye Choyse of A Com: Counselman
Tho: Blagrave }
Rich: Kemm } Quest men
Tho: Russell Constable
Richard Kem Scavinger

St Christophers March 26th 1668

At a Meeting as a Vestry then holden, in ye Ward of Broadstreete there were Chosen for ye yeare ensueing Mr Thomas Lambe senior Churchwarden and Mr John Elliott Junior Churchwarden And Mr Thomas Saywell and Mr Samuell Powell Sidesmen And it is Ordered that Mr Thomas Lambe senior Churchwarden shall Enter into Bond of 300li penalty with two Sufficient Suretyes for giving a Just and true Accompt of what Plate monyes Materialls vtensills &c belonging to ye Parish when he shallbe therevnto required. And the Auditt day for Auditting Mr Peter Aylworths Accompt is appointed ye last day of Aprill next ensueing being Assention day And Thomas Culling & Thomas Colclough Esqrs Mr Stephen Skynner Mr John Adrian Mr Nathaniell Brookes Mr Stephen Gey Mr William Walker Mr John Webb Mr Thomas Hooton & Mr Robert Watkins or any ffive of them are appointed Auditors of the said Accompt And it is further Ordered That Thomas Culling Esqr Mr John Adrian Mr Thomas Colclough Mr William Bainbrigge Mr Nathaniell Brookes Mr John Webb Mr Peter Aylworth Mr Thomas Hooton Mr Robert Watkins & Mr Jeremiah Gregory shallbee a Comitee to Assist ye Churchwardens in Carrying on ye Affaires of ye Parish And that they or any ffower of them with one of ye Churchwardens shall Act as a Comittee in ye behalfe of ye said Parish

Robert Watkins	Tho Culling
Tho: Russell	John Adrian
Peter Aylworth	Tho: Colclough
Nath: Brooke	Tho: Hooton
Will: Horsey	John Webb
Tho Kemble	Rich Kinsey
John West	

St Christophers Aprill 30th 1668

At a Meeting then holden in the Ward of Broadstreete, at a Vestr[y] of the said parish, Mr John Elliott formerly Chosen for junior Churchwarden was Excused for holding ye sd Office vpon his promise that if he shall hereafter Inhabit in ye said parish, he will freely performe & hold ye same Office of Churchwarden. And then and there was Chosen for ye yeare ensueing Mr William Horsey Junior Churchwarden in ye place of ye sd John Elliott

	Joh: Hall late Rector
Robert Watkins	Tho Culling
Jerimie Gregory	John Adrian
Saml Harwar	Tho: Colclough
Tho Russell	Nath: Brooke
Tho: Hooton	John Webb
Samuel Powell	Peter Aylworth
Rich Kinsey	Steph: Skynner
	Edward Godman
	Tho: Lambe
	John West

St Christophers Aprill 16th 1669

At a Meeting then holden in the said parish, as a Vestry of the said parish there were Chosen for the yeare ensueing Mr William Horsey senior Churchwarden and Mr Robert Kerrington junior Churchwarden. And Mr Thomas Russell & Mr Richard Barwell Sidesmen And it is Orderd That Mr William Horsey senior Churchwarden shall enter into Bond of 300li penalty with twoe sufficient Suretyes ffor giving a Just and true Accompt of what Plate Monyes Materialls Vtensills &c doth belong to ye parish when he shallbe therevnto required And the Auditt day for Auditting Mr Thomas Lambs Accompt is appointed the 20th day of May next ensueing being Ascension day. And Thomas Culling Esqr Mr Thomas Colclough Mr John Adrian Mr Nathaniell Brookes Mr John Webb Mr Peter Aylworth Mr Thomas Hooton & William Bainbrigge Esqr Mr Stephen Gey or any ffive or them are appointed Auditors of the said Accompt

Peter Aylworth	Tho: Colclough
Tho: Ru sell	Tho: Blagraue
Charles wellings	John Webb
Richard: Kenn	Rich. Kinsey
Joseph ffrancklin	Tho: Kemble
Wm Hasellwood	Nath: Brooke
John West	Tho: Hooton
	Tho: Lambe

St Christophers June 11th 1669

At a Meeting as Vestry then holden in the parish aforesaid It was Ordered That Mr John Adrian Mr Thomas Colclough Mr Nathaniell Brookes Mr John Webb Mr Thomas Hooton Mr

Peter Aylworth Mr William Drope Mr Thomas Kemble Mr Samuell Powell Mr Edward Butterfeild Mr Stephen Gey Mr Thomas Pearcehurst shallbe a Comittee to Assist the Churchwardens in Carrying on the Affaires of ye Parish And that they or any fower of them with one of the Churchwardens shall Act as a Comittee in the behalfe of the said parish This to Continue vntill the next Easter. And further Mr George ffrancklyn was Chosen Clarke and Sexton of ye same parish.

Samuell Powell	Joh: Hall
Tho. Persehowse	Tho: Colclough
John West	Peter Aylworth
John Bowyer	Stephen Gey
John marriott	Tho Hooton
John: Whitter	Wm Drope

William Horsey } Churchwardens
Rob: Kerington }

ffebruary 7th 1667

At a Meeting with ye Parish Tenants It was Offered that they should pay halfe their Rents Have their p'sent Leases made vp 61 yeares And to begin their tyme at Lady day come Twelve month They desire tyme to Consider till Monday come Sennight to give their Answeare which was Ordered to be given to the Churchwarden there was p'sent at this Meeting Thomas Culling Esqr Mr Adrian Mr Brookes Mr Skynner Mr Webb Mr Gregory Mr Aylworth Mr Lambe.

St Christophers June 11th 1669

The parish Tenants viz. Mr William Wheatley Mr William Smyth Mr Richard Scrivener and Mr John Sharpe haveing since ye said Proposall of the 7th ffebruary 1667 and before the said Lady day 1669 Accepted of ye same Proposall And severally declared they were willing to Build and Hold their severall Houses for Threescore and one yeares At halfe their respective Old rents At a Meeting as a Vestry holden in ye said parish ye day abovesaid The Parishoners Confirmed and Allowed of ye Agreement made by ye Comittee and ye parish Tenants touching the said Houses

		Joh: Hall
	Sam: Powell	Tho Colclough
	Tho. Persehowse	Peter Aylworth
William Horsey } Church	John West	Stephen Gey
Rob: Kerington } Wardens	John Bowyer	Tho: Hooton
	John marriott	Wm Drope
	John Whitter	

St Christophers March 25 1670

At a Vestry then holden it was ordered that twoe hundred Pounds be taken vp for the vse of the Parish of Christophers in the repair of the Church and that four men of the said Parish giue in Personall Security in behalfe of the Parish to those that lend it, the ffour Persons chosen by the Vestry are mr William Horsey Robert Kerington mr Thomas Colclough mr Peter Aylworth and it is further ordered that these Persons shall be indemnified and saued harmelesse by the Parish for soe doeinge.

Joh: Hall
Tho: Colclough
Peter Aylworth
Tho: Blagraue
Tho Persehowse
John Elliott
John Whitter

Joseph Lem
Joseph ffrancklin
Robert Todd
John Williams
Charles wellinges
Church Wardens { William Horsey
{ Robt: Kerington
Wm Drope

St Christophers Aprill ye 7th 1670. 67 a

Att A vestry holden the day aboue written there was Chosen for sen' Churchwarden of ye parish for ye yeare Ensuing mr Robert Kerington & for Jun' Churchwarden mr Jno Ellyott & for Sidesmen mr Tho Blagraue & mr Edw: Buckerfeild, and it is agreed that next Ascention day be ye auditt day for ye Acc° of mr Wm Horsey late vpper Churchwarden, & it is alsoe ordered mr Robert Kerington the p'sent vpper Churchwarden giue a bond of 300li penalty wth 2 sufficient Securytyes for giueing a Just & true Account of what plate monyes Materialls vtensills &c doth belong to ye parish when he shall be thervnto required, the Auditors appoynted for mr Horseys Account are mr Jno Hall rector, Tho: Colclough Nath Brooke peter Aylworth, Wm Drope, Tho Russell, Sam: powell, & Tho: Kemble or any 5 of them. It is lastly agreed yt the Comittee formerly chosen to manage the parish busines be continued till ye next Auditt day, mr Wm Horsey & mr Tho Russell being added to them.

Joh: Hall
Tho: Colclough
Nath: Brooke
Peter Aylworth
Wm: Drope
Tho: Russell
Tho: Kemble
Edw: Buckerfeild
Edward Godman
Henry Joyce
Charles Wellinges
John Williams
John Daniell
Richard Kenn
William Horsey.

St Christophers 1° Junij 1670 67 b

At a Vestry then holden in the Pish Church there It was Ordered and Consented to That a Provisoe in ye Lease intended to be granted to Mr Horsey of pte of ye lands belonging to ye parish for forfeiture vpon letting or Assigning without Lycence may be left out & ye fforfeiture altered And instead yt of a Nomina Pœna inserted of One hundred pounds And that he may Demise ye p'mises to ffernelius Clarveato Vintner now in Possession thereof And yt ye Parsone & Churchwardens may proceede to Seale & Execute Three Leases to ye Three Tenants in fleetestreete for 61 yeares in pursuance of a former Order to yt purpose Making such Alteracōns in all of them as aforesaid (if required) And Measuring all ye Estate of ye Pish in fleetestreete And insert ye same in ye severall Leases as they shall see Cause

Joh: Hall Rector
Tho: Colclough
Stephen Gey
Peter Aylworth
Tho: Russell

Will: Allen
Sam: Powell
Tho Persehowse
John Bowyer
Joseph ffrancklin
Robert Tod
Siluester Deane
John Williams

Church Wardens { Rob: Kerington
John Elliott }

68 a. St Christophers 23^the Novemb 1670

Att a Vestry then Holden in the Parish Church there it was ordered and consented to that the taking down of the East End of the Church bee freely left to the Judgment and consideration of ye Lords Commissioners and the surveyo^rs to act therein as they shall think convenient

Tho. Persehowse	Joh: Hall Recto^r
John Williams	Tho: Colclough
John Bowyer	Peter Aylworth
Jasper Holt	Samuel Powell
ffra Lucy	Tho: Russell
Edward Willoughby	Stephen Gey
	Will: Allen

Rob: Kerington } Church Wardens
John Elliott }

Ordered by the persons above named y^t Mr Colclough Mr Aylework Mr Brooks Mr Horsey Mr Kemble Mr Drope Mr Powell Mr Russell Mr Allen Mr Persehowse and the two Churchwardens for the time being bee appointed a Committee to treat wth Mr Buckeridge or any other persons concerning the Interest of the Parish and to prepare matters thereto relating for the consideration of ye vestry any three of them with one of the Churchwardens being of the Quorum

68 b. St Christophers Lond: 26th December 1670

At a vestry then holden in the said p̄ish Church in pursuance of an Order made by the Com̄ittee appointed by Com̄on Councell to Consider the Bill for the Citty & Ministers Maintenance Pursuant to their Order of Referrence Wee of the vestry whose names are Subscribed Have Considered of the Matters conteyned in the said Order And wee doe Conceive That our p^rsent Tyths or Contribucōn for Tyths for a Competent Maintenance for our Minister being at p^rsent 70^li p annū may be raised and Augmented 30^li p an̄n Soe as to make the same for ye future One hundred pounds p annū ffor that improvements of Rents are made in severall places in our said p̄ish And p̄ticulerly in that parte of the Royall Exchange that Stands in our said P̄ish In the Buildings of the Ground of the late generall Pesthouse And the Buildings of Grice Esqr neare the Royall Exchange:

Thos Persehowse	Richd Booth
Edw: Buckerfeild	Tho: Colclough
John Bowyer	Peter Ayleworth
Jno Watts	Will Allen
ffra Lucy	Wm Drope
Henry Joyce	Samuell Powell
John Williams	Tho: Blagrave
Robert Todd	Edward Willougby
Charles Wellinges	Edward Godman

George Varney	Samuell Parker
	Silustcr Deane
	Tho Russell

Robert Kerington } Churchwardens
John Elliott }

St Christophers Parish

Mr John Hall Rector

Tyths before the fire were	70^li	p an̄
Glebe besides dwellinge house	30	
Perquesitts Com^bus Annis about	2. 10^s	
To the Curate that shall officiate at prayers euery morneinge at six of the clock (giuen by m^r Kenndrick) ...	20^s	
Glebe and dwellinge house let at ...	24^l	
Except a garden		

The aboue written is coppy of what was deliuered to the Comitte of Adermen & Comon Counsellmen at Guild Hall the 27th December 1670.

St Christophers London 26 of Jan. 1670.

Att a Vestry then holden in persuance of an order made by the Committee appointed by the Common Councill to consider the Bill for the City Ministers maintenance it was agreed between the Minister and the Inhabitants of the sayd Parish that the Tythes of the sayd Parish formerly about seventy Pounds a year bee rais'd and advanc'd to one Hundred and twenty pounds a year to bee setled by Act of Parliament

present & Consenting to the abovesayd order

Rich: Booth Esqr	Tho Pearcehowse	Jno Williams	Joh: Hall Recto^r
Nath: Brooke	Jno Cross	ffra: Padget	Peter Aylworth
Wm: Horsey	ffrā: Lucy	Rich: Kenn	
Edw: Godman	Jos: ffrancklin	Corne: Glover	
Tho. Kemble	George Verney	Rob: Todd	
Step: Jey	Sam: Powell	Sam: Parker	
Wm. Drope	Oliver Conyer		

Rob Kerington } Church
John Elliot } Wardens

St Christophers London: March: 23rd 1670

At a Vestry then holden in the Parish Church it was ordered that ye Minister & Church Wardens shall let a lease of Seuenty one yeares to m^r Nicholas Buckridge of soe much ground as can conveniently be Spared out of the passage on ye North side of the Church at the rate of Sixpence p foote square p̄ an̄.

At ye same time it was ordered that m^r Samuell Brewster shall be suffered to make lights in the west side of his house in consideration whereof the Parish shall haue the vse of his wall to build against or to fasten any buildinge to it.

At ye same time it was ordered that the Churchwarden shall get the great branch y^t was giuen by m^r Kendrick repaired & that all ye old brasse and Iron belongeinge to ye Church shall be disposed off for y^t vse.

At ye Same time it was ordered that m^r Colclough m^r Brooks m^r Aylworth m^r Horsey m^r Kemble m^r Drope m^r Powell m^r Russell m^r Allen m^r Persehouse m^r Booth m^r Houblon m^r Blagraue m^r Buckerfeild m^r Conyar and the twoe p^rsent Church Wardens be a Comitte and seuen to be a quorum (whereof one of the Church Wardens to be one) to consider of a way to build a Parsonage house & to giue their opinions to ye Vestrey.

	Joh: Hall Recto'
Tho: Colclough	Peter Aylworth
Nath: Brooks	Jn° Houblon
Will: Allen	Wm Drope
Tho. Kemble	Tho: Russell
Oliver: Conyers	Will Horsey
Rob. Kerington } Church-	Tho: Blagraue
} Wardens	Tho: Perschowse
	John Byrows
	Charles wellinges
	Robert Todd
	George Varney

St Christophers London Aprill 27th 1671

At a vestry then holden in the Parish Church was chosen m^r^ John Elliot vper Church Warden m^r^ Thomas Kemble vnder Church Warden m^r^ Joseph ffrancklin & m^r^ Edward Godman Sidesmen for the yeare insueinge. And it is ordered that next assention day be the time to audite the accoumpt of Robert Kerington late vper Church Warden: And that the p'sent vper Church Warden giue bond of 300^li^ wth One sufficient security for giueinge a iust & true acco^ts^ of what plate moneys materialls and vtensills that belongeth to the Parish when he shall be therevnto required and that m^r^ Peter Aylwourth shall keep the bond on behalfe of the Parish. the Auditors apointed for Robert Keringtons accoumpt Are m^r^ Hall m^r^ Colclough Majo^r^ Brooks m^r^ Aylworth m^r^ Gey m^r^ Horsey Ald^r^ Booth m^r^ Allen or an fiue of them:

Will: Allen	Joh: Hall Recto'
Edw: Buckerfeild	Peter Aylworth
Thomas Lee	Samuell Powell
Siluester Deane	Rob. Kerington
Samuell parker	Rich: Barwell
George Varney	Tho: Perschowse
Will Woodbridge	Will Banks
Laurence Aggar	Rob Kerington

May ye 16th 1671

At a Vestry then holden in ye p̃ish Church it was this day ordered y^t^ ye two Churchwardens and m^r^ Horsey shall take a Surueyour to veiw ye grounds in fleete streete concerning m^r^ Sharpes & m^r^ Smiths houses in reference to treate & make an end with the Citty aboute the Melioration ground:

Edw. Buckerfeild	Joh: Hall Recto'
Joseph ffrancklin	Peter Aylworth
ffra Lucy	Jn° Houblon
Corn^s^ Glover	William Horsey
John Elliott } Churchwardens	John Crosse
Tho Kemble }	Edward Godman
	Thomas Lee
	Michaell Dunwell
	Samuell Parker

St Christophers London July 14: 1671

At a Vestrey then holden in the Parish Church it was agreed and concluded that a com̃utation be made with the Parish of St Bartholomews and that the Parish accept of the front of a house adioyninge to m^r^ Blagraue now buildinge by m^r^ Rooks in exchange for the front of those buildinges belongeinge to ye Exchange which stand vpon ye soile of St Christophers. And it is further ordered at the same Vestrey that the reserued rent for the houses in ffleet street be mortgaged for the sum̃e of fiue hundred pounds more or lesse as the Parish occasions shall require, twoe hundred and fifty pounds of which is to be aplied to the building of a Parsonage house and the rest for the peweinge ye Church: prouided that m^r^ John Hall the p'sent Incumbent grant a lease to ye said Parish or to trustees for there vse for the terme of ffourty yeares at the ground rent of fiue pounds p an̄

Joh: Hall Recto'
Peter Aylworth
Rob̄ Kerington
Joseph ffrancklin
Rob̄: Weddell
Charls wellinge
Lawrence Agar
Henry Lascoe
Robert Todd
George Varney
Samuel Powell
Joseph Lem
Tho: Blagraue
Tho: Russell
John Elliott } Churchwarden

St Christophers London August 8 1671 70 b.

At a Vestry then holden in ye said Parish Church it was ordered that Richard Booth Esqr Peter Aylworth Nathaniell Brooks William Horsey William Allen John Houblon Robert Kerington William Drope Thomas Russell Joseph Lem̃e Thomas Blagraue Samuell Powell and the twoe p'sent Church Wardens be a Com̃itte fiue besides one of the Church Wardens to be a Quorum to treat wth any Person or Persons about morgageing the ground rent in ffleet street for such a sum̃e of money as the Parish shall haue occasion for as alsoe to treat wth Joyners and other wourkmen and agree wth them for peweinge the Church repaireinge the Vestrey or doeinge such other thinges relateinge to the Church as the Surveyours shall leaue vndone and that the Church Wardens take the assistance of a solisitour for draweing conveyances and consulting lawyers in order to that affair the power of this Comitt^e^ to continue vntill Easter and noe longer:

And it is further ordered that the Clerks wages shall be Sixteen pounds P̃ an̄ to be assessed on the Inhabitants of the said Parish by the abouesd Comitt^e^ and if any Parishoner findes himselfe agreiued by ye assesment that he may haue liberty to apeale to the next Vestrey after demand by the said Clerke.

And it is further ordered that Nathaniell Brooks Peter Aylworth John Potter Stephen Jeye William Horsey Robert Kerington John Elliot & Thomas Kemble be trustees in behalfe of the Parish to take a lease in their names for the vse of the Parish from John Hall p'sent Rector of the Glebe land to be built vpon on the termes already agreed vpon:

Joh: Hall Recto'
Stephen Gey
Nath: Brooke
Peter Aylworth
Will: Allen
William Horsey
Rob Kerington

Wm Drope
Tho: Russell
John Bvrowes
Richard: Kenn
Charls wellinges
George Varney
Samuel parker
Lawrence Agar
Nicholas day
John Elliott Churchwarden

a. St Xpofers London October 10th 1671

At a Vestrey then holden in the said Parish Church In pursuance of a Referrence made by Mr Sharpe & Mr Smyth Tennts of 2 of the Pish Houses in ffleetestreete vnto the said Vestry touching the ffynes to be by them respectively paid in regard of ye Ground by them Gained on ffleete streete to Enlarge their Houses The said Pishoners demanding of the said Mr Smyth Tenne pounds Eighteene shillings & Nyne Pence And of ye sd Mr Sharpe Twelve pounds Eight Shillings & fower pence Being the sume demanded for the Inheritance of ye same Ground at 5s for each supficiall foote And it was then Ordered That ye said Tennts should each of them be abated One Tenth parte of ye respective sumes of them demanded as aforesaid And that they should pay the other nyne partes by way of ffyne & Seale ye Counterptes of their Leases to them to be Tendred out of hand And doe further Order That Mr Kerringtons Accompts shallbe Auditted on or before Tomorrow Sennight And Auditors for Mr Kerringtons Acct are Mr Nath: Brookes Mr Peter Aylworth Mr William Horsey Ald: Booth Mr William Allen Mr John Houblon Mr Thomas Russell Mr William Drope Mr Samuell Powell Mr Edw: Buckerfeild & Mr Edw: Godman or any ffive of them And further it was Ordered & Confirmed That the Clerkes Wages be Sixteene Pounds Thirteene Shillings & ffower Pence P annum According to a Roll for that purpose made being ye Sixth Parte of ye Tyth

Nath. Brooke
Peter Aylworth
William Horsey
Ed Buckerfeild
Ed Godman
Silustr deane
Samuel parker
Charles wellinges
Will Millman
Robeart Todd
George Varney
Lau. Agar
John Elliott } Churchwardens
Tho Kemble }

b. St Christophers London October the 20th 1671

At a Vestry then holden in the said Parrish Church Many things being debated for the Explaining an Order of the 14th of July past touching the Building of the Parsonage house. It was resolued And agreed That in Consideracon of Two hundred and ffifty pounds to bee paid towards the Building the said Parsonage House, That Mr Hall the present Incumbent doe grant a Lease of the Toft and Parsonage House to Trustees for the said Parrish for fforty yeares from the Sealing thereof At the Rent of ffyve pounds per Annũ Cleare of Taxes Vppon Trust and Confidence That the Trusees for the said Parrish for the time being shall from time to time Grant a Lease of the said Parsonage House to the said Mr Hall and his Successors Parsons of St Christophers ffor all the said Terme Except one Weeke (if hee or they shall soe longe live). Provided Hee and They shall time to time during the said Terme Reside and dwell therein Att the Rent of Twenty pounds per Annũ Cleare of all Taxes. And that the said Trustees shall accordingly Seale such Redemise to Mr Hall

Will: Allen	Joh: Hall Rector
Tho: Russell	Peter Aylworth
Samuel Powell	William Horsey
Henry Lascoe	Rob Kerington
John marriott	Wm Drope
Siluester Deane	John Elliott } Church Wardens
	Tho Kemble }
	Rob: Weddell

St Christophers London November 28th 1671

At a Vestry then holden in the Parish Church of the said Parish It was Ordered and Agreed That Mr Stephen Skynner Mr Nath: Brooke Mr Xpofer Marsham Mr Peter Aylworth Mr Thomas Lambe Mr John Rouse Mr John Elliott Mr John Pointer & Mr Rich: Kensey being ye remaining Trustees for the Pish Land in ffleetestreete Doe & shall Convey ye same Lands & yr Interest therein To ye Vse of Rich Booth Esqr & John Houblon of London Merchant Wm Allen Vpholder Nathaniell Brooke Stacõner Peter Aylworth Clothworker William Horsey Cordweyner Robert Kerrington Merch'taylor John Elliott Leatherseller Thomas Kemble Draper Edward Buckerfeild Leatherseller Edward Godman Merch'taylor Joseph ffranklyn Plumer Thomas Russell Haberdasher Sam: Powell Grocer Henry Lascoe & ffrancis Lucy Grocers & their heires in ye same maner as ye sd former Psons were Trustees And likewise That ye Conveyance for ye Land in ffleetestreete taken out of the Streete there And such other Conveyances Leases & other Deedes as are or shallbe neceassary to be made for ye Vse or Accompt of the said Pish shallbe granted & made to ye said Psent Trustees

Joh: Hall Rector
Nath: Brooke
Peter Aylworth
Rob Kerington
Edward Godman
Joseph ffrancklin
Jno: Watts
John marriott
George Varney
Samuell parker
John Elliott } Church
Tho. Kemble } Wardens

St Christopher 11th Aprill 1672

At a Vestry then holden in the said Pish were Chosen for ye yeare ensueing Mr Thomas Kemble Vpper Churchwarden & Mr Willm Drope lower Churchwarden Mr John Bowyer and Mr Richard Kenne Sidesmen And it is Ordered that next Ascention day be the tyme for Auditting ye Accompt of Mr John Elliott ye late Vpper Churchwarden And that the p'sent Vpper Churchwarden doe forthwith give Bond of 300li penalty with one sufficient Surety for giving a just & true Accompt of ye money Plate

Vtensills & other things of ye said Pish yt shall come to his hands wn thereto required And that Mr Peter Aylworth keepe the same Bond And Auditors for ye said Mr John Elliotts Accompt are hereby appointed Mr John Hall Mr Nath: Brookes Mr Peter Aylworth Rich Booth Esqr Mr Wm Allen Mr Wm Horsey & Mr Robert Kerrington or any five of them And it is hereby Ordered yt the Persons next herevnder named or any Sixe of them whereof one to be one of ye Churchwardens be a Comittee to Act & doe on the behalfe of the said Pish in all their Affaires for the yeare ensueing viz. Mr John Hall Rectr Rich: Booth Esqr Mr William Allen Mr John Houblon Mr Nath: Brookes Mr Peter Aylworth Mr Wm Horsey Mr Robert Kerrington Mr Moses Goodyeare Mr John Elliott Mr Thomas Russell Mr Sam: Powell Mr Thomas Blagrave Mr Edw: Buckerfeild Mr ffrancis Lucy Mr Edward Godman Mr Joseph Lem and Mr Oliver Conyers And Mr Thomas Kemble & Mr Willm Drope ye p'sent Churchwardens

And it is lastly Ordered That the Churchwarden be allowed for or towards ye Entertainemt & other necessary charges of Ascention day next And his Auditt dinner ye sume of ffive pounds & noe more

	Joh: Hall Rectr
Samuel parker	Nath: Brooke
Oliver: Conyers	Peter Aylworth
Robert Moody	Moses Goodyeare
Joseph Lem	John Elliott
John Bowyer	Tho: Russell
Thomas Scott	Fra: Lucy
	Tho: Blagraue
	Edw: Buckerfeild
	Edward Godman
	ffrancis Pagett

July 2d 1672

At a vestry then holden in the said Pish Church Vestry of St Christophers it was Agreed yt Tho: Kemble uper Churchwarden should dispose of Jno Michaell a nurse Pish boy to a Master yt should giue bond to discharge ye Pish from him: & to bind him apprentice to Learne his Art & trade of a painter and that he should Agree with his said Master as cheape as hee could for his soe doeing not exceeding seauen pounds. It was alsoe then ordered yt ye said Churchwarden shall dispose of an old man Tho. Day lately throwen vpon ye Charge of the parrish as cheape as hee can, to bee putt out to Nurse: And that ye said Pish shall keepe harmeless & indempnified ye Pish where hee shall bee bestowed. And that Goodwife Stratford shall haue fifty shillings giuen her ouer & aboue her wages for her former Charge with the said boy: it was then alsoe Agreed yt shall take ye aboue said Tho: Day att three shillings & sixpence p weeke: And it was then alsoe Agreed yt A poores tax Extraordinary for one yeere shall bee rated & giuen to ye Carying on & defrayeing ye necessary expences for ye finishing of ye Remajnder of the said Church

Joh: Hall Rectr
Richd Booth
Peter Aylworth
Jno Houblon
Will: Allen
Daniel Mercer
Edward Godman
ffra Lucy
Samn Brewster
Rich Barwell
Thomas Lee
Edw: Buckerfeild
Thomas Scott
Josiah Mitchell
Tho: Kemble } Churchwards
Wm Drope }

St Christophers 1st Aprill 1673 73 b.

At a Vestry then holden for the said Pish were Chosen Mr William Drope vpper Churchwarden Mr Richard Barwell vnder Churchwarden And Mr William Barker & Mr Thomas Pearsehouse Sidesmen for ye yeare ensueing And it was Ordered that next Ascension day be the time for Auditing Mr Thomas Kemble's Accompts the late vpp Churchwarden And that Mr John Hall ye p'sent Rectr Mr Nathaniell Brookes Mr Peter Aylworth Mr William Horsey Mr Robert Kerrington Mr John Elliott & Mr William Allen or any ffower of them be the Auditors of the said Accompts And that the p'sent vpper Churchwarden Give Bond of 300li penalty, with one sufficient Surety ffor giveing a true Accompt of the Moneyes Plate & Vtensills belonging to ye same Parish when thereto required And that Mr Peter Aylworth keepe the said Bond on behalfe of ye Parish And lastly it's Ordered That from time to time hereafter the Churchwarden for the time being shallbe allowed ffor or towards the Entertainement Dinner Points & other things & Charges of Ascention day And for ye Auditt dinner the sume of ffive pounds & noe more, And that all the Auditors of ye Accompts of Mr Kemble be Assistant to the Churchwardens in Placeing ye Parishoners in ye Pewes of ye sd Church And ye sd Mr Thomas Kemble be Added to the said Assistants.

Joh: Hall Rectr
Nath: Brooke
Peter Aylworth
Will: Allen
Will Horsey
Rob: Kerington
John Elliott
Tho: Russell
Edw: Buckerfeild
Tho. Persehowse
Will. Parker
Edward Godman
Siluester Deane
Robert Moody
Thomas Lee
Will Banks
ffra Lucy
Samn Brewster
Tho Short
Geo: ffulford
Tho: Kemble

St Christophers 20th of Novembr 1673 74 a.

Att a Vestry then holden in the Vestry house of the said Parish it was ordered thatt two Taxes bee made upon all inhabitants of the said Parish the same with the Poor's Roll for discharging the debts of the Parish to workmen the one of wch Taxes is to be Levied presently the other to bee Levied six month's after the Date of this Order.

Samuel Powell	Bn Billingsley	Joh: Hall Recto'
Tho: Russell	John Groue	Richd Booth
Will: Allen	Michaell Dewing	Tho: Blagraue
	John Morris	Peter Aylworth
	George Varney	Tho: Kemble
		Witt Horsey
		Will Barker
		Samll parker
Wm Drope } Churchwards		Samll Brewster
Rich: Barwell }		Ed Buckerfeild
		Daniel Mercer
		Thomas Lee
		Robert Moodij
		Richard Nicoll
		Rob Todd

Memorandum that Wm: Bancks was present at this vestry And consented to this order, by makeing noe Objection.

S' Christophers Aprill ye 20th 1674

At a Vestry then Holden M' Richard Barwell was Elected for upper Church warden in the Roome of m' Wm: Drope, but desiering to fine and be Discharged from the sayd Office it was admitted by the Vestry, and he haveing served one yeare Alreddy, should be Excused from the sd Offis, paying the sume of Six pounds to m' Wm: Drope, the last Church warden At the same time m' Samuel Powell was Elected Church warden for the yeare Ensewing and he Desiering to fine for the same was fined at Twelve pounds to be payd to M' Wm: Drope, and he to be Discharged from the same offis.

At the same time m' Edward Buckerfeild was Elected for Cornhill side, upper Churchwarden for ye yeare Ensewing

At the same time m' Tho: Russell was Elected under Church warden and he desiering to fine for the sayd place was fined at fourteene pounds to be payd to m: wm: Drope & to be discharged from the sd place for Ever

At the same time m' Tho: Blagrave was Elected under Churchwarden, for the yeare Ensewing.

For Sidesmen were Elected for the Church side m' Silvester Deane and for Cornhill side m' Robert Mordant.

It is ordered that M' Wm: Dropes accoumpt shall be Auditted the 27th day of May next Ensewing

And that m' Edward Buckerfield upper Church warden shall give bond of 300ll penallty with one suffitient suerty to give a true acc°. when therunto Required of all Muñy plate &c belonging to the sd parish

And it is Ordered that M' Nath: Brookes Peter Aylworth m: Wm: Horsey m' Rob. Kerington m' Jn° Elleott m' Tho. Kemble M' Rich: Barwell M' Samuell Powell and M' Tho Russell, or any five of them shall be Auditers of m' wm: Dropes Accoumpt

It is farther Ordered that the fines above mentioned shall be payd Downe upon Demand

		Joh: Hall Recto'
	Samll Brewster	Nath: Brooke
	Will Barker	Peter Aylworth
Samuel Powell	Witt Wood	John Elliott
Tho Russell	Witt Meriden	Witt Horsey
Ed Buckerfeild	Bn Billingsley	Tho. Kemble
	Wm Drope	Edw: Godman
	Rich Barwell	Jn° Houblon
	Saml parker	

It is farther Ordered by the sd Vestrey that M: Wm: Drope shall cause pipes of Lead to be brought Downe by the side of the Church, according to a late Act of Parlayment.

S' Christophers 4th March 1674 75

At a Vestry then holden It was Agreed and Ordered That the ffower Hundred pounds Subscribed by Severall persons for Purchasing a Revenue to ffind Evening Prayers for ever in this Parish Church. Shallbe receaved of M' Aylworth ye Treasurer for that Money, ffor ye Vse of this pish to be Paid and Applyed towards the discharge of ye Debt of 500ll and Interest due on Accompt of this Parish to M' John Brewer And for which the Houses in ffleetestreete belonging to this Parish are Mortgaged And that in Consideracōn of ye said ffower hundred pounds a Rent Charge Añuity or yearely Suñe of Twenty pounds shall be Charged on and Payable out of the said Houses in ffleetestreete ffor ever ffor ffinding Evening Prayers in this Parish Church as above, To be Setled in such mañer as Councell shall Advise.

And to ye End the said Houses in ffleetestreete may be Discharged of the said Incumbrance by Mortgage, And the residue of ye said Debt to M' Brewer being about 100ll may be paid off, It is further Agreed & Ordered That if M' Peter Aylworth & M' Thomas Kemble thinke fitt to Enter into Bond to M' Brewer ffor One hundred pounds & Interest y'of They ye sd M' Aylworth & M' Kemble are & shallbe for ever Saved harmelesse & Indempnifyed for ye same. And that the said One hundred pounds and Interest shallbe paid on Accompt of this Pish as a proper debt of this Parish.

	Joh: Hall Recto'
Rob: Kerington	Peter Aylworth
Tho: Kemble	Will: Allen
Samuel Powell	Moš. Goodyeare
John Morris	Witt Horsey
Will Barker	John Bvrowes
Richard Nicoll	Samll parker
Nicholas Day	John Groue
John Williams	Rob' Morden
Edward Woolner	
Robert Moody	
Witt Meriden	
Edw: Buckerfeild } Churchwardens	
Tho: Blagraue }	

S' Christophers Aprill 5th 1675 75

At a Vestry then holden M' Edward Buckerfeild was Chosen Vpper Churchwarden for ye yeare ensueing. And M' Thomas Blagrave was Chosen Vnder Churchwarden for ye same yeare, But Desiring to ffyne he ye said M' Blagrave (having served one yeare) was Admitted to ffyne for ye Office of Churchwarden ffor ye suñe of Six pounds which was Ordered to be paid to ye other Churchwarden M' Buckerfeild forthwith, Wherevpon M' William Allen was Chosen Churchwarden And he desireing to ffyne, was Admitted to ffyne for Churchwarden this yeare And Vpper Churchwarden ye yeare following & for ye said Place for ever ffor fifteene pounds which was accordingly Ordered to be Paid forthwith to M' Edward Buckerfeild, Wherevpon Richard Booth Esq' was Chosen Churchwarden for ye Church side for ye yeare ensueing. And M' Samuell Brewster being P'sent & desiring to ffyne for Churchwarden & all pish Offices, & Offering ye Parish ffifteene pounds for such ffyne It was Accepted And

Ordered to be paid p'sently to Mr Edward Buckerfeild. And Mr Joseph Lem being also p'sent desiring to ffyne for ye Office of Churchwarden & sydesman for Twenty pounds was Admitted And ye ffyne accepted & ordered to be paid likewise forthwith to Mr Edward Buckerfeild

And Sydesmen were then Elected Mr William Banks for Cornehill side And Mr Samuell Parker for Churchside.

Auditors appointed to Audit mr Edw: Buckerfeilds late Churchwardens Acct are

	mr Jno Hall
Richard Boswell	Nat. Brooke
Tho: Blagrave	Peter Aylworth
Jno Powell	wm Horsey
Tho. Russell	Robert Kerrington
Wm Allen	Jno Elliott
Sam: Breuster	Tho: Kemble
Josh Lemm or	Wm Drope

any fiue of these two Collumes

The Auditt day to bee on ye thirteenth day of May next

Joh: Hall Rector
Peter Aylworth
Rob Kerington
John Elliott
Tho. Kemble
Wm Drope
Tho. Perschowse
Edw: Godman
Robert Moodÿ
John Williams
Samll. Brewster
William Banks
Robt Morden
Bn Billingsley
John Morris
ffrancis pagett
Josiah Mitchill
ffurley Barton
Edw Buckerfeild
Church Warden

St Christophers Aprill 14th 1675

At a Vestry then holden at the Instance of Richard Booth Esqr he the said Richard Booth desired to be admitted to a fine for the office of Church Warden for this and the ensueinge yeare the said Vestry agreed to accept of his fine and to excuse him from the aforesd office of Churchwarden at the same time it was ordered by the Vestry that his fine shall be twenty pounds to be forthwith paid to mr Edward Buckerfeild the p'sent vpper Church Warden att the same time Mr William Barker was Chosen vnder Church Warden for the yeare ensueinge

Joh: Hall Rector
Nath Brooke
Peter Aylworth
Rob Kerington
Will: Allen
John Elliott
Tho: Kemble
Wm Drope
Edward Godman
Samll Brewster
Robt Morden
ffrancis pagett
Robert Moodÿ
Edw: Buckerfeild } Church
Will Barker } Wardns

Bee it Remembered That at a Vestrey holden within the Parish of St Christopher London the Twentieth day of October One thousand Six hundred Seaventy and ffive It was ordered and Agreed That the Churchwardens and Parishioners of St Giles without Criplegate London are and shall be from henceforth for ever saved defended and kept harmelesse by the Parishioners of this Parish of St Christopher of and from all Costs Charges and expences that shall or may Arise and happen vnto them or any of them by reason of Samuell Acres his wife and Three Children of theirs or any of them dwelling or Residing within the said Parish of St Giles Criplegate (in Case any such Charge shall happen) their last place of Legall Settlement being in our said Parish of St Christopher And also That the Churchwardens of our said Parish of St Christopher (for the time being) shall and may (if any such Charge shall fall or happen to the Parishioners of the said Parish of St Giles Criplegate for or by reason or meanes of the said Samuell Acres his wife and Three Children or any of them residing or Inhabiting in the said Parish as aforesaid) well and truely pay to the Churchwardens of the said Parish of St Giles Criplegate All such Charges from time to time within Three dayes next after demand thereof made

Peter Aylworth
Tho: Kemble
Michael Danwell
Edward Woolmer
Richard Nicoll
John Williams
Rob Todd
Robert Moodij
Thomas Scott
John Morris
Wm Bythell
Edw Buckerfeild
Will Barker
Church Wardens

St Christophers 77 a.

At a vestry holden ye 18th day of Nouembr 1675 it was agreed that Joana Varny should bee allowed for and towards her maintenance two shillings p weeke to bee paid her p ye Churchwardens for ye time being dureing her naturall life except ye Pish shall find hereafter any reason to ye Contrary and alsoe that ye said Churchwarden send to the widdow Mathewes tenn shillings towards her p'sent releife and two shillings p weeke dureing her sickness being not able to helpe herselfe.

Joh: Hall Rector
Peter Aylworth
Tho: Kemble
Wm Drope
Samuell Powell
Samll Brewster
John Morris
Rob Todd
William W woodbridge his mark
John Groue
Will Wood
Bn Billingsley
Edwd Buckerfeild
Will Barker
Church-Wardens

St Christopher 77 b.

At a vestry holden ye twenty seauenth day of March 1676 mr Wm Barker was chosen Senior Churchwarden and mr Edw: Godman was chosen Junior Churchwarden for the yeere ensueing, at ye same tyme was chosen sidesmen for the same yeere mr John

I

Williams for Church side and m^r John Cross for Cornhill side. At ye same tyme it is ordered that m^r Edw: Buckerfeild late Churchwarden his Accts shall be Auditted on the Ascention day next ensueing, Mr John Hall m^r Nat. Brooke m^r peter Ayleworth m^r John Elliott m^r Wm Horsey m^r Robt Kerrington Tho: Kemble m^r Rich: Barwell m^r Tho: Blagraue m^r Wm Allen m^r Wm Drope m^r Sam powell m^r Tho Russell m^r Jos. Lemm m^r Sam: Brewster are appointed Auditors of the said Acc^t or any fiue of them: it is alsoe ordered y^t Wm Barker senior Churchwarden shall forthwith giue one Sufficient Security with himselfe in three hundred pounds Bond, to giue a true Accompt of all such stocke plate and utensills belonging to ye said parrish that shall come to his hands when thereunto required, And that m^r peter Ayleworth keepe the said bond in behalfe of the parrish being a 300^li bond

Joh: Hall Recto^r
Peter Aylworth
Will: Allen
John Elliott
Tho: Kemble
Wm Drope
Rich: Barwell
Samuel Powell
Thō: Blagraue
Tho Short
Rob Todd
John Williams
Will Banks
John Morris
Will Wood
Edward Woolmer
Robt Morden
Wm Bythell
Edwd Buckerfeild
Will Barker
Edw: Godman
Church- }
Wardens }

a. St Christophers 22th August 1676

At a Vestry then holden It was Ordered That if Mrs Adryan doe pay ye Churchwarden for the vse of the Parish Twenty pounds That shee shall have liberty at her Charge to take downe ye Wall at ye West End of ye Vault in ye Church wherein ye Body of her late Husband Mr John Adryan Merchant lately an Inhabitant of this Parish lyes And to Build ye same Vault Westward ffower foote & a halfe or thereabouts. And of such breadth as Conveniently to Conteyne Two Coffins in breadth: And that ye same shall be vsed from henceforth for ye Interring ye Bodyes of such psons as the said Mrs Adryan or her Children shall Appoint: Paying Customary Dutyes

Peter Aylworth
Wm Drope
Sam^ll Brewster
John Morris
Silvester Deane
Fra: Lucy
Tho: Short
Rob Todd
Joseph Heywood
John Groue
Richard Nicoll
Will Barker
Edward Godman
Church Warden

St Christopher Lond 7

At a Vestry holden ye Eleauenth daij of Decemb^r 1676: it was ordered, y^t whereas Jno Hieron late seru^t to m^r Nathaniel Brooke of this pish being lunaticke, and it being endeauered p some to Cast the said lunatick upon this pish, for the preuention whereof, the Churchwardens of this pish take the Aduice of m^r Simpson & m^r Lane ye Comptroller or such able Cunsell as they can gett, to defend the said pish from the Charge of ye aboue said lunaticke att a Tryal att Sessions, And in case the lunaticke bee cast upon ye said pish then the said Churchwardens shall enter into bond to the Masters of Bethlehem att the rate of fiue shillings p weeke for his keeping

Joh: Hall Recto^r
Peter Aylworth
Wm Horsey
Tho: Kemble
John Graue
Siluester Deane
Sam^ll Brewster
Will Wood
William Banks
Robt Morden
Rob Todd
John Morris
Will Parker } Church
Edward Godman } Wardens

St Christophers London 7

At a Vestry holden the 8 of January 1676 It was ordered that John Mathews be Sexton of this parish and shall receive all such fees as belong to that place and that the sd John Mathews shall give such security to the Churchwardens for the time being as the Church orders doe in that behalfe appoint And it was then further ordered that the Churchwarden shall pay into the hands of Mr Ayleworth the sume of Tenne pounds sterling for the use and accomodation of M^rs ffranklin widow of George ffrankling late Clerke and Sexton of this parish decd

	Joh: Hall Recto^r
Sam: Powell	Peter Aylworth
Tho Short	Jno Houblon
Sam^ll Brewster	Will: Allen
Edw: Buckerfeild	Wm Drope
William Banks	John Elliott
Siluester Deane	Tho Kemble
Arthur Myles jun^r	Micha: Dewing
	John Williams
	Will Barker

St Christophers London 7

At a Vestry held this 20th of March 1676/7 It was consented to by all the parishoners of the said parish that the right of nominateing and declareing the Clerke for the said parish was undoubtedly in the parson and that the Precedents entred into this Vestry Booke of Clerks chosen by the Vote of the Parishoners are noe

Barre or Prejudice to the right of the present Incumbent or his successors.

Vpon clearing of which point the present Incumbent Mr John Hall did declare that he would admitt of him to be Clerke whome the Major part of the parish should nominate and thereupon the most of the Parishoners agreed to nominate Israel ffolgate Inhabitant of the said parish to be Clerke thereof who imediately thereupon was nominated by the parishoners and approved of by Mr Hall

Joh: Hall Recto'
Jno Houblon

John Williams
Rob Todd
Wm Pepys
William Gloster
Tho: Rea
Wm Nicholson
Josiah Mitchell
Richard Instars
marke R I
James Lambert
Will: Allen
Arthur Myles junr

William Hawke
Mos: Goodyear
John Elliott
Wm Drope
Micha: Dewing
Silu ster Deane
ffra Lucy
Saml Parker
Nicholas Day
Randal Stathan
William Barker }
Edward Godman }
Church Wardens

St Christophers London

At a Vestry holden the Sixteenth day of Aprill 1677 Mr Edward Godman was chosen Senior Church Warden. And whereas Richard Booth Esqr was formerly fined twenty pounds for the Office of Church Warden, which fine he hath hitherto refused to pay, the said Richard Booth is chosen Vnder Church Warden for the yeare ensewing. And at the same Vestry was chosen Sidesmen for Cornhill side Thomas Lee and for Church side Mr Robert Todd. At the same time it is ordered That the day for the Auditing of the Accompts of Mr William Barker shalbe on Assention day being the 24th of May next ensewing. And that the Auditors for the said Accompt shalbe Mr John Hall, Rector, Mr Peter Aylworth, Mr Jon Elliot, Mr Willm Horsey, Mr Thomas Kemball, Mr Will Drope, Mr Richard Barwell, Mr Will Allen, Mr Sam: Powel, Mr Tho: Blagraue, Mr Samuel Brewster, Mr Jos: Lem, Mr Edward Buckerfeild, or any five of them. And it is also Ordered that Mr Edward Godman Senior Church Warden shall forthwith give one sufficient Security with himselfe in a Bond of Three hundred Pounds penalty To give a true Accompt of all such Stock Plate and vtensills, belonging to ye sd Parish as shall come into his hands, when he shalbe therevnto required, And that Mr Peter Aylworth, keep the said Bond in behalfe of the same Parish

Joh: Hall Recto'
Peter Aylworth
Will: Allen
John Elliott
Samuel Powell
Edw Buckerfeild
Mos: Goodyeare
ffra Lucy
Saml Parker
Robt Morden
John Williams
Wm Bethell
John Morris
Wm Fashion
Sam: Bennet
Samue: King
Will Barker

St Christophers London 80 b.

At a vestry holden this 25th of Aprill 1677 it was agreed that Richard Booth Esqr should bee excused from serueing Churchwarden upon the paymt of twenty pounds to mr Wm Barker late churchwarden, And at ye same time mr Wm Haukes was chosen iunior Churchwarden, and upon a proposition made & in regard of his greate Age it was agreed p ye said Vestry that hee should bee excused for the paymt of fiue pounds to ye p'sent Churchwarden, from serueing the office of Churchwarden. And then was chosen mr Siluester Deane in mr Hawkes his stead junior Churchwarden, And then it was alsoe agreed and ordered that noe person shall bee excused from the office of Churchwarden p way of fine till such time as the party hath paid his fine according to order nor any other person shall bee chose in his roome till hee hath paid his fine as aforesaid

Joh: Hall Recto'
Will: Allen
Tho Kemble
John Elliott
Wm Drope
Samuel Powell
Saml Brewster
ffra Lucy
Edw Buckerfeild
Will Wood
John Williams
Rob Todd
Latimer Burroughs
Samuel King
Will Barker
Edward Godman }
Church Warden }

St Christophers London jmo Aprilis 1678 81 a.

At a vestry then holden Mr Sylvester Deane was chosen Churchwarden for Churchside and Mr Robert Morden Churchwarden for Cornehillside and Mr John Houblon Sydesman for Churchside and Mr Simon Cole sidesman for Cornehill side and it was then and there ordered that the accounts of Mr Edward Godman the Churchwarden for the last yeare shall be audited on Tuesday the Seaventh day of May next by Mr John Hall Rector Mr Peter Aylworth Mr John Elliott Mr Wm Horsey Mr Thomas Kemball Mr Wm Drope Mr Richard Barrwell Mr Wm Allen Mr Samuel Powell Mr Thomas Blagrave Mr Samuel Brewster Mr Joseph Lemm Mr Edward Buckerfield & Richard Booth Esqr or any five or more of them, and alsoe that the said Mr Sylvester Deane shall on or before the said Seaventh day of May now & next ensueing give one sufficient security togeather with himselfe to be bound in a bond of Three Hundred pounds penalty to be conditioned to give a true account of all such stock plate and utensills belonging to the said parish as shall come into Mr Deanes hands at any time or times dureing his Churchwardenship and that Mr Peter Aylworth shall keepe the said Bond in trust for the said parish. And alsoe that the Bearers for the dead shall be from time to time appointed by the upper Churchwarden for the time being unles the Relations of the deceased shall appoint them.

Joh: Hall Rectoʳ
Peter Aylworth
Will: Allen
Tho: Kemble
ffra Lucy
William Banks
Will Wood
Edw Buckerfeild
Tho Short
Edward Godman
Nichᵒ Buckeridge
Latimer Burroughs
Thomas Taylor
William Gloster
Arthur Myles junʳ
Nicholas Day
Siluester Deane } Church wardens

b. Sᵗ Christophers 21° Aprilis 1679

At a Vestry then holden Mʳ Robert Morden was chosen upper Churchwarden for Cornehill side and Mʳ Samuel Parker under-churchwarden for Churchside and Mʳ Henry Lascoe Sidesman for Cornehill side and Mʳ ffrancis Lucy Sydesman for Churchside And it was then and there ordered that the Accounts of Mʳ Sylvester Deane the Churchwarden for the last yeare shall be audited on Tuesday the Seaven and Twentieth of May next by Mʳ John Hall Rector Mʳ Peter Aylworth Mʳ John Elliott Mʳ William Horsey Mʳ Thomas Kemball Mʳ Wᵐ Drope Mʳ Richard Barrwell Mʳ William Allen Mʳ Samuel Powell Mʳ Thomas Blagrave Mʳ Samuel Brewster Mʳ Joseph Lemm Mʳ Edward Buckerfield Richard Booth Esqʳ and Mʳ Edward Godman or any five or more of them. And alsoe that the said Mʳ Robert Morden shall on or before the said Seaven and Twentieth of May next give one sufficient security togeather with himself to be bound in a bond of Three Hundred pounds penalty to be conditioned to give a true Account of all such stock plate and utensills belonging to the said parish as shall come into Mʳ Mordens hands at any time or times dureing his Churchwardenship And that Mʳ Peter Ayleworth shall keepe the said Bond in Trust for the said parish And it was alsoe then and there ordered that the Churchwarden from time to time being shall prosecute and sue according to Lawe from time to time such person and persons shoppkeepers and others (and in respect of their shopps and otherwise) as shall from time to time refuse to pay what is and shall be respectively charged on them for the Poore of this parish

Joh: Hall Rectoʳ
Peter Aylworth
John Elliott
Tho: Kemble
Edw: Godman
Thomas Lee
Josiah Mitchell
William Wood
John Prittyman
Nicolas Skinner
Willᵐ Gloster
John Williams
Silvester Deane
William Blunt
Arthur Myles junʳ
Tho Short
Tho. Collins
Wᵐ Bythell

Sᵗ Christophers. Aprill 12ᵒ 1680

At a vestry then holden was chosen upper Churchwarden for Churchside mʳ Sam: parker and under Churchwarden for Cornehill side mʳ Wᵐ Banckes, and for sidesmen mʳ Nich Day for Church side & mʳ Humphrey Bradley for Cornhill side, And it was then & there ordered that the Accompts of mʳ Robᵗ Morden late Churchwarden for yᵉ last yeere shall bee Audited on Wednesday yᵉ nineteenth day of May next by mʳ Jnᵒ Hall Rector mʳ peter Aylworth mʳ Jnᵒ Elliott mʳ Wᵐ Horsey Tho: Kemble mʳ Wᵐ Drope mʳ Richard Barwell mʳ Wᵐ Allen mʳ Sam. powell mʳ Tho Blagrave mʳ Sam Brewster mʳ Joseph Lemm Rich. Booth Esqʳ & mʳ Siluester Deane or any fiue of them. And alsoe yᵗ the said mʳ Sam. parker shall att or before the nineteenth day of May next giue one sufficient security togeather with himselfe in a bond of three hundred pounds penalty to giue a true Accᵗ of all such stocke plate & vtensills belonging to yᵉ said pish, as shall come to yᵉ said mʳ parkers hands, And that mʳ Peter Aylworth shall keepe yᵉ said bond.

Joh: Hall Rectoʳ.
John Elliott
Tho Kemble
Samuel Powell
Henry Lascoe
Rich: Barwell
Will Barker
Tho Short
Thomas Lee
Thomas Groue
Latimer Burroughs
Michaell Dewing
John Williams
Wᵐ Bythell
Isaac Hancock
William Gloster

Sᵗ Christophers the 4th day of April 1681

At a Vestry then holden were chosen churchwardens for the year insuing for Cornhill side upper Churchwarden mʳ William Banks and for Churchside under Churchwarden Mʳ John Williams then alsoe were chosen Sidesmen for Cornhill side Mʳ William Bythell and for Churchside Mʳ Daniel Mercer. And it was then ordered that the accounts of Mʳ Samuel Parker late Churchwarden shall bee Audited on Tuesday the tenth day of May next ensuing By Mʳ John Hall Rectoʳ Mʳ Deputy Peter Aylworth Mʳ John Eliot Mʳ William Horsey Mʳ Thomas Kemble Mʳ William Drope Mʳ Richard Barwell Mʳ Wᵐ Allen Mʳ Samuel Powell Mʳ Thomas Blagrave Mʳ Samuel Brewster Mʳ Joseph Lemme Richard Booth Esqʳ Mʳ Silvester Deane Mʳ Robᵗ Morden or any five or more of them. And alsoe that the said Mʳ William Banks shall on or before the said tenth day of May next give one sufficient security together wth himself to be bound in a bond of three hundred pounds penalty to give a true account of all such stock plate and utensills belonging to the said Parish as shall come into his hands and y^t^ Mr Peter Aylworth shall keep the said Bond in behalf of the s^d^ Parish It was alsoe ordered that Mr Banks the upper Churchwarden shall dispose of Elizabeth Christopher to Edward Everett of ffarnham and give five pounds wth her hee the said Edward and Mr John Eliott wth him giving bond to the Parish to discharge them of her and to keep her wth good usage and all necessaries till shee shall bee able to work for her living.

Joh: Hall Recto^r^
John Elliott
Rich: Barwell
Samuel Powell
Siluester Deane
Tho Short
ffra Lucy
Robt Morden
Sam^ll^ Parker
Will Winne
Isaac Hancock
Wm Bythell
Josiah Mitchell
Tho: Collins
Humph Bradly
Andrew Keepe

St Christophers Nouemb^r^ ye 25 1681.

At a vestry then holden Wm Dalton was Chose Sexton dureing his good behauiour, and it was then ordered y^t^ Israel ffolgate & ye said Wm Dalton shall giue their seuerall bonds with one security for each of ffiffty pounds each bond to the present Churchwardens for their tyme being, for the safety & forthcomeing of all such goods & vtensells & mony as shall come to their hands respectiuely belonging to ye parrish, pursuant to ye first Article in ye Table of orders of vestry bearing Date eleauenth day of Aprill 1664. both which bonds are to bee sealed & delūed att or before the 20th day of December next ensueing.

Joh: Hall Recto^r^
Peter Aylworth
Tho. Kemble
Rich: Barwell
Samuel Powell
Robt Morden
Sam^ll^ Parker
John Groue
Samuell Bennet
Grif Vincent
Tho Short
James Ashwood
Tho Collins
Toby Chapman
Will Winne
Richd Chauncy
William Scott
Gerrard Harris
William Banks
John Williams Churchwarden

St Christophers The 17th of Aprill 1682

At A vestery then holden were Chosen Churchwardens for ye yeare insewing for ye Churchsid vpper Churchwarden Mr John Williams and ffor Cornehill sid vnder Churchwarden Mr John Cros. And Allso ware Chosen sidsmen for ye Church sid Mr John Groues and for Cornhill sid Mr Thomas Collins and it was then ordered that the Accounts of Mr William Banks Late Churchwarden shall be Audited one Tuesday ye Twenty third of May next Ensuing by Mr John Hall Rector Mr Deputy Peter Aylworth Mr John Eliot Mr William Horsey Mr Thomas Kimball Mr William Drope Mr Richard Barwell Mr Samuell Powell Mr Thomas Blagraue Mr Samuell Brewster Mr Joseph Lemme Richard Booth Esqr Mr Siluester Deane Mr Robert Morden Mr Samuell Parker or Any fiue or more of them and Allsoe that ye saide John Williams shall one or before the said twenty third day of May next giue one sufficient security togeather with him selfe to be bound in A bond of three hundered pounds penall to giue a trew Account of All such Stocke plat and Vtensills belonging to ye said Parrish as shall Come to his Hands And that ye said Peter Aylworth shall keepe ye said bond in behalfe of ye said parrish. Mr John Cros desiring to fine for Churchwarden it was putt to the vote and it was Carried in ye Negatiue. Memorandum.

W^r^ Horsey
Sam^ll^ Parker
Thomas Manton
Samuel Welles
Isaac Hancock
Jeremiah mitchell
Sam^ll^ Brewster
Tho Short
John Prittyman
Daniell ffranklyn
Wm Bythell

Joh: Hall Recto^r^
Peter Aylworth
Tho. Kemble
Rich: Barwell
Tho: Blagraue
Robt Morden
Wm Pepys
Arthur Myles jun^r^
Will Banks
Churchwarden

St Christophers London The 16th of May 1682 It was agreed

At a Vestry then holden that John Cross should be Excused from the serving ye office of Churchwarden upon the payment of sixteen pounds to Mr Wm Bankes late Churchwarden, and att the same time Mr Thomas Lee was chosen Junior Churchwarden for the year Ensueing

Memorandum the same time Mr John Cross paid the said summe of Sixteen pounds to Mr Wm Bankes aforesaid.

William Glaister
Isaac Hancock
Jere mitchell
Samuel Welles
John Groue
William Winne
William Banks } Church
John Williams } wardens

Samuell Powell
Sam^ll^ Brewster
Sam^ll^ Parker
Constable Wheeler
Micha: Dewing
Will Barker
Rob Todd
Nicholas Day
James Cornwall
Siluester Deane
William Scott
Js Puller
Josiah mitchell

St Christophers 24 May 1682

At a Vestry then holden upon the instance of Mr Lee who was of opinion that he was not regularly chosen Churchwarden and Mr Crosse excused it was debated whether we should proceed upon that matter againe and upon Mr Crosses referring himself to the Vestry it was put to the Question and carried in the affirmative that we should take that matter into Consideracōn and debate whether Mr Crosse shall be excused on a fine and another person chosen Churchwarden and afterwards twas voted by the Major part of the Vestry that Mr John Crosses fine should be Sixteene pounds and at the same time Mr Banks did deliver the 16li in his hands to Mr John Williams present upper Churchwarden Vpon which the Vestry proceeded to a new Choice and chose Mr Thomas Lee Churchwarden for the yeare ensueing for Cornehill side who alsoe desireing to be admitted to fine and withdraweing it was carried in the Negative

Joh: Hall Recto'
Wm Horsey
Tho. Kemble
Rich: Barwell
Samll Parker
Constable Wheeler
Samuel Powell
Grif Vencent
Micha: Dewing
William Banks
Isaac Puller
Toby Chapman
Wm Bythell
John Lawrence
John Groue
Tho Collins
Humphry Bradly — Josiah Mitchell
Jno Brinkley — Jere Mitchell
Arthur Myles junr — John Williams

a. St Christophers Aprill ye 9o 1683

At a vestry then holden mr Thomas Lee was chosen upper Churchwarden for Cornhill side & mr Robert Tod under Churchwarden for Churchside, and mr Jno Hopkins sidesman for Cornhill side & mr Tho: Scott sidesman for Churchside for the yeare ensueing And it was Then ordered that mr John Williams his Accounts late Churchwarden shall bee Auditted on Tewsday ye fiueteenth day of May next ensueing. p mr John Hall Rector mr Deputy Peter Ayleworth, mr Wm Horsey Tho: Kemble, mr Wm Drope, mr Richard Barwell, mr Sam̃ Powell, Capt. Tho: Blagraue, mr Sam̃ Brewster, mr Joseph Lemm, Richard Booth Esq: mr Robt Morden, mr Sam. Parker, mr Wm Banckes, or any fiue or more of them, And alsoe that mr Thomas Lee shall on or before the said 15th of May giue one sufficient security togeather with himselfe to bee bound in a bond of three hundred pounds penall, to giue a True Accot of all such plate stocke & vtensells belonging to the said parrish as shall come to his hands, And that the said Deputy Ayleworth shall keepe ye said bond on behalfe of the said parrish, it was then Agreed yt a parchmt of the parishoners names intitled the Clarkes Wages Bearing date this day shall bee confirmed and paid According to the Rates there inserted.

Joh: Hall Recto'
Will Barker — Peter Aylworth
Robt Morden — W. Horsey
John Groue — Tho: Kemble
Samll Parker — Tho: Blagraue
Micha: Dewing — Sam̃ll Brewster
Wm Pepys — Jno Houblon
William Scott — Wil̃l Banckys
Gerrard: Harris — Josiah Mitchell
Wm Bythnell — Jere Mitchell
John Lawrence — Tho: Scott
James Ashwood — Isaac Hancock
Samuel Welles

St Christophers 31o July 1683 85 b.

At a vestry then held. It was declared by the Church Wardens that they had putt out Apprentices the Parish Children following vizt: Philip Chrestopher baptized May the 4th 1673 to John Sawyer of Leytonstone in the parish of Lowe Layton in the County of Essex Black Smith the said Master to have wth his said Apprentice Seaven Pounds and tenn Shillings & such Clothes as he now hath and not more, and to give Bond in twenty Pounds penalty to save the said Parish of St Christophers harmelesse, Izabella Christopher baptized 22d July 1673, to John Elliot Currier & Marie his wife of the Parish of St Giles Criplegate London the said Master & Mrs to have with their said Apprentice Eight Pounds & such Clothes as shee now hath and not more. And Mr Robert Watkins Citizen & Leatherseller of London to giue bond with the said John Elliot in Twenty Pounds Penalty to save harmlesse the said Parish of St Christophers. All which agreement is ratified and confirmed by this Vestrey

Joh: Hall Recto'
Peter Aylworth
Tho: Kemble
Rich: Barwell
Samll Brewster
Tho Short
To: Chapman
John Williams
Wm Fashion
Samuel Puller
Jere mitchell
James Ashwood
John Lawrence

St Christophers ffebruary 6th 1683 86 a.

Att a Vestry then holden It was Agreed and Ordered That whereas the Parishoners of St Christophers Did by Order of Vestry Dated ffowerth March 1674 Agree to Indempnifie and Save harmelesse Mr Peter Aylworth and Mr Thomas Kemble if they thought fitt to Enter into Bond to Mr Brewer for Security of One hundred pounds Which said Mr Peter Aylworth and Mr Thomas Kemble did accordingly become bound to the said Mr Brewer for the said One hundred pounds and Interest And whereas the said Mr Peter Aylworth is since removed out of the said Parish and the said Mr Kemble is since dead Soe that the said Mr Aylworth desires to bee Discharged from the said Obligacon Now Therefore it is Ordered & Agreed that if Mr William Drope and Mr Richard Barwell thinke fitt and doe enter into bond to Mr John West for One hundred pounds and Interest thereof ffor Paying off of the said Debt to Mr Brewer They the said Mr William Drope and Mr Richard Barwell are and shall bee for ever Saved harmelesse and Indempnified for the same And that the said One hundred pounds and Interest shall bee paid on Accompt of this Parish as a proper Debt of this Parish

	Witt Banks	Joh Hall Recto'
Tho Blagraue	John Ashwood	Wm Drope
Richd Booth	John Lockyer	W Horsey
John Dunton	Constable Wheeler	Jno Houblon
Witt Glaister	Micha: Dewing	Daniel Mercer
John Prittyman	Samuel Puller	Samuel Powell
	Isaac Puller	Sam^ll Brewster
	Peter Capelin	Sam^ll Parker
	Robert Morden	Rich: Barwell
	John Lawrence	Wm Fashion
	Wm Bythell	John Williams
	Cha: Robinson	Tho: Rea
	Wm Pepys	Toby Chapman
	Tho Short	John Hopkins
	Isaac Hancock	Hen: Wellington
	Thomas Lee Rob Todd	church wardens

St Christopher 31° March 1684

At a Vestrey then held Mr Robert Todd was chosen vpper Churchwarden for Church side, and Mr Humphrey Bradley vnder Church Warden for Cornehill side and Mr Thomas Shorte Sidesman for Church side and Mr Tobias Chapman Sidesman for Cornehill side, And it was then ordered That Mr Thomas Lee his Accompts as late Church Warden shalbe audited on Tuesday the Sixth day of May next p Mr John Hall Rector Mr William Drope, Mr Witt Horsey, Mr Richard Barwell, Mr Samuel Powel, Capt Thomas Blagrave, Mr Samuel Brewster, Mr Joseph Lemm, Richard Booth Esq, Mr Robert Morden, Mr Samuel Parker, Mr Witt Bancks, Mr John Williams, or any five, or more of them; and also that the said Mr Robert Todd shall on or before the said 6th day of May next, give one sufficient Security together with himself to be bound in a Bond of Three Hundred Pounds penalty, to give a true Accompt of all such Plate Stock vtensills & things belonging to the said Parish as shall come to his hands, And that the said m^r William Drope shall keep the said Bond on behalfe of the said Parish

Joh: Hall Recto'
Wm Drope
Jno Houblon
Will Barker
Witt Banks
John Groue
Robt Williamson
Tho: Rea
Wm Pepys
Ger^d Harris
Sam: Bennet
Wm Fashion
Nicha: Dewing
Tho: scott
John Williams
Jere mitchell

St Christophers March 2^d 1684

Att a Vestry then holden It was Ordered that the Present Churchwardens bind Samuell Christopher Apprentice to William Palmer Cittizen and fframeworke Knitter for Eight yeares and that Six pounds bee given to his M^r vpon that Consideracon hee giveing Security to the Parish to Save the same harmelesse from the said Samuell. It was then likewise further Ordered that the Expences vpon the Tennants for Receiving the Parish Rents for the future shall not exceed Tenn shillings for one whole yeare. It was then further Agreed and Ordered by the said Vestrey That Capt Thomas Blagrave Shall have the Vse of a Vault in the South Isle of the Parish Church and that hee may Remove thither the Corps of his Relacons that lye else where and that it bee left to him the said Capt Blagrave and his Civillity what Consideracon hee shall give the Parish for the said accomadation

	Joh: Hall Recto'
Jno Houblon	Wm Drope
Tho Short	Rich Barwell
	Will Barker
	William Banks
	Robt Morden
	Sam^ll Parker
	John Williams
	Thomas Lee
	Tho: Scott
	Josiah mitchell
	Tho: Collins
	Rob Todd } Church Hump^h Bradley } wardens

St Christophers 15° Aprill 1685

At a vestry then held It is agreed That this parish Church be repaired and beautified and that such persons as were auditors of the last Church Wardens Accompts together with Mr Jo^n Houblon, Mr Tho: Short, Mr Jo^s Grove Mr Tho: Scott, Mr Robt Todd Mr Tho: Lee Mr Willm Bythell & Willm Fasheon be a Comittee with ye Church Wardens for the time being, or any five of them whereof one to be a Church Warden To ~~agree with Workemen~~ order & direct what is fitt to be donne and to agree with the respective workemen. It is further agreed That the monies to be paid for the said works shall be raised forthwith by way of a poores rate

Joh: Hall Recto'
Wm Drope
Rich: Barwell
Samuel Powell
Sam^ll Brewster
William Banks
John Williams
Thomas Lee
Will Barker
Robt Morden
Tho. Short
Tho: Scott
Wm Merriden
Wm Fashion
Robt Williamson
Witt Glaister
Jos Cressett
Wm Bythell
Rob Todd } Church Warden

St Christophers. 22° Aprill 1685

At a vestry then held Mr Humphrey Bradley was chosen vper Church Warden for Cornehill side, and Mr John Houblon Church

Warden for Church side, but Mr Houblon desireing to Fine for the said Office and offering twenty pounds, it was accepted and he discharged frō the said office for ever. And whereas Mr Michael Dewing freely offring fowerteen pounds for a Fine to be excused from the Offices of Sidesman and Church Warden for ever, the same was accepted and he discharged, which said two Fines to be paid to Mr Robert Todd. The Vestry proceeded to another choice, and did elect m^r Nicholas Day for Church Warden for Church side, also was chosen Sidesmen For Cornehill side Mr Isaac Puller, and for Church side Mr Josiah Mitchell. It was then ordered, That Mr Robert Todd his Accompts as late Church Warden be audited on Tuesday the Six & twentieth day of May next by Mr John Hall Rector, Mr William Drope, Mr Willm Horsey, Mr Rich. Barwell, Mr Sam: Powel, Mr Samuell Brewster, Mr Joseph Lem, Rich: Booth Esqr, Mr Robt Morden, Mr Sam: Parker, Mr Will Bankes, Mr Jo^n Williams, Mr Tho: Lee, Mr John Houblon, Mr Michael Dewing, or any five or more of them. And also that ye said Humphrey Bradley shall on or before the said 26° day of May next give one sufficient security together wth himselfe to be bound in a bond of 300^ll Penalty to give a true Accompt of all such Plate Stock Vtensills & things belonging to the said Parish as shall come to his hands. And that the said Mr Willm Drope Shall keep the said Bond on behalfe of the s^d Parish

Will Banks
Arthur Myles
John Williams
Will Barker
Rob Todd Church-warde

Joh: Hall Recto^r
Wm Drope
Rich: Barwell
Jno Houblon
Samuel Powell
Thomas Lee
Sam^ll Brewster
Tho Short
Dauid Heywood
Will Glaister
Wm Bythell
Sam^ll Parker
Tho: Scott
Charles Robinson
Robt Morden
Jere mitchell
Wm Fashion
Josiah mitchell

St Christophers Maij 11th 1685

Att a vestry then held m^r w^m Bithell was chosen Church-warden for Cornehill side in ye Roome of Humphry Bradley deceased, ye same vestry did alsoe Approue of wch Mr Todd hath done in bindinge Tho. Christopher to Jno Bell Barber-chirurgeon & payinge six pounds to ye s^d Bell of whome he hath rēd bond for to save ye Parish harmelesse

Robt Morden
Wm Pepys
Robt Williamson
Ger: Harris
Isaac Hancock
William Glaister

Joh: Hall Recto^r
Wm Drope
Rich: Barwell
Sam^ll Brewster
Thomas Lee
Tho Short
John Williams
William Scott
Toby Chapman
Isaac Puller
Rob Todd
Church warden

St Christophers Maij ye 25th 1685

Att a vestry then holden It was then ordered y^t m^r Nic: Day on or before ye 4th of June next doe give one sufficient securety wth him selfe to be bound in a bond of 300^ll penalty to give a trew acc^t of all such plate stock & vtensils belonginge to ye Parrish of s^t xtopheres as shall come to his hands & y^t m^r Drope doe keepe ye s^d Bond

Tho: Collins
henry Chūch
Rob Todd
Churchwarden

Sam: Harris Curate
Wm Drope
Will Barker
Sam^ll Brewster
Robt Morden
Will Banks
Tho Short
Toby Chapman
Isaac Hancock
Andrew keepe
Gerrard Harris
Samuel Puller
John Lockyer

St Christophers December the 2^d 1685

Att a Vestry then holden, It was Ordered that Mr Samuell Brewster Mr John Crosse Mr Michaell Dewing Mr John Grove Mr William ffashion Mr Thomas Rea Mr Thomas Collins Mr Thomas Scott (Mr Nicholas Day and Mr William Bethell Churchwardens) bee appointed as a Cōmittee to enquire after examine and inspect all Bookes Writings and Accompts relating to or concerning the Parish of St Christopher And to Report to the Vestry of the said Parish how, wherein, and by whome, the said Parish is any way prejudiced or Damnified Of which Cōmittee five to bee a Quorum the Vpper Churchwarden of the said Parish then being to bee one. It was also Ordered at the same time that the Parishioners of St Margarett Lothbury shall have the Accomodacōn of the Church of St Christopher to meete vpon Lord's Dayes and Holy dayes till their owne Church bee Rebuilt If the Vestry of this Parish shall not see cause to otherwise Order it

Joh: Hall Recto^r
Wm Drope
Samuel Powell
Sam^ll Brewster
William Banks
John Williams
John Groue
H. Coningesby
Dauid Heywood
Samuel Puller
Tho Short
Robt Williamson
Jere mitchell
Will Glaister
Josiah Mitchell
Constable Wheeler
Nicholas Day } Church
Wm Bythell } wardens

S[t] Christopher January 17 1685

At a Vestry then holden D[r] John Mapletoft lately Chosen Minister of S[t] Lawren e Jury was unanimously Chosen Lecturer for this Parish to Preach every Lords day in the Afternoone for One yeare To Commence at Lady day next. And It was then likewise Ordered that Richard Booth Esq[r] M[r] John Houblon M[r] Samuell Brewster M[r] Richard Barwell M[r] Thomas Lee M[r] John Grove and Nicholas Day and William Bythell Churchwardens Or any two of them with the Churchwardens Doe goe about the Parish to gett Subscriptions of the Severall Inhabitants for his Incouragement

Joh: Hall Recto[r]
Richd Booth
Jn[o] Houblon
Sam[ll] Brewster
Samuel Powell
Rich: Barwell
Thomas Lee
W[m] Merriden
Rob[t] Morden
Micha: Dewing
Tho: Rea
Dauid Heywood
Arthur Myles
Rob[t] Williamson
Jos: Cleare
Jn[o] Batton
Jos Cressett
Cha: Bysshopp
Tho: Jacks
Nicholas Day } Church wardens
W[m] Bythell }

S[t] Christopher March 24th 168$\frac{5}{6}$ 90 a.

At a Vestry then holden It was Ordered and Agreed that such Agreement as M[r] William Bythell has made with M[r] John Page concerning a Parish Child shall noe wayes bee any Obligacon or tye vpon the Parish And that the Bond given by the said John Page to M[r] Day and M[r] Bythell Dated the 23th Instant for the Saveing the Parish harmelesse against Katherine Christopher wee doe protest against and noe wayes accept of the same, the same being made and taken without the Knowledge or Consent of the said M[r] Day

William Banks
Samuel Puller
Jere Mitchell
Nicholas day Churchwarden

APPENDIX.

These beth the ꝑsellis of the Juellis Goodis and Ornamentis of the churche of Seynte Cristofre of london founden in the Same Churche the xxvj day of the monethe of marche the yere of the reigne of oure lurde god m[lo] cccc° lxxxiij takyn into the warde and kepyng of william Brown and Robt Eyzyk wardens of the same Churche the which juellis goodis and ornamentis that Richard Croke and John Jacoby haue Receyued into theire warde and kepyng the xxvj daye of the moneth of marche A° dñi m[lo] cccc° lxxxviij as apperith by a bille

In primis a grete Crosse with mari and john of Siluer and ouergilde weyenge iiij[xx] xj vncis of the gifte of william Gardyner draper and a foote therto of Copur & gilte

* *the Same crose Rd agayne ij knopys lakyng*

Itm̃ a nother Crosse of Siluer and ouergilde without mari & john havyng therin a plate of iron the whiche Crosse weyeth with the iron lxxix owncis

Itm̃ a Chales with a patent of Siluer and ou'gilt w[t] a Trinite weyng —— xxj ownes *w[t] the cruciffix in the fote & mary & john*

Itm̃ a Chaleys with the patent of Siluer and ou'gilde with a Crusyfix & T & S theruppon & an hande vppon the patent the whiche Chaleys weyeth —— xvj ownes

Itm̃ a Chaleys with a Crucifix and mari & john vppon the foote and the Coronacion of oure lady vppon the patent weyng —— xxv ownes di

Itm̃ a Chaleys with a Crucifix and too hartis hedis vppon the foote and the jugement of god Sittyng vppon the patent the whiche Challeys weyeth —— xliij ownes di

Itm̃ a Chaleys with a vernacle vppon the patent weyng vj owncis

Itm a Chaleys off the gifte of henry walter & the said name graved vppon the ffote

Itm̃ a grete mustraunce of Silner & ou'gilde with the Pixt of Cristall weyeng —— lxviij owncis

soulde to thomas mostyan by the consent of a vestre for to pay the nessysarye chargs of the sayd cherche as aperethe by the cherche wardyns akownte

Itm too Sensers of Siluer ꝑcell gilte weyng j[c] and ij ownes

bought by master jaks cherche wardyn in the yeire of o[r] lord 1536 j sencers of selver ꝑcells gylt weyng xxv oz coste iij[s] viij[d] the oz & thomas hylton was cherche wardyn w[t] hym ... ... } *iiij[li] xj[s] viij[d]*

* The portions in italics are additions in later handwritings of various dates, as may generally be gathered from the context.

† Itm̃ ij Basons of Siluer with leggys armes weyeng lix ownes & di

† Itm̃ too Candelstikks of Siluer with leggis armes vppon them weyng bothe —— lxv ownes

Itm̃ a Coupe of Siluer & ou'gilde with a Crucifix vppon the hed to put in the Sacrement weyng —— xxxj owncis *sold*

Itm̃ a Crismatorie of Siluer and gilde w[t] ij imags oon of oure lady the other of Seynt Cristofre the Same Crismatorie weyng xxix ownes di *the same cresmetore broken & consertcd w[t] a chales to make a comen comynyon cope gilte xl oz by me thomas groschampe one of the cherche wardenes wythe the consentt of the same paryes*

Itm̃ a Shippe of Siluer ꝑcell gilte for the ffrankensence that weyeth —— viij owncis

Itm̃ a mustraunse of Siluer & gilde w[t] an image of Seynt Cristofre therin weyng the same mustraunce —— vj ownes di

Itm̃ a pelar of Siluer with a Cristall theron gilt w[t] c'tayne relikks weyng all to gedur —— v 'ownes

Itm̃ a Sepulture of Siluer with ij crosses theruppon and with certayne Relyquees therin weyeng all to gedur —— iiij ownes

Itm̃ a Sepulcre of siluer and ou'gilde with the ffleesshe of Seynt Cristofre therin that weieth with the fflesshe xi ownes di

N.B.—Here is an addition made in 1518 which has been erased with the word "sold" written at a subsequent date. It is illegible.

Itm̃ a paire of Siluer feete belongyng to the image of Seynt Cristofre weyeng both —— xviij owncis

Itm̃ a Pax of Siluer and ouergilte weyeng —— vj ownẽs lakkyng ~~a~~ [ij] knop of ~~a~~ [ij] corner beneth *on knop more lakyng 3 in all.*

Itm̃ ij rownde Crewetts of Siluer ꝑcell gilte weyng both —— xij ownẽs.

Itm̃ ij Square Crewetts of Siluer ꝑcell gilte weyeng bothe —— iij owncis. *sold*

Itm̃ ij Shone of Siluer with a Stone that s'ued somtyme for an image of oure lady that weyed bothe with the Stone an ounce di

the Sho w[t]oute the stone lakking the scho w[t] the stone sold by

Itm̃ a Crosse of Siluer the foote and the hed Cristall that weyeth an ownce & a halff.

† Probably the gift of Thomas Legge, who, by his will dated 31 Edward the Third, gave various bequests to the Parish of St. Christopher. A copy of the will is in the Book of Records. He apparently increased the churchyard.

Itm̃ ther is a Crosstaffe of Copur and gilte that is for the best Crosse that cost the pisshons —— xvij *s.*

Itm̃ a Sewte of Crymysyn veluet the Orpharies of blewe cloth of Tissew and flowres of gold, for preist dekyn and subdeakyn wᵗ stole and ffanons and iiij Coopes of the same sewte that sewte was bought of my lady Stockdon. *Wherof one is cloth of golde blewe Tyssewe the orphers of the said cowpe is of redde golde the whiche cowpe of red gold was of the gifte of my lady stokton abouesaid.*

Itm̃ a Coope of blewe cloth of tyssewe the Orpharies of Red cloth of golde of the gifte of my lady stokdon *scriptũ vt supᵃ*

Itm A Coppe of clothe of gold the Orpharies wᵗ ymegery All of Broderes werke gyffe be dame Thomasyn peyvall

Itm̃ a Sewte of Red veluet for Preist dekyn & Subdeakyn browderid with Griffons of golde with the armes of legge with too Stooles & iij ffanons and with iij Coopes of the Same Sewte and a Cloth of the Same to hange before the high altar with a ffrontell of the Same armes and a cloth for the lectarũ of the Same Sewte *lackyng a lectory clothe of this sewt wyche mʳ chambers hathe in kepyng by the parsons Request*

Itm̃ a Sewte of vestements of Red Saten with Orpharies of blewe Bawdekyn for Preist dekyn and Subdeakyn with ij Stooles and iij ffanons and a Coope of the same Sewte

Itm A vestement of purpull veluet wᵗ Orpharies of Brodre werke and yᵉ vestemēt ffull of fflerédelys of gold wᵗ yᵉ albe and all thᵉto belongyng gyvyn by mʳ Roger acheley late mayre of London yᵉ ffyrst day of Novemb aᵒ 1513 *

Itm̃ a Sewte of vestements of blewe Satyn with Birdes of goolde and lyons and the Orpharies of Red Bawdekyn the grownde Powdered with white fllowres for Preist dekyn and Subdeakyn ij Stooles and iij ffanons and a Coope of the same wᵗ Sterres in thẽ Orpharies

Itm̃ a Sewte of vestements of white Bawdekyn with libbards of gold Crowned abought theire nekkis and Rooses of Red Silke for Preist dekyn and Subdekyn with ij Stooles iij ffanons & a Coope of the same suyte & ij aulter clothes for the high Alter of white Saten Steyned wᵗ the same libardis and ij Ridels of the same and a ffrontell of white Bawdekyn with iij platis of blewe bawdekyn and ij pendauntis therto to hange at iche ende of the cloth to eke hit for the cloth is or [o'er] Shorte for the alter

Itm̃ a nother Sewte of vestements of white Bawdekyn with Rooses of goolde and Orpharies of Red Bawdekyn full of the same Rooses for Preist dekyn and Subdeakyn with ij Stooles and iij ffanons and iij Coopes and a cloth of the Sewte to lye vppon a forme vppon the high alter vndre the juellis

Itm̃ ij Coopes of white Bawdekyn & the grounde of the Orpharies Red wᵗ libardis of goolde havyng in theire mouthes Rolles

Itm̃ a Sewte of Blak vestementis of damaske and the Orpharies browdred with images and Trayfoyles of grene Silke in the hed, & the grownndes of Siluer with a Scripture therin and the Armes wᵗ Rynges of goolde for Preist dekyn and Subdeakyn with ij Stooles and iij ffanons and with iij Coopis of the Same Sewte

* This was written in 1518. Sir Roger Achely (Draper) was Mayor of London 1511. Stowe says he was a careful Magistrate for corn, which he caused to be stowed up in Leaden Hall. He lived in Cornhill, and was buried in St. Christopher's church.

Itm̃ a Sewte of Blak bawdekyn browderid with treis of goold and the Armes whyte with mones of Blewe for Preist dekyn and Subdeakyn and a Coope of the Same Sewte

Itm̃ a vestement Syngle of worsted with Crownes m with Goolde the grounde of Blak Syngle vestments

Itm a vestment of Bawdekyn white and Red with the Orpharies of Blewe with Crownes & Sterris of golde

Itm̃ a vestement of Red Bawdekyn full of Braunches of goolde and blewe Sterris of Silke the Orpharies of blewe playne bawdekyn vestements

Itm̃ a vestement of whyte Bawdekyn and the Orpharies of Red with lambes and Rooses of goolde, with Stoole and fanon

Itm̃ a vestement of Cloth of goolde ffebull full of flowres delyes & the Orpharies of blew Red and Grene with Strypus of whyte for Preist dekyn with Stoole and fanon & a Coope of the same

Itm̃ a vestement Syngle of Clothe of goolde febull wᵗ Stoole and fanon & the Orpharies of dyu's Colours and an egle Splayed of blew.

Itm̃ a vestement Syngle of Red and the Orpharies of blewe worsted with stoole and ffanon. vestements

Itm̃ a vestement Syngle of Silke full of Ray and of Chekkis of dyuers Coloures and the Orpharies of blew veluet

Itm̃ a vestement Syngle paled of Purple and grene and the Orpharies of blewe with dyuers birdes of golde therin

Itm̃ a vestement Syngle of whyte Cloth browderid wᵗ Jhesus

Itm̃ a vestement Syngle partie oon Side Red and grene and the other side blewe and lyons of siluer with longe tailes and the Orpharies of blak with Crownes and Sterrys vestements

Itm̃ a vestement of Grene and Red Single with whyte flowres and the Orpharies of blewe veluet wᵗ Images and Sterres of goolde

Itm̃ a Cope feble of grene the Orpharies of Red wᵗ flowres of whyte and grene

Itm̃ ij Coopis of blewe Rayes

Itm̃ a Cope of Cloth of gold ffeble for a Child Bisshop

Itm̃ a vestement of blewe Saten the Orpharies grene damaske with blewe garters Stole and fanon

Itm̃ a Cope ffeble for a Childe of dyuers Coloures and iij Copes of white Bustyan and the Orpharies of grene thise iij Copes byn Smale coopes for Children

Itm̃ a Cloth of blewe Rayes with a ffrontell theron of blewe damasque with other pecys of the Same Rayes that belonged Som tyme to the Alters and nowe ben Spente and made a Certeyne forto cloose aboute the founte and another about oure lady of Pytie of the Same Rayes

Itm̃ a Cloth of ffeble Silke to Serue at Weddyngs for a care cloth

Itm̃ a Cloth of Gold fyne Bawdekyn wᵗ a valance aboute of Silke called a vertaine that Serueth to bere ouer the Sacrement with iiij Staves and iiij bellis longynge therto

Itm̃ ij Awbes of Ray for Children of oon Sewyte

Itm̃ vj Spare Amytes of the whiche oon is browdered with gold and iij Images therynne John kateryne and Antony. Another is of Red veluet with Sterres of goold. The thirde of white damaske. The iiijᵗʰ of Red veluet with letters of T. & C. of golde. The vᵗʰ of grene Bawdekyn with whyte and Red fflowres. The vjᵗʰ of dyuers Coloures Rayes

Itm̃ ij Clothes Steyned whyte for thappostellis Aulter aboue with the Trynyte and beneth with oure lady and ij Riddelles therto

Itm̃ ij Clothes for the high Alter Stayned with the xij appostellis

Itm̃ ij Aulter Clothes of Red and grene paled and ij Riddellis and a ffrontell of the Same

Itm a Clothe of Red damaske with armes at every ende and wᵗ fflowres of golde to hange aboue the Table ou' the Alter and ij clothes of the Same to hange before the Alter and ij Riddels of Red Tarteron and an Altercloth of diapre with a ffrontell of the Sewte of the best Cope of blewe cloth of gold of my lady Stokdons gifte

Itm̃ a banercloth for the Crosse of grene Tarteron with the Trynyte theryn of my lady Stokdons geyfte

Itm̃ ij Clothes for oure lady Alter oon to hange aboue the Alter and another to hange before the alter havyng the vij Sacraments vppon hem Steyned & leide with golde and ij Curteyns of the Same with Shepe theryn that beth of master whits gifte

Itm̃ ij Riddelles of Lawne that renne behynde in the Quere that beth of Johnsons wiffs gifte

Itm̃ ij longe and ij Shorte Riddels of Red Silke with griffons and T. of gold and Crownes that Serue in the Quere at tymes

Itm̃ a lectarne Cloth grownde blewe with Red Strypes ou'thwarte that is but feble cloth

Itm̃ ij Riddels for an Alter White Stayned wᵗ Roses of gold

Itm̃ ther beth viij pillowes of dyuers Coloures beside other that beth Suspent & dampned for bad as apperith in the p̃cellis of the Suspent wares

Itm̃ a gheton of Silke betyn with golde and iiij baners wᵗ liberts hedis ij baners with the armys of london and vj smale baners with dyuers armes and iiij ~~Smale~~ baner clothes ~~of master ffosters gyfte and a banerclothe for the Crosse of oure lady of Silke~~

Itm̃ iiij longe grene baner powlles and iiij Shorte Standarts Staves

Itm̃ xxiij Aulter Clothes good and badde the most parte Symple and vj hussyllyng Towellis Therof and playne feble oon the Remlaut diapre of whiche is oon longe of my lady Cookes gifte & a litell oon that was gevyn in lent A° 87 by Reynold Rutters wiffe.

*Itm avlter Clothe off porpull veluet wᵗ fflowre delys of Gold gytyn by master Roger Acheley late mayre of Thys Cetie of london.**

Itm̃ a Sewdarie of grene Tarterne ffringed with Silke on bothe endis and a Canape of knyt warke and ij kerchiffs of Silke oon Red and a nother whyte for the Sacrament

Itm̃ ij *large* paire of longe laton Candelstykks Standards oon paire to Set before the high aulter and the other paire to Serue for Obites to Setton the Tapers bothe the paire weyenge

Itm̃ ~~iij~~ ii Candelstykks of a Sewte to Sett on Smaller tapers vppon the Alters and to bere Tapers vppon of laton weyng all

Itm̃ ~~iij~~ ij laton Candelstikks with ij Noses to Set Inne Talowe Candell for the Alters. ~~And a Candell braunche wᵗ ij Noses and a Pyke sett at the ffounte of laton~~ weyng ~~all~~

~~Itm a payre of Candelstikks of copur gilte of whiche oon is~~ broken

Itm̃ a payre of Candelstykks greate standards for grete tapers of Tynne, and a paire of lesse of Tynne that beth parte brent

Itm̃ ij payre Peautre Crewetts that Seruen daily the Preists

* Written in 1518.

Itm̃ ij Crosses of ~~Tynne~~ Copur on that hath had Marie and John that is gilte and another without Marie and John that is blak

Itm̃ ij Copur disshes to gedre offryng Inne and iij Sacryg bellys and an haly water Stop̃ and the Spryngell of laton therto

Itm̃ ther beth iij Sup̃ Altarces of the Churches a large & A middell and a lytell oon that ben Clothed in cloth

Itm ther beth xx Corpores cases that longe to the Churche and iiij heeris to ley vppon the Alters & iiij Canvase to Couer the Alters

Braunches of laton longyng to the Churche

Itm̃ ther beth longyng to the Rode loft xxxᵗⁱ bolles of laton

Itm̃ in the Quere before Seynt James a braunche with vij fflowres that weyeth

Itm̃ before oure lady in the North Chapell a braunche of vj fflowres laton weyng

Itm̃ before oure lady and Seynt Anne in the Same Chapell is a braunche of v fllowres of laton weyng

Itm̃ in the South Chapell before the Trynyte is a braunche of laton with v fflowres weyng

Itm̃ before oʳ lady a braunche of laton wᵗ v branchys

Itm̃ before oure lady of Pytie in the body of the Churche is a braunche of iij fllowres of laton weyng

Itm̃ before the Pytie of Seynt Gregorie in the body of the Churche is a braunche of iij fllowres weyng

Itm̃ ther is a lavmpe hangyng before the Rode in a basyn of laton and a basyn with Cheynes and a Sterre of laton for to hange Inne the Pascall at the Season of Esterne

Itm̃ ther beth ij olde grete braunches of laton that beth eche for oon Tapur that s'ued before oure lady & before Seynt Anne

Itm̃ for the high Aulter ij Clothes of whyte Stayned with the Some vppon them and a Crosse with Scorges vppon the other

Itm̃ ij Clothes for the postellys Aucter Steyned with the Crosse and Scorges to hange on aboue and the other before the Aucter

Itm̃ ther beth for ij Aucters of the Same Sewte both for a boue and beneth

Itm̃ there beth iiij Clothes of the Same Sewte that s'ue for Riddellys in the Quere in the lentyn Season

Itm̃ ther is a Vaile Clothe to hange before the high aucter and therto longeth ij weyghts of leed iche of xxviij li

Itm̃ a Cloth for the lectarne of the Same Sewte for lente

Itm̃ a Cloth to hange before the Roode with the passion Story

Itm̃ ij Clothes with the Imags of Seynt Cristofre to couer Seynt Cristofre

Itm̃ ij baners of vexilla and a Cloth to cou' wᵗ Seynt John

Itm̃ viij Clothes Stayned to couer wᵗ other Images marked

Itm̃ iij Symple vestements of whyte bustyan and the Orpharies of Red veluet to s'ue in the lente Season

Itm̃ ij Clothes for the Sepulcre oon with the passion and the other Steyned full of whyte leves,

Itm̃ afore the Rode lofte beth ij Curteyns of lynnen cloth wᵗ ffrynges of grene vppon hem of lynnen Syngle yaron

In primis A grete Antifoner of master Gedneys gyfte begunyng in the secounde leeff hoc modo durᵃ

Itm an Antifoner begynnyng in the secounde leeffe memorie que ꝑcedit

Itm a nother Antifoner begynnyng in the Secownd leeffe Allia hec ant' dicatur

Itm a nother antyfory that begynnyng in the thyrd leefle Campanis more selito

Itm an olde antyphoner that begynneth in the Secunde leeffe paries quidem filii

Itm v masbokes of the whiche oon begynneth in the Secunde leeff Et in Ramys palmar

Itm a nother in the Secunde leeff, Et finiat' hoc modo hitaculo

Itm a nother in the Secunde leeff, Te pater Supplices

Itm a nother in the Secunde leeffe factoribz istius loci

Itm a nother in the Secunde leffe Reprimis qz inimici

Itm oon begynneth in the Secunde leeff P totu aduentu

Itm a nother in the Secunde leeff Cumque dicat' missa

Itm a nother in the Secunde leeffe In diebz illis

Itm the iiij[th] begynneth in the Secunde leeff Spontanea gra

Itm v Pressessionaries of the whiche oon begynneth in the ij[de] leeffe. Infande

Itm in a nother in the Secunde leeff begynneth Eradicare

Itm in a nother in the Secunde leeff begynneth Propicius inuocacoibz

Itm in a nother in the Secunde leeff begynneth Oem potestatem

Itm in a nother in the Secunde leeff begynneth Paufu Suof

Itm ij manewelles oon begynnyng, in the Secunde leeff Inimici et ipm, Another begynneth in the Secunde leeff mundi Spus

Itm ij bokes on called a legende and a nother called a Tempall oon begynnyng in the Secunde leeff Cecitatem quanda And the other in the Secunde leeff begynneth In quæ immaculatus

Itm ij Portewos oon begynnyng in the Secunde leeff dei credim[us] and the other with Brigitts legent begynnyng in the Secunde leeff Ipo die et cotidie

Itm A lectonarie w[t] a martelage therin begynnyng in the Secunde leeff Relacio p'ui

Itm a Colectori in the Secunde leeff begynnyng Sibi in nob etc'

Itm an ymner and a Sequencer noted bothe in oon boke begynnyng in the Secunde leffe Carnem qui viuis

Itm an Ordinall begynnyng in the Secunde leeff festum Sci marcij

Itm ij Queyres oon of Corpus Cristi with legende therin The of Seynt Cristofer

Itm a Pryk Songe boke of paper Royall with dyuers masses therin begynnyng in the first lyne of the Secunde leffe Ne filii vni

Itm a miter for a Bisshop of the lord Pyggs* gifte of whyt damaske with marie and Gabriell & petyr & poule theron of golde ymags and a Case of leder therto & a Croyser staffe hed gilte therto

Itm on the Est Side and on the west side in the vestrarie beth on iche an Alter joyned and vndre theme they be full of Closetts to ley Jnne vestments and Surplecys that beth daily occupied to kepe them clene and closse

* Perhaps the gift of John Peche, Lord Mayor of London, 1361, or his predecessor Henry Pycard, 1356.

Itm ther Stondeth the xxvj daie of marche A° 88 in the Churche yarde a deske ioyned of Estryche burde with an Almery and ij durres and iiij paire of Stronge garnetts and a lok therto

Itm ther beth the Same daie in the Store hows xix Imags of Tymbre and an Image of oure lady in a Tabernacle of Tymbre with many Aungellis therabought — olde ymags

Itm in the Churche yarde ther beth iij longe ladders lokked in a Cheyne oon of xxxj staues and a nother of xxv anoth' xxiiij — ladders

Itm ther be in the Rode loft a paire of Orgons with the ij peire blewers the Orgons closse to be shitte w[t] clos leffes — Orgons

Itm ther beth vj Judas Staves for Torches peynted havyng iche a Castell gilded to set Inne Torchetts to bere with the Sacrement on Corpus Cristy daye & other tymes — Judas Staves

Itm ther be ij letterns of tre Stondyng in the Quere — letternes

Itm ther is a Standyng letterne of yron, and ij Stondyng letterns of tre in the Rode lofte, and a grete deske lettarne for the grete boke, and ij smaller deske lettarnes for the quere and iij letternes of tre for the iij alters

Itm ther be xij Tables in the Churche the xxvj daie of the moneth of marche A° 88 of the whiche is oon of the x comaundements, A nother hangyng vndre oure lady of Pitie with dyuers good prayers of oure lady and the Sauter of Charite, And a nother of Seynt Gregories pitie of James Wellis gifte, A nother of Seynt Erasynus, A nother of Seynt kateryne of dyuers good prayers, A nother of Seynt Anne, A nother of Seynt Jamys, and iij of Seynt Cristofre, and ij of Seynt Sebestian — Tables in the Churche

Itm a Sensers of laton and a Ship of laton therto for thensense and a fire Shofell of yron for to sette with ffire to Sense with

Itm ther longeth to the Churche the same xxvj daie of marche A° 88 a Crowe of yron a whele barowe a Shofull and a matok

Itm ther beth longyng to the Churche ij Carpetts a more and a lesse of the whiche the more longeth for the high Aulter and the lesse to the Trynyte Aulter — Carpetts

Itm ther beth longyng to the Churche the xxvj daie of march A° Dni m[l] cccclxxxviij vij Chestis and a forcer of the which Stonde in the vestrarie iij therof oon is plated all ouer with platis and bondes of yron to kepe in the Juellis, A nother that is playne Chest boundyn with bandis of Iron to put in necessaries, Another litell Chest to put Inne evidencs and ther is a Stronge bownden fforcer with evidence, And in the Rode loft is a grete Shipchest, And in the body of the Churche stond ij longe smale Chestis, And in the Churche yarde Stondeth a longe deske Chest for Torches — vij Chestis

Itm in the vestrarie Stondeth on the North Side a grete closet wherin beth certayne fframes to hange on Copes And in the Same beth c'tayne Smale Closetts with lokkys and keyes to Shit Inne the Clerks chargs that beth daily occupied — in y[e] vestrary

Itm on the South side of the vestrarie Standeth a grete library with ij longe lecturnalles theron to ley on the bokes

Hoc Inuentar' q' in p'dcis xxxiiij ffolijs exhibit' erat coram me Johne Calipolen epo Archno london p'mo die mensis ffebruarij Anno dni m[l] quigentesimo xviij†

+ Jo Calipolen

† This is a later addition to the older list, and was probably made on the occasion of an Archidiaconal visitation at the time when the addition of the things given by Sir Roger Acheley was made.

Memorandum these beth the Specialteis that I Robt Fyryk delyuered vnto master Croke and John Jacoby the Churche Wardens as apperith by a bille delyuered to me by master Croke the xxvj daie of marche A° dñi m^{l} cccc° lxxx viij°

In primis iij endentures of leses of the whiche oon was of the leese of the vernacle with the tenauntry therby to William Browne for the t'me of xx yerys, begynnyng at midsomer A° 88 by Couenaunte to paie yerely to the Churche iij li xiij s iiij d clere he to bere all maner chargs and reparacions therof

Itm a nother of the Cok and Sterre leten to George Venables for xij yeris after iij li xiij s iiij d by yere begynnyng at midsomer A° dñi m^{l} cccc° lxxxv

Itm the iij^{de} of the Aungell in ffletestrete with the ij tenntries therby leten to John Cok for the terme of l yerís begynnyng at Cristemas A° dñi m^{l}cccc^{o}lxxxvij to paie yerely to the churche iij li x s and bere all maner reparacions of the houses & vessellys

Itm v obligacions therynne bownden John Wanton and Thomas Wayte in the Sm of viij li vj s viij d wherof is paied as apperith vppon the bak of oon of the obligacions xiij s. iiij d Rest

Memorandum these bethe the pcellis of lyuelode pteynyng to Seynte Cristoferes Churche Showyng at the xxvj daye of marche A° 88 howe they stonde leten

Furst the house that John Jacoby holdeth and dwellith Jnne payeng by yere vj^{li} and the tenements next hit on the west side payeng by yere xl s that is vacant from oure lady daie in lente last passed vnto midsomer. And the tenement next on the est side that John a Ridis holdith for xxvj s viij d by yere the whiche grete house and the ij tenements beth letyn vnto John Jacoby by endenture for t'me of his liff & a yere after payng for theyme yerely ix li vj s viij d. The whiche lyvelode is of the gifte of my lady Nerford,* for the whiche the Churche wardens beth bounden by her testament

---

A trew Coppie of the length & bredth of that pte of the Royall Exchaunge both wthout on the streat side & also wthin the Exchaunge as the same was measured before ye exchaunge was builded & as is now Recorded in Chamber of London to be Cituat & lying wthin the prish of St xpofers by ye Stocks & registred this xxiiijth of June 1590

The length of the soyle of the prish of St xpofers on the streat syde of Cornehill ffrom the late new allye gate on the Easte pte vnto the howse late Jaques on the west pt Conteyneth — xlvj foote — vj Inches of Assise

The bredth of the same streete on the South pte wherin on Scother dwelt & the ground late of Christe Churche in Caunterbury on the North pte Conteyneth — Lxxiij foote — vj Inches of Assise

p me Johnẽ Thorp Rectorẽ
Ecclie Sti xpofori p le stocks

Memorandũ y^{t} ye pson & churchewardens the 2^{d} of Julye 1590 dyd fynde an old date in ye north glasse wyndowe in the vestry howse of ye prysh churche of St xpofers in pieces of glasse disseuered bearing ye date of 1462 & because ye same was broken in sondry pieces we the pson & Churchwardens ioyning each piece together haue found the date afore seyde haue therefore subscribed ou' hands & names as aboueseyd

p me Johnẽ Thorp in Artibus Mgrũ
et Ecclie Sti xpoferi Rectorẽ

Memorandũ these beth the articles concluded at A vestry ye vj day of Janyver in anno 1507

ffurste it was agreed & fully concluded by ye psun by ye alderman and by ye pisshens of Seynt xpofers pisshe that for certen cawses and consideracions, in thextchewyng of suche p'els as hath happed to be w^{t} ynne the cherche yerde, And as myght happe to be in tyme to com to the cherche, & vnto them y^{t} beth dwellyng wynne ye cherche yerde and other, that ther shalbe set a sewer lok vppon ye weket of the alle gate of ye cherche yerd, that shalbe bothe w^{t} a spryng & a stok lok in on stok the whiche weket shalnot be shytte w^{t} ye stok lokke from myhelmas vnto candilmas before y^{t} ye clarke of this cherche hath Rongun curfew after viij of the clok, noder from candilmas vnto myhelmas before ye owre of ix of ye clok at nyte, but oonly w^{t} ye spryng lok, vnto ye whiche spryng lok every inhabitant dwellyg w^{t}ynne ye gate may have a key, to have his fre comyng ynne & goyng owte, before & vnto the seid owres & not after exsepte for a resonable cawse, and y^{t} to ye stok lok ij keyes to be made whiche shall open bothe the spryng & ye stok lok, & therof the õn key to be in ye kepyng of ye p'sun of this cherche or of his debyte dwellyng w^{t}ynne the church yerd, And ye other key to be in ye kepyng of ye pisshe clarke dwellyng w^{t}owte ye gate, w^{t} ye whiche key he to have his goynge ynne & his comyng owte at all nedefull tymes, And to shyt ye seyd stok lok at the seyd owres

Itm that ye chaplyn or chawntry prest y^{t} shall serve & syng in owre cherche for John Whateler & suche as bethe expressed in his wille & testament, and to have ye mancion appteynyng thervnto shalnot from hensefurth grawnt noder lete that mansyon nor no chamber nor parte therof vnto no strawnger nor prest w^{t}owte ye willes & ye consents of the psun and the wardens of this cherche

Itm it is concluded the day aboveseid that owre lady masse shall be done solemply by note in owre cherche by owre prests & clarkes every saterday in the yere beyng werkeday exsepte in the lente seson, And that iche and every on of owre prests chapelyns and owre pisshe clerke or pisshe clerkys shalbe attendaunt and helpyg vnto the same dewly and w^{t}oute faylyng & at ye begynyng therof exsept a Resonable cawse be ther lettyng, provided alwey so y^{t} ther be in nomber iiij prests oder chawntry prests or sell prests servyng in this cherche, & on pisshe clerke to be attendaunt & helpyng vnto ye same

Itm that every werkeday in the lent seson the hye masse the evensonge shalbe done in this cherche by note And ye cõplyn in lyke wyse at ye after none by owre seid chapelyns prests & clerks, and that everyon of them to be attendawnt & helpyng thervnto day & dewly to be at ye begynyng & ye endyng exsept that a Resonable cavse be ther lettyng therfrom.

Itm that the antem or salve shalbe done dayle by owre chaplyns prestis & clark or clarks and that every on & iche of them to be attendant & helpyng therto dayle exsepte that a Resonable cavse be ther lettyng ther from.

* Lady Margaret Nerford was a cousin of the rector of St. Christopher's in the year 1417, in the reign of King Henry V.; she lived in the Parish and gave bequests to it and to other Parishes in the city. She was buried in St. Christopher's, and a copy of her will, which is very curious, is among the Records. She was a friend of Sir John Oldcastle, Lord Cobham.

Itm that the morow masse be kepte & done in this cherche dayle frō myhelmas vnto owre lady day thannōciacon before ye owre of vij of ye clok and frō owre seid lady day vnto myhelmas before the owre of vj of ye clok, and y^{t} it shalbe kepte & done by owre seid prests & chapelyns by covrse and y^{t} that preste y^{t} seith it shall have that weke that iij pence of ye yefte of benet harlwy and he to sey therfore acordȳng to the will & so to iche of thē

Itm that non of owre chaplyns shall go vnto eny trental or place and leve this cherche but dewly to kepe this cherche & herynne to sey ther masse & pray for ther benefactors and fownders dayle exsepte a lawfull cawse be ther lett and els to be Rebated acordyng

Itm that owre seid chapelyñs prestis shalnot on the werke dayes go to ther masse too at ones exsepte for a lawfull cawse shewed vnto the p'sun or vnto his debyte, and by them admytted but that they shall disspose them among themselfe that they go to ther masses immediatly the oñ after the other, so that betwene the morowmasse and the hye masse ther masses may be done in gud order to the plesure of god, & to the consolacion of the pepull that shall come therto, And y^{t} the clarke shall leyfurth to them every werke day ij masse bokes ij chalesses ij awbes & on chesebull exsepte that he be otherwyse cofīanded by ye p'sun or by his debyte & the cherche wardens.

a Itm to that entent and for that these forseyd Articles shalbe ferme and stable holde & contenewe from hensefurth w^{t}oute eny varyaunce or contradixion of any of the seid ꝑsones, or other herafter we y^{e} ꝑsun the alderman and the ꝑisshens before seyd have subscribed owre names hervnder w^{t} owre owne handes the yere and the day beforeseyde

---

a Memorand that the xj day of December in the yere of our lord god m^{l} v^{c} xxiiij and in the xvj yere of the Raigne of King Henry the viijth There was assembled in this vestry m^{r} Richard Reynolds m^{r} John ꝑnell henry Walter Will'm Hertwell Will'm Seintpier Thom's fflude John pierson John Bulkeley peter ꝑson George Wyng laurence Solly Robert Johnson Richard kytwythe John Horspole xpōfre Bowlyng Will'm Sprynget Will'm mach'm Will'm hardwyke Jamys Turner henry Johnson Robert Whitechurche and Richard Romsey, and than and there by the hole voyce and comon assent of all the aforenamed ꝑsones being in nombre xxij^{ti} ꝑsones of the moost substanciall and honest ꝑsones of the parisshe It was condiscended and agreed for a ꝑpetuall quyetnes to be had among all the ꝑisshens. That the clerks wags shuld be sessed by the pyews bothe yn the chapels and in the body of the churche Wherevpon by all their hole assent were than and there chosen for Sessours of the same Pyews henry Walter Will'm hertwell Thomas ffiude John Bulkeley Peter ꝑson George Wyng Robert Johnson John horspole William Sprynget and Will'm hardwyke to sesse eu'y piew seu'ally at a certain sm^{a} as they be in order yndifferently after their discrestions And moreou' that the same sessours at their assemble for the said sessyng shuld appoynte to sit in eu'y piew of the piews of the said churche suche ꝑsones as by their discrestions shuld be thought most cōuenient aswell men to the piews ordeyned for men as the Women to the piews ordeyned for Women And yf any ꝑsone be rebell so that he will not syt or pay according as he is now appointed by the same sessours, or as herafter he shalbe appoynted by the churchwardeyns than being, that than the churchwardeins shall furst shew his Rebellyon to the parisshens in the vestry Where yf he Will not be reformed by the furst monycōn gyuēn vnto hym openly in the vestry by the ꝑisshens there assembled Orells if he refuse to come afore the ꝑisshens there assembled when he is warned by the church wardeins That than the churche wardeins for that tyme being shall complayne of hym that so rebellith vnto the ordynary there to sue hym at the church costys vntill suche tyme as he be reduced vnto a good order and hath paid bothe the costys of the sute and the chargs that he owith vnto the church Prouyded alway that the order that the aforenamed ꝑsonys now being sessours haue takyn in sessyng and appoyntyng of the ꝑisshens in the piews be nother in all or any ꝑcell therof revoked aduychilat or broken in tyme comyng except it be done by viij sessours and the ij churchwardens thervnto elect chosen and appoynted openly in the vestry by xxij ꝑsones in nomb̄ of the moost substanciall and honest ꝑsones of the ꝑish withoute contradiccōn or any agaynsaying of any ꝑsone of the said nombre that than shalbe p'sent but that they than be as hole and fully agreed vnto the breking of this order as the xxij ꝑisshens aforenamed Were vnto the making of this order, all the which were consentyng to the making heroff and no ꝑsone of the said nomb of xxij abouereherced said nay but all were agrecabill therto and to the Writing hereoff.

Hereafter ensueth the Sessyng of the pyews in the ij Chapells that is 117 b. to say in the Chappell of the blessed Trynyte and our lady and in the Chappell of oure lady and saint Anne and of the pyews in the body of the church and the appoyntment of the same pyews which is formest and furst in order which ij^{de} and whiche iij^{de} soo descending frome the highest piew vnto the lowest in the churche Where any housholder or their wyves haue vsed in tymes past to syt sessed and appoynted by the sessours abouenamed In witnes whereoff the same sessours haue vndernethe a Rolle conteynyng all the sessyng and appoyntyng of the said pyews seu'ally sette their namys the day and yere aboue writen

The pyews in the chappell of the blissed Trinite ~~and our lady~~

The furst and formest piew ys in the Trinite chapell before our lady for oon man alone to pay a quarter	ij^{s} iiij^{d}
The iij^{de} piew ys the formest piew before the Trynite for ij ꝑsones eche of them to pay a quarter xxij^{d}	xxij^{d}
The vth piew is the ij^{de} piew before our lady for ij ꝑsons eche of them to pay a quarter xvj^{d}	xvj^{d}
The vijth piew is the second piew before the Trynyte for ij ꝑsones eche of them to pay a quarter xij^{d}	xij^{d}
The ixth piew in ordre is the iij^{de} piew before our lady for ij ꝑsones eche of them to pay a quarter x^{d}	x^{d}
The xjth piew in order is the iij^{de} piew before the trinite for too ꝑsons to pay a quart' viij^{d}	viij^{d}
The xiijth piew in order is the iiijth piew before o^{r} lady for ij ꝑsones eche of theym to pay a quart' vj^{d}	vj^{d}
The xvth piew in order is the iiijth piewe before *ye trenyte* our lady for iij ꝑsonys ech of them to pay a quart' iiij^{d}	iiij^{d}

The pyews in the chappell of our lady and saint Anne 118 a.

The ij^{de} piew in order is the formest piew before saint Anne for ij ꝑsones ech of them to pay a quart' ij^{s}	ij^{s}

The fourth piew in order is the formest piew before o^r lady for ij psones eche of them to pay a quart' xx^d ... } xx^d

The vj piew in order is the second pewe before saint Anne for ij psones eche of theym to pay a quarter xiij^d ... } xiij^d

The viij piew in order is the second piew before our lady for ij psones eche of theym to pay a quarter xj^d ... } xj^d

The xth piew in order is the iij^de piew before saint Anne for ij psonys eche of theym to pay a quarter ix^d ... ... } ix^d

The xij^th piew in ordre is the iij^de piew before o^r lady for ij psones eche of theym to pay a quarter vij^d ... ... } vij^d

The xiiij^th piew in order is the iiij^th piew before saint Anne for iij psones eche of theym to pay a quarter v^d ... } v^d

The xvj^th piew in order is the iiij^th pew before our lady for ij psones eche of them to pay a quart' iiij^d ... ... } iiij^d

The pyews in the body of the churche
The South side

The litill piew on the southside of the church vnder saint Gregoryes petre ij psones ech of them to pay a q^rt' ij^d } ij^d

The litill piew in the body of the church on the southside of saint Gregories petre for oon psone to pay a quart' ij^d } ij^d

The long piew on the southside for v psones eche of theym to pay a quarter ij^d ... ... } ij^d

The pyews in the body of the churche
for women of the parisshe

The iij^de pew is the formest piew on the south side

The vth piew in order is the ij^de piew on the south side

The vij^th piew in order is the iij^de piew on the south side

The ix^th piew in order is the iiij^th piew on the south side

The xj^th piew in order is the vth piew on the south side

The xiij^th piew in order is the vj piew on the south side

The xv^th piew in order is the vij^th piew on the south side

The xvj piew in order is the viij piew on the south side

The xvij piew in ordre is the ix^th piew on the south side

The North side

The litill piew in the body of the church vnder the pulpet for oon psone to pay a quarter ij^d ... ... } ij^d

The litill piew on the northside of the pulpet for oon psone to pay a quarter ij^d ... ... } ij^d

The long piew on the northside for iiij psones eche of theym to pay a quarter ij^d ... ... } ij^d

The piewe for women

The furst and formest piew in the body of the churche for the women is the piew next on the north side to the table of Jhūs

The ij^de piew is on the north side next pew before the shryving hous

The iiij^th piew is the formest piew on the North side

The vj piew in order is the second piew on the north side

The viij piew in order is the iij^de piew on the North side

The xth piew in order is the iiij^th piew on the north side

The xij^th piew in order is the vth piew on the North side

The xiiij^th piew in order is the vj piew on the North side.

Memorandum the xviij^th daye of december in The yere of our Lorde god m^li v^c xlvj it was agreyd by the worshipfull of the peryshens of this perryshe of saynt Christoffers assembled in a vestrie. That wheare as oon ffraunces Merye hath ben putto great Costes and Charges in the reparing of a certen Tenement wherin the same ffraunces nowe dwellethe, being in this perryshe of saynt Christoffers and belonging to the same Churche. In Consideracōn whereof Thaforsaide whorshipfull peryshens withe oon Comen voise and consent haue condiscended and agreed that John Dogget nowe Churche warden of this saide Churche shall delyver and paye vnto the aforsaide ffraunces or his assignes Towardes his saide Charges at the Daye of the Delyvering vppe of his Accompte fyve Markes sterlinges of suche money as the saide John Dogget receyved of the rentes and profetes of the saide Churche. And farther that the same ffraunces nor his Assignes shall paye no rent vnto the saide John Dogget nowe Church warden nor his Assignes for this p̄nte yere of A m^li v^c xlvj for his said dwelling howse, nor vnto his Successors Churche wardens nor thier Assignes vnto the tyme of iiij yeres then next ensuing be fully complet and ended which shalbe at the feast of the Nativite of o^r Lorde in the yere of o^r Lorde god A m^li v^c xlix And frome Thensforthe to paye his saide rent as afore tyme hathe been Accostomed.

The Second daye of Maye 1561. And in the Thirde yere of the Reign of o^r sovereign Lady Elizabeth by the grace of god quene of england ffraunce and Ireland Defender of the faythe etc. Hereafter ensuithe a note of suche goods and ornaments as were in the churche of Saynt xpofer at the stocks in London at the tyme of the enteraunce of John Jakes into the churchewardenshippe, p'vsed in the presence of Thomas Laurence wylliam wyngat Richard Meryt and Thomas Curtys prissheners of the same prisshe, And lefte in the custody of John Mynte Sexton then of the same churche viz.

In primis a table clothe for the commynon table of nettell clothe and two towells of the lyk clothe

Item one playne table clothe and two playne towells.

Item one olde table clothe of dyaper

Item a vestment w^t two tunicolls of clothe of golde, pte broken and ript

Item a red vestment of satten of brudges broken in peces

Item a cope of blew velvet w^t flowers of golde.

Item a hersse clothe of clothe of golde pte & olde velvet

Item an olde hersse clothe of olde sore wome silk

Item thre table clothes narrowe one of velvet, tawney, another of fustyan a napes, and one of red velvet

Item a pvlpit clothe of red damaske w^t flowers of golde

Item an olde turque carpet

Item vij olde broken surpleses.

Item a wrytinge Indented vpon John Younge m'cer for certayne money due longe past the some of iij^li vj^s viij^d

Item a Desk of latten w^t a fawken

Item a communyon cuppe of sylver and gilte weinge xij ounces & half a quarter

Item certayne peces of latten taken of graves

Note that the xv daye of Maye 1561 there was chosen six of the prissheners, that is to saye Mr Becher, Mr fforman, Mr Laurence, Mr Basford, Mr Whithed & Mr Banester, to cease wt the churche-wardeyns those that ar not cest for the clarcks wages, aswell in the new pewes as other, And those six to take order for the sale of suche things as myght well be solde of the churche goods, and all other matters nedefull to be done from yere to yere those six or other in their steads to be chosen to take order therein

The names of those por folkes of the prisshe as ar appoynted to haue vjd a weke out of the money geuen to the por

Baune
Henley
Carlell
Hillton

Collectors for the poore

John Younge
Richard Merryet

A ceasment made for the Clarcks wages the vth daye of June 1561 by Harry Becher, George fforman, Thomas Banester, Thomas Laurence, John Jakes, Thomas Basford, John Whytched, and John Overton, and this rate to stond vntill consent of the prisshe by a vestry it be altered, and is quarterly xls xd

Sir Willm Garret knight and Alderman … …	iijs iiijd	James Bentley … …	ijd
Thomas Wylkes … …	viijd	Thomas Laurence … …	viijd
willyam Colle … …	iiijd	John Baker … … …	iijd
Edward Sotherik … …	xijd	Richard Meryt … …	vjd
Thomas Monds … …	iiijd	Thomas Basford [124 b.]	viijd
Robert ffox … … …	ijd	Adam Wormall … …	vjd
Thomas Brayfelde … …	ijd	Stephen Barrowe … …	vjd
John Hawkins … …	jd	John Whytched … …	viijd
Willyam Tompson … …	jd	John Overton … …	vd
willm Yertyngeton …	iiijd	George fforman … …	xviijd
Christofer Goodrik and his ptes … … …	xxd	John Barrow … … …	xvjd
		John Barrow … … …	xiiijd
		Willyam heckmans plumer	viijd
John Cery … … …	jd	Misteres Thorowgood …	iiijd
Misteres Casse wydowe …	iiijd	Robert Horne … …	xiiijd
Thomas Beson … …	jd	Willyam Thorowgood …	iiijd
Richard Howson … …	jd	John Smithe … … …	vjd
Thomas Curtys … …	jd	Willyam wyngat … …	xijd
Willm Weldon … …	xviijd	John Younge … … …	viijd
John Whyte … … …	xxd	Thomas Bannester …	xviijd
John Kelk … … …	vjd	Gyles Evenyt … … …	viijd
Harry Bechar … …	xxijd	Misteres Saterley … …	iiijd
Thomas Lancaster …	ijd	Misteres Person … …	xd
Misteres Compagny …	iijs iiijd	Thomas Raynam … …	ijd
Thomas Garret … …	iiijd	Thomas Curtys … …	iiijd
Robert Holfourthe …	ijd	John Jakes … … …	xvjd
Robert Thorneton … …	iijd	Willyam Poole … …	iijd
John Egilsfelde … …	ijd	Richard Rusheall … …	xd
Thomas Adams … …	vjd	Anthony Whyte … …	xvjd
Adam Whetley … …	vjd	Misteres Jakes Wydowe	vjd

Some quarterly — xls xd

It was determyned the same vth daye of Junie 1561 that the foure keys of the por mens box sholde remayne in the custody of theis psons followinge that is to saye [illegible] a.

Mr Becher one key
The Parson a nother
Mr fforman a nother
The churche wardeyns a nother

Also ijd ob is to be gathered euery sundaye by the Sexton wch was wont to serve for holy breade, And nowe to serve for wyne for the comunyon table, And if any overplus be left then the same to be geuen to the por of the prisshe.

An Inventory of Goods and Ornaments belonging to the Church and Parrish of St Christophers London saved and p'served at and after the Burning of the said Church by the dismall ffire happening in London in September 1666 Robert Watkins and Peter Ayleworth then Churchwardens 127 a.

	c	qr	li	oz	
Imprimis Old Burn'd Brasse belonging to a large Branch and Gravestones … …	iij	oj	xviij	—	Sould by Mr Horsey pt of it, ye rest pad dd to mr Kerington
Course Burn'd Bell Mettle … … …	iiij	oj	xxij	—	sould by mr Horsey & accounted for by him for 24. 14. 7 [illegible]
One Bell broken and burn'd mixt with Iron Lead and Stones … … … …	v	iij	xij	—	
One great whole Bell Weighing … …	ix	—	ij	—	Hanged in ye steeple
Copper belonging to St Peter Lameeres Monnument … … … … …			lxxxviij		These are affixed to the Church Wall Near the Vestry Doore
Out of which a deaths Head left in the Custody of Mr Robert Watkins of the same Mettle weighing … … … …	—	—	ij:	xij	

Goods preserved by William Bate Clerke of the said Parrish as followeth

One Box with a small brasse Branch
ffower brasse Candlesticks
Three Trenches
Two Old Service Bookes
Six Tinn Sconces 127 b.
One other Box with a Master of Arts hood
One Communion Cloth
Two Surplices
One Velvet Carpet wth Gold and Silke ffringe Lost
One Velvet Pulpitt Cloth wth Gold & silke ffringe
Two Pulpett Cushions one of them Velvet
One Black Cloth for a Hearse
One Greene Cloth Carpet
ffower Pewter Basons
One Old Carpett
Three Service Bookes
One Booke of Homilies
One Booke of Cannons
Severall small service Bookes for p'ticuler Occasions
One Church Bible
One large Bible
One Booke against Popish Errors
One Booke of Peter Martirs Conc. Plases 126 a.
Two Bookes of Erasmus Comentaryes on the new Testament
Three Vollums of the Booke of Martirs

Not found since Mr Horsey's time of being Church-warden

The Guift of Mr George Goodday

Register Bookes

ffower Tables that hang'd in the Vestry concerning the Parrish Lands Church dutyes and other Matters

[illegible margin note]			ℭ	q^r	li
	Six large Iron Casements weighing ...		—	—	lxxviij
	One large Curtaine Rodd weighing	...	—	—	xix
		Tunns	ℭ	q^r	li
	Lead	x	ij	iij	vj
	One large Iron Casement weighing	—	—	—	xxxix

Plate for ye Cōmunion

		oz	d.	gr.
The Guift of Mr Gilbert Morewood	One Silver fflagon weighing	xliiij	v	—
	One Bason weighing	xxij	—	—
	One Plate weighing	viij	xiiij	—
The Guift of Mr Thomas [illegible]	One fflagon weighing	lj½	wanting 1d waite	
	One other fflagon weighing	lij½	oj	—
	One Silver and Gilt Cupp and Cover	xxvj	xij	xij
	One other Gilt Cupp and Cover weighing ...	xxvij	ov	—

One silver and Gilt Salver the Gift of Madam Jane Bainbrigg relict of Wm̄ Bainbrigg Esq. 1691

137 b. Bookes of Parrish acc^ts: &c

One Booke of Records
One Booke of Assessm^ts for the Poore and Scavenger
One Old Booke of Churchwardens Acc^ts:
One new Booke of Churchwardens Acc^ts
One Vestry Booke
One Old Chest bought since the ffire

---

138 b. Conveyance from Mayor Cominalty & Cittizens of London granted to the Trustees of St Christophers Parish on the behalfe of the same Parish of a Slipp of Ground Added to the Front of the Houses in Fleete Streete

This Indenture made the Eight and Twentieth day of November in the Three and Twentieth yeare of the Reigne of our Soveraigne Lord Charles the second by the grace of God of England Scotland ffrance and Ireland King defender of the ffaith etc Betweene the Mayor Coialty and Cittizens of the City of London on the One part And Richard Booth Esqr John Hubland Merch^t William Allen Vphold^r Nathaniell Brooke Stacōner Peter Ayleworth Grocer William Horsey Cordwayner Robert Kerrington Merchanttaylor John Elliott Leatherseller Thomas Kemble Draper Edward Buckerfeild Leatherseller Edward Godman Merchanttaylor Jos. ffrancklin Plumer Thomas Russell Habdasher Samuel Powell Grocer Henry Lascoe & ffra Lucy Grocers Parishioners of the Parish of St Christophers London Trustees for and on the behalfe of the said Parish on the other pte Witnesseth that the said Mayor Coīalty and Cittizens for and in Consideracon of the Sume of Twenty Three pounds Six shillings of Lawfull money of England to them paid the Receipt whereof they doe hereby acknowledge and thereof and of every pte and parcell thereof doe acquite and discharge the said Parishioners their heires and Assignes Have granted bargained sold released and confirmed And by these p'sents doe grant bargaine sell release and confirme vnto the said Richard Booth John Houblon William Allen Nathaniell Brooke Peter Ayleworth William Horsey Robt Kerington John Elliott Tho Kemble Edw: Buckerfeild Edw Godman Jos ffranklin Tho Russell Sam Powell Henry Lascoe and ffrancis Lucy All that their late Wast and Comon Ground or Soyle now taken laid or added vnto Two new built Messuages or Tenements belonging to the said Parish scituate and being in the Parish of St Dunstans in the West on the north side of the same Streete in the severall Tenures of William Smith and John Sharpe and lying in the ffront or ffore pte of the said Tenem^ts next the said Streete Conteyning in Length from East to West Ninety Three foote ffive inches of Assize little more or Lesse and from North to South ffower ffoote of Assize or thereabouts at one End and Three ffoote at thother End And all thestate right title Interest Clayme and demande whatsoever of them the said Mayor Coialty and Cittizens of in and to the same ground To have and to hold the said late wast and Comon ground or soyle herein before mencōned and intended to be hereby given and granted and every parte and parcell thereof vnto the said Parishioners their heires and Assignes to th' onely proper vse and behoofe of them and their heires for ever And the said Mayor Coialty and Cittizens for them and their Successors the said late Wast and Cōmon ground or soyle and every pte and pcell thereof vnto the said Parishioners and their heires against them the said Mayor Coialty and Cittizens and their Successors and against all and every other pson and psons whatsoever lawfully Clayming or which shall or may lawfully Clayme by from or vnder them shall and will warrant and for ever defend by these p'sents In witnes whereof the said Mayor Coialty and Cittizens to these p'sents their Cōmon Seale haue caused to be affixed the day and yeare above written 139 a.

Primo die Januarii Anno Primo Regni Regis Edwardi Sexti 139 b.

The Cytye of London and the County of Middelsexe } That is to say { A breefe declaracōn made by vs Sr Roger Cholmeley Knight Cheefe Baron of the Kings Maties Exchequer, Nicholas Hare, Wymounde Carewe and John Godsalue Knights, Richard Goodricke, John Carrell, Richard Morrison and Hewe Losse Esquiers Cōmissioners of our Soveraigne Lord the King, within the City of London, and the County of Middelsex, Assigned for thexecution of an Acte made in the first yeare of his Highnes Reigne, Concerning Colledges, ffree chappells, Chaunteries, ffraternities, Gildes, Brotherheddes and other Lands whatsoever, geven for or towardes the findinge of anny Preestes, Obits, Leightes or Lampes and such other like those, as in the Kinges Commission vnto vs directed in that behalfe more plainely appeareth declaring as well the trew valew of all such Colledges, ffree chappells, Chaunteries, ffraternities Brotherheddes, Gildes and such other, with thyerelie Repriss and Annuall deduccons goinge out of them as also of all suche Somes of Money comeinge and growinge to the Kinges saied Maiestie by reason of the forenamed Acte of Parliament, as hereafter more plainely may appeare

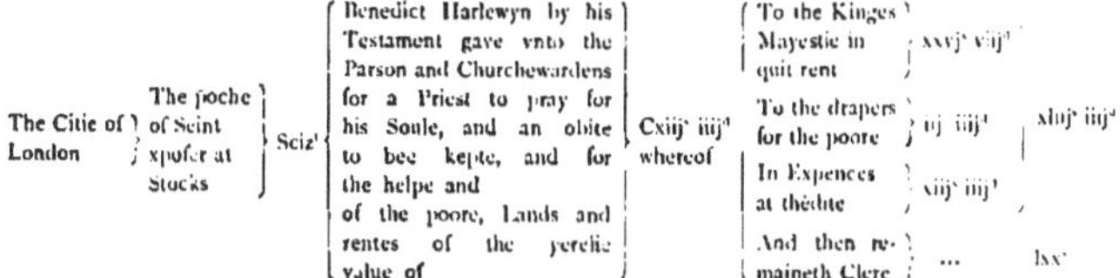

The Citie of London — The poche of Seint xpofer at Stocks — Sciz' — Benedict Harlewyn by his Testament gave vnto the Parson and Churchewardens for a Priest to pray for his Soule, and an obite to bee kepte, and for the helpe and of the poore, Lands and rentes of the yerelie value of — Cxiij^s iiij^d whereof

To the Kinges Mayestie in quit rent	xxvj^s viij^d	xliij^s iiij^d
To the drapers for the poore	iij iiij^d	
In Expences at thédite	xiij^s iiij^d	
And then remaineth Clere	...	lxx^s

This is a true Copie, and Examined in the Augmentaĉon Office at Westminster

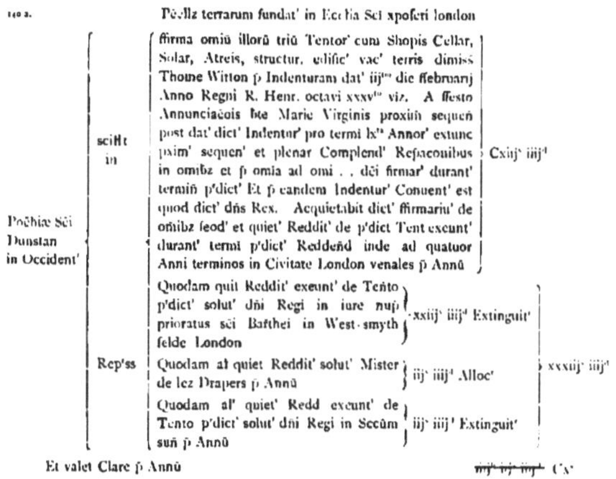

140 a. Pĉells terrarum fundat' in Eccl'ia Sci xpoferi london

Poĉhiæ Sĉi Dunstan in Occident'

sciHt in — ffirma omiũ illorũ triũ Tentor' cum Shopis Cellar, Solar, Atreis, structur, edific' vac' terris dimiss Thome Witton p Indenturam dat' iij^{tio} die ffebruarij Anno Regni R. Henr. octavi xxxv^{to} viz. A ffesto Annunciaĉois bte Marie Virginis proxiñ sequeñ post dat' dict' Indentur' pro termi lx^{ta} Annor' extunc pxim' sequen' et plenar Complend' Refpacoibus in omibz et p omia ad omi . . dĉi firmar' durant' termiñ p'dict' Et p eandem Indentur' Conuent' est quod dict' dñs Rex. Acquietabit dict' ffirmariu' de omibz feod' et quiet' Reddit' de p'dict Tent exeunt' durant' termi p'dict' Reddeñd inde ad quatuor Anni terminos in Civitate London venales p Annũ — Cxiij^s iiij^d

Rep'ss —

Quodam quit Reddit' exeunt' de Teñto p'dict' solut' dñi Regi in iure nup prioratus sĉi Bafthei in West-smyth felde London	xxiij^s iiij^d Extinguit'	xxxiij^s iiij^d
Quodam al quiet Reddit' solut' Mister de lez Drapers p Annũ	iij^s iiij^d Alloc'	
Quodam al' quiet' Redd exeunt' de Tento p'dict' solut' dñi Regi in Secûm suñ p Annũ	iij^s iiij^d Extinguit'	

Et valet Clare p Annũ ~~iiij^{li} iij^s iiij^d~~ Cx^s

Memorandũ those Tẽnts were given by Benedicte Harlewyn towards the finding of Preists, and to keepe an obite for his Sole for ever

p me Hugonem Losse

xvj^{to} die Junii Anno Secundo Regs Edri vj^{ti} pro Johne Crooke de Chilton in Com' Bucks Armig' —

The clere yearelie value of the p'misses	Cx^s
Which rated at xvj yeres purchase Amounteth to	iiij^{xx} viij^{li}
To bee paid in hand	

The kinges Maiestie to discharge the Purchaser of all incumbrances excepte Leases and the Covenants of the same, and the rent before allowed.

The tenure in Socage or free Burgage

The Purchaser to have th'issues from Easter last

M^r p Thomam Goueld Wa: Mildmay

Robt Keylwey

Memorandũ That I John Croke of Chilton in the County of Bucks Esquier, doe require to Purchase of the Kings Highnes by virtue of his Graces Commission of Sale the Lands Tenements and hereditaments Conteyned and specified in the particulers and Rate herevnto annexed, being of such clere yerelie value as in the same particulers and rate is expressed. In witnes whereof to this Bill subscribed with my hand I have put my Seale the xvj^{th} day of June in the Second yeare of the Reigne of our Soveraigne Lord Edward the Sixth by the grace of God King of England ffrance and Ireland Defender of the ffaith, and of the Church of England and also of Ireland in Earth the Supreme Hedde

p me J. Croke

This is a true Coppie and Examined in the Augmentacon Office at Westm'ster

Parish of St Christophers London 1681 An Assessement made within the said Parish of Money to bee paid yearely by Quarterly Payments in Liew of Tythes to the Parson of the said Parish for the time being over and above the Glebe Perquisites Guifts and Bequests According to an Act of Parliament Intituled an Act for the better Settlement of the Mainteinance of the Parsons Viccars and Curates in the Parishes of the Citty of London Burnt by the late dreadfull ffire there diverse Appealles haveing been made to and heard and determined by the Lord Mayor and Court of Aldermen According to the direccõn of the said Act. Beginning at the West Corner of Princes Streete neer to the Poultrey.

No		li	s	d
1	ffrancis Lucy	01	12	00
2	Silvester Deane	00	17	04
3	Griffith Vincent	00	17	04
4	Samuell Bennett	00	17	04
5	John Hemingway	00	17	04
6	Nicholas Skinner	01	12	00
7	Richard Booth Esqr	02	14	00
8	David Heywood	00	14	08
9	Thomas Scott	00	15	00
10	Elizabeth Davis	00	08	00
11	Joseph Lem	01	08	00
12	John Clare	00	12	00
13	William Barker	00	12	00
14	James Cornwall	00	12	00
15	Michaell Dewing	00	17	04
16	Robert Adams	00	17	04
17	John Grove	00	17	04
18	Thomas Rea	00	17	04
19	Constable Wheeler	01	05	00
20	Richard Lightwood	00	06	08

Thredneedle Streete North side

No		li	s	d
21	Nicholas Day	00	16	00
22	Mary Croxton	00	11	=

Three Nunn Alley

No		li	s	d
23	William Blunt	00	08	08
24	John Williams	00	14	08
25	Robert Crosse	00	08	08
26	John Elleott	00	08	08
27	Anne Clarke	00	08	08
28	William Dalton	00	08	08
29	Jonathan Platte	00	08	08
30	Richard Marchant	00	06	00
31	Robert Todd	00	13	04
32	Thomas Manton	01	07	00

Church Alley next the Church doore

No		li	s	d
33	Sarah James	00	13	00
34	Jeremie Mitchell	00	14	08
35	Samuell Wells	00	14	08
36	Israell ffalgate	00	15	=
37	Benjamin Billingsley	00	13	00
38	William Scott	00	13	00
39	James Ashwood	00	08	08
40	Gerrard Harris	00	08	00
41	Nicholas Buckeridge	00	17	04
42	The Parsonage house	00	00	00
43	Mabell Roland	00	08	08
44	Josiah Mitchell	00	12	00
45	Gerrard Harris Office of Intelligance and Two Stalls	00	02	04

Thredneedle Streete North side

No		li	s	d
46	Samuell Brewster	01	12	00
47	Thomas Short	01	12	00
48	William ffashion	01	12	00
49	John Houblon	04	06	00
50	Samuell Powell	01	07	00
51	Daniell ffrancklin 1^li^ 5^s^	01	05	00
52	Anne Craven	00	05	04 148
53	Capt Tho. Blagrave	04	06	00
54	Andrew Keepe	00	08	08
55	Henry Browne	01	01	08
56	Henry Wellington	01	16	00

Bartholomew lane

No		li	s	d
57	Daniell Mercer	02	00	00

Castle Court Broadstreete Ward

No		li	s	d
58	Hannah Herring	00	06	08

Castle Alley

No		li	s	d
59 60	Henry Boone — 16^s^ both in one 16	01	12	00

Thredneedle Streete Southside

No		li	s	d
61	John Prettiman	00	13	04
62	William Winn	00	13	04
63	Arthur Miles	00	16	08
64	Isaac Hancocke	01	01	08
65	William Gloster	00	12	00
66	William Pepes	00	16	08
67	Samuell Parker	00	13	00
68	William Meriden	00	13	00
69	Peter Aylworth	01	07	00
70	Deborah Woodbridge	00	12	00
71	William Drope	01	07	00

Cornhill side and Ward

No		li	s	d
72	Peter Caplin	01	00	00
73	Isaac Puller	02	16	00
74	John Crosse	02	08	00
75	Henry Lascoe	02	14	00
76	Robert Mordant	01	02	00
77	Arrabella Bobert	01	00	00
78	John Hopkins & Partner	02	03	04
79	William Bancks	01	12	00
80	Thomas Collins	02	08	00
81	John Lawrence	01	12	00
82	Charles Robinson	01	00	00
83	William Bethell	02	14	00
84	Thomas Kemble	01	04	00
85	Tobit Chapman	02	00	00
86	Thomas Lee	02	00	00
87	Richard Barwell	01	00	00

Castle Alley Cornhill Ward

88 William Horsey the Corner House … … 01 17 04
89 Humphrey Bradley … … … … 00 16 00
90 Simon Cole … … … … … 01 04 00
91 Henry Moss in Castle Court … … … 00 06 08
92 William Newman … … … … 00 16 04

100 00 00

Exchange Shopps in Castle Alley

1 Humphry Cuningsby an Office … … … 00 08 00
2, 3, 4, 5 } John Cave Stationer … … … 01 15 00

Cornhill Piaza

6 Edward Browne … … … … 00 11 02
7 Benjamin Billingley … … … 00 11 02
8 Samuell Hodgkins … … … 00 19 00

New Pawne above North Row of South Pawn

1 Dorothy Hervy … … … … … 00 07 00
2 & 3 } John ffencell … 00 14 00

West side of the West Pawne

6 ffoote Samll Bathurst being ⅔ of his Shopp 0 06 02
10 8 ffoote … … … … 00 05 00
11 11 ffoote … … … … … 00 06 10
12 12 ffoote … … … … 00 07 06
13 8 ffoote Thomas Smith … … … … 00 06 02
14 9 ffoote ffronting Old Pawne Dudley … 06 06
15 A Large Roome in Southwest Corner Severall Shopps Mr Dudley … … } 0 12 06

South Pawne South Row

16 Joseph Cooke 17 ffoote Mr Richardson A Closett and Roome over it … … … } 0 16 00
17 ffoote Sarah Nicholls … 0 08 04
18 ffoote Mrs Alsopp … … 0 08 00
19 ffoote Peter Way … … 0 07 00
20 6 ffoote being ¾ Mrs Denhams … 0 04 08

Old Pawne & Pepper Cellar

1 8 ffoote Mrs Browne … … 00 12 00
2 12 ffoote ffrancis Webster … 00 18 00
3 12 ffoote Mrs Lockyer … 00 18 00
4 9 ffoote Mrs Shaw … … 00 13 06
5 12 ffoote Dorothy Lacon … … 00 18 00
6 6 ffoote But ½ St xpfers Mrs Humlock … 0 04 06

West side

7 8 ffoote Mrs Goff … … 00 12 00
8 8 ffoote Andrew Turner … 00 12 00
9 16 ffoote John Spillet … 01 04 00
10 8 ffoote Thomas Jellan … … 00 12 00
11 6 ffoote & ½ Tho Symonds … 00 09 09
12 5 ffoote Anne Randell … … 00 07 06
13 8 ffoote William Badham … 00 12 00
14 10 ffoote Mrs ffoster … … 00 15 00
ffor the Pepper Cellar … … 00 11 09

20 00 00
100 00 00
120 00 00

Wm Pritchard Ald'man
Peter Aylworth Depty & Pishonr
Michaell Rolles } Com Councell
Robert Watkins } men for Broad
Geo Cole } streete Ward

1681

Nics Bendy Depty } Corn hill Ward
Leonard Bates }
Tho Kemble Pishonr }

Will Bancks } Churchwardens
John Williams }

Jno Houblon }
Samll Brewster } Parishonrs
Samuel Powell }
Wm Drope }

Ano 1556 the 10 of may 216 a.

by the consent of the holle vestry ffor the order of the pwes and sesement thereof ffor the clarkes wages to tacke payns therein
mr Jackes
Mastar bechere
Mastar krampton
Mastar fforeman
Mastar Grovare
Mastar Banestar
Mastar Mousteau
Mastar Raynesby
And the ij cherche wardens
And To be ffeneshed By Wysson day ore afore
And to be vj ore iiij at the leste by Syd the cherche wardens
beynge Cherche wardens at that pressente tyme Wyllyam laker and thomas lawrns

---

This order taken by asseste of this pares the fferst daye of nofember 1551 for the pore of this paress quarterly the names of them Rd of mr westcott the same daye for mykellmas qr is now xvijs viijd 217 b. mr westcotts

The good man hawkes … … … xvjd
The ffather cossen … … … xvjd
mother linton … … … … xvjd
goodman claybroke … … … xvjd
Jhon anssell … … … … xvjd
ffather bauwne … … … … ijs
good wyfe waren … … … xvjd
mothe corlell … … … … xvjd
good wyfe sshayn … … … xvjd
dafe poyntt maker … … … xvjd
Rychard brayffeld … … … … xvjd

one qr'ly som xvs iiijd

Jhon som … … … … … … … … xvjd
~~It mother costen … … … … … … xvjd~~
~~Remayneng in mr yowengs handes the daye aforesaid … iiijd~~

~~Remayneng in mr somethes handes in his Resette … … vjd~~

~~Remaynes in mr Miesehompe handes of the resette of mychellmas qr the daye aforsaid of mr wescotte qr som } iis iiijd~~

Rd of m^r^ dokette the xxvj daye of desember 1551 for crest-mas q^r^ ... ... } xvij^s^

Rd of m^r^ fforman the xij day of Apprell for the pore ester q^r^ som is ... ... } xxx^s^

Rd of m^r^ amyas the x day of July for the power for thys q^r^ that is from our lady day to mydsommar ... } xxx^s^ vij^d^

browght in by m^r^ amyas the wyche was gyuyn by a wyddo xx^s^

browght in by me thomas lawrons & harry pekyns the fyrst day of nouembyr for the power & hyt remenes in the box ... ... } xxvj^s^ x^d^

---

m^d^ the x day of may an^o^ 1532 where there ys v kayes wher of iij of thē belongythe to the grett chest in the Rod loft & the other ij ys for the lytell chest wher in ys apors [a purse] w^t^ iij^li^ xij^s^ iiij^d^ wher of on of thē ys in m^r^ Reynold hands & ~~the Rest of thē~~ lawrens sowley hathe another and the Rest of thē m^r^ thron hathe cherche wardyn

m^d^ payd to manewell lucar vj li xiiij s j d for a Rest of accowmpte geven vp be hem in presens of owre curet m^r^ kyng & wyllm kent John askeve churche wardens, & m^r^ semp larans solley Robert Jennyns willm machen & be the consent of m^r^ Reynolds m^r^ p'nell the iij day of apryll the xxiiij yere of keng henry the viiij^th^ a^o^ 1533

Itm the vij day of may an^o^ m^l^ v^c^ xxx^o^ the cherche of synt crestovers ow^t^ onto wyllym chamber goldsmythe of london for that he layd out in redy mony for the sayd cherche besynes as yt aperethe by the akovnte som xiiij^li^ xviiij^s^ v^d^ iij q^r^ sterlyng and for the plege of the same I wyllym chamber hathe Resayued in to my hands the viij day of July in the yere aforsayd as yt was agred by a vestre of the hole preshe thys pcells folowyng

Itm monester of selver and gylte & ij crewetts of selver and pcells gylte and a pakes of sylver & gelte the lgys & the otter pte therof, tyll the mony be payd aforsayd

p me wyllym chamber

thys mony was p^d^ agen to the sayd chambe by the hands of m^r^ Jaks 1536 & all thys pcells of plat was clerly delyuerd agen in to the cherche wardyns

THE END.

ΕΝ ΤΗ ΒΑΣΙΛΕΙΑ ΣΟΥ ΜΝΗΣΘΗΤΙ ΚΥΡΙΕ ΤΩΝ ΔΟΥΛΩΝ ΣΟΥ ΕΔΟΥΙΝΟΥ ΦΡΕΣΦΙΕΛΔ ΚΑΙ ΖΩΗΣ ΤΗΣ ΓΥΝΑΙΚΟΣ ΑΥΤΟΥ ΚΑΙ ΕΔΟΥΙΝΟΥ ΤΟΥ ΥΙΟΥ ΑΥΤΩΝ.

www.ingramcontent.com/pod-product-compliance
Lightning Source LLC
Chambersburg PA
CBHW021423090426
42742CB00009B/1227
* 9 7 8 3 3 3 7 8 4 8 6 0 6 *